WEEKENDS in and around CAPE TOWN

Peter Joyce
Jill Johnson
Ashley Joyce

STRUIK TIMMINS

Struik Timmins Publishers
(A member of the Struik Group (Pty)Ltd)
Struik House
80 McKenzie Street
Cape Town 8001

Reg. No.: 54/00965/07

First published 1991

Text © Peter and Ashley Joyce 1991

Editor: Geoffrey Payne
Designer: Robert Meas
Cover Designers: Abdul Amien and Robert Meas

Typesetting by Struik DTP, Kerry Hall
Cover and map reproduction by Fotoplate (Pty) Ltd, Cape Town
Printed and bound by Unique Press (Pty) Ltd, Cape Town

Front cover photography: The late Percy Sargeant

All rights reserved. No part of this publication may be reproduced, stored in a retrieval system, or transmitted in any form or by any means, electronic, mechanical, photocopying, recording or otherwise, without the prior written permission of the copyright owners.

ISBN 0 86978 467 6

CONTENTS

CAPE TOWN: City and Suburbs
5

THE PENINSULA
53

THE WINELANDS
72

THE WESTCOAST
112

THE OVERBERG
125

VISITORS' ADVISORY
146

INDEX
155

Maps

Cape Town Central 24, 25
Peninsula 52
Western Cape (Regional) 84

AUTHORS' NOTE

We have tried, in these pages, to suggest some of the more pleasant ways in which prospective visitors to the western Cape, and indeed Capetonians themselves – those in need of a break – can enjoy this most inviting segment of southern Africa.

The book is divided into five chapters, each covering a particular part of the region and each of which has two distinct but closely related components: an introductory overview that highlights the relevant area's more notable tourist attractions and, secondly, profiles of some of its hotels, lodges and guest farms.

Our approach to the latter coverage, entitled 'Where to Stay', was selective rather than comprehensive. The ingredients we looked for were comfort, good food, friendly service and genuine hospitality, and in this context we have included a number of places that are unpretentious, even unsophisticated, but which offer good value. Conversely, we have ommited a number of notable and popular establishments – the Holiday Inns and City Lodge, for example – simply because they belong to well-known groups that give the travelling public an excellent but fairly uniform service.

We spent many weeks on tour, visiting a bewildering number and variety of places, and our final choice – some 75 recommended establishments – was the product of a great deal of careful thought. Nevertheless, the overall selection and the individual assessments are, by definition, highly subjective, reflecting our personal preferences rather than a set of formal criteria, and the book should be read as such. There is no claim here to any special expertize or authority: we have simply written about what impressed us most, in the hope that other people share our likes and (a far less prominent element) our dislikes.

The tariffs that appear in the 'in brief' summaries appended to the profiles were those quoted in mid-1991. We found it impractical to give full details of the various rates – they differed markedly, according to season and to the type of accommodation on offer. In order to avoid confusion, the standard daily charge for a double room in season (bed and breakfast) is represented by a letter of the alphabet, as follows: **A**: up to R100 **B**: R101 – R150 **C**: R151 – R200 **D**: R201 – R250 **E**: R251 – R300 **F**: Above R300.

The scale, however, provides a broad indication only. There are permutations in between and, as mentioned, seasonal and other variations.

This is the first edition of *Weekends in and around Cape Town* but, hopefully, not the last: we intend updating the work on a regular basis to produce biennial editions, perhaps even a new volume each year, and will shortly be embarking on a series of refresher tours to see what changes have taken place, and to seek out new places to profile. Again the approach will be subjective, but rather less so if we could persuade readers to contribute to the exercise – by letting us have their own asssessments. If you've been a recent guest at one of the establishments featured, or at one that isn't covered here but which you feel should be, please would you write to us with your impressions. These we shall use to supplement our own. Letters should be addressed to The Editor, Cape Weekends, Struik Timmins Publishers, P.O. Box 1144, Cape Town 8000.

For the rest, we must record our most appreciative thanks to those many managers and members of staff who extended their hospitality to us. Throughout our journeys we were received, almost without exception, with the utmost kindness and courtesy.

PJ JJ AJ

CAPE TOWN

City and Suburbs

❏ WHAT TO SEE AND DO

❏ WHERE TO STAY

❏ WHAT TO SEE AND DO

South Africa's 'Mother City' lies on the shores of Table Bay at the southern extremity of the African continent. It is the country's legislative capital, second largest city and by far the oldest urban centre: it was established in 1652 by Commander Jan van Riebeeck and his small party of settlers as a victualling station for the fleets of the Dutch East India Company's thriving maritime empire.

Greater Cape Town, which has a population of about two million (a figure that will rise by another million before the end of the decade, if the present pattern of 'urban drift' is sustained), fills the amphitheatre formed by Table Mountain and its flanking peaks. It stretches on either side of the Peninsula and inland, the suburbs hugging the lowest slopes of the mountain range and then extending southwards along the line of rail. These Southern Suburbs, several founded as farms during the 1650s, are the oldest of the outlying residential areas. Central Cape Town is small by international standards, its potential for expansion limited by sea and mountain.

To the north and east are what are known as the Cape Flats, a region that once lay beneath the ocean, so separating the Peninsula from the mainland. But over the millennia the waters receded to expose a low, sandy, flat area known to the early Dutch colonists as 'Die Groote Woeste Vlakte', or Great Desolate Plain – a nightmarish region of drifting dunes and a serious obstacle to communications between Cape Town and the developing hinterland. Eventually, during the 19th century, the sands were stabilized by planting out hardy wattles and hakeas and, most notably, Port Jackson willows. These last, a species of acacia imported from Australia, served their purpose only too well: in due course they spread far and wide and are now regarded as thoroughgoing pests. (Incidentally, though, justice of a perverse kind was served when the Cape bietou bush found its way, in ships' ballast, to Australia around 1908 and, lacking 'biological checks' to its distribution, spread alarmingly in that country, blocking access to beaches, damaging beach-planting programs and posing a major threat to the natural flora.)

Today the northern plain is intensively cultivated in some parts, otherwise dense with suburbia. Among the larger of its many components are the municipalities of Milnerton and Parow, the city of Bellville and, farther south, close to the shores of False Bay, the vast new township of Khayelitsha. The latter, whose name means 'new home', is a largely black residential township established in the later 1980s, initially to house residents of the 'squatter camps' (including the notorious Crossroads settlement) that had mushroomed around the city. It is now linked by rail to the central area, has a huge, modern shopping centre, an industrial complex for 100 factories and is intended to accommodate 250 000 people in reasonable comfort.

Popularly termed the 'Tavern of the Seas', Cape Town owed its prominence and prosperity over three centuries and more to its strategic position astride the ocean lanes, and to its harbour, South

CAPE TOWN: CITY AND SUBURBS

Africa's second biggest. Today the port is quieter than it was in the heyday of the passenger steamer, and other harbours, much closer to the northern industrial markets, have siphoned off much of its traditional freight traffic. There are splendidly imaginative plans to revitalize the under-used parts of the dockland area (see page 14).

Nevertheless, Cape Town remains a substantial port city. The harbour boasts some of the world's most extensive pre-cooling stores (they handle the western Cape's huge export-fruit harvests); ship repair is a major industry (the dry dock, well-used by tankers in need of maintenance, is the southern hemisphere's largest graving facility); marine and mercantile enterprises still contribute a lot to the local economy, and the cruise ships are coming back.

The city's wider economic base includes marine fishing (about 40 per cent of the national catch is brought into Table Bay), petroleum refining, cement, chemicals and fertilizers, motor assembly, food processing, wine-making, electronics and light engineering, the manufacture of plastics, textiles, clothing and footwear, printing and publishing, and the service industries (many of the larger banking and insurance companies have established their headquarters in Cape Town, mainly, it seems, because it is such a pleasant place in which to live).

And tourism. Cape Town is one of South Africa's premier holiday centres; the mountain, the beaches, the lovely Peninsula countryside and the winelands just to the north, the history in the stones of the buildings, the lively calendar of arts, the eating and drinking places, and the undemanding, unhurried lifestyle are powerful attractions. Many affluent people retire to, or near to, the city.

Climate The western Cape – the City, the Peninsula, the coastal extensions and the hinterland – is unique within the southern African context in its Mediterranean character.

The region has dry summer months with long, cloudless days that are sometimes – in what are known as 'berg wind conditions' (hot air blowing in from the northern interior) – perfect in their somnolent stillness, at other times disturbed by a gusty, unnerving, occasionally vicious 'black' south-easter that often reaches gale force and can last up to a week or more and which, when it comes to one's enjoyment of the outdoors, can be thoroughly disruptive. Without it, though, Cape Town would be as steamily enervating as Bombay. Its freshness is said to cleanse the city of sickness (this may well have been so in earlier and less sanitary days), and for this reason it's known to locals as the 'Cape Doctor'.

Winter is the green season, wet and cool, downright cold at times (snow falls on the nearby mountains), but the periods of driving rain – brought in by moist air from the north-west – are interspersed with crisp, sunlit days of magical quality.

The best Cape months are those of its brief spring (September and October) and autumn (March to May), when the sky is clear, the colours change and the fragile delicacy of the air lifts and sustains the spirit.

TABLE MOUNTAIN

South Africa's, and one of the world's, best-known landmarks, the mountain's rugged majesty dominates the Peninsula's northern skyline. It towers 1 086 metres above the city; measures nearly three kilometres from end to end; on clear days it can be discerned from 200 kilometres at sea. From its summit there are dramatic views of Cape Town, its harbour and Table Bay below, of Lion's Head and Devil's Peak to either side, of Cape Point far to the south, and of the blue-hazed Hottentots-Holland range of mountains to the east.

Very often, though, the heights are hidden from view. The clouds that billow across its rim to tumble down the massively precipitous northern face are known as the 'tablecloth', and are the product of the south-easter. The wind, which can reach speeds of over 100 km/h for sustained periods, collects water as it blows around False Bay, collides with the mountain barrier and rises, cooling as it does so, the moisture condensing to form thick cloud over the mountain that then cascades down, dissipating as it reaches the warmer levels of air. It is a continuous and spectacular process, and a source of endless fascination to the watchers in the city below.

The mountain has had many names: the one that endured was given it by the first white man to climb the heights – Antonio da Saldanha, who made the ascent in 1503. The buttresses that guard the range's Atlantic flank were named Gewelbergen (Gable Mountains) by Jan van Riebeeck, but are today known as the Twelve Apostles. Saldanha had to beat his own way to the top; today, there are more than 350 charted paths to the summit, some of them suitable only for experienced climbers.

Those who venture onto the slopes, through the wooded krantzes and over the heavily watered central plateau, can find almost every one of the 2 600 species of indigenous flora known in the Cape Peninsula, including the sparkling silver tree (*Leucadendron argenteum*) and the wild orchid (*Disa uniflora*), commonly known as 'the Pride of Table Mountain'. Among the fauna are baboons, dassies (rock-rabbits), small buck species, civet cat and lynx, porcupine and tortoise, and an exotic species called the Himalayan tahr, descendants of a pair that escaped from Groote Schuur Estate in the 1930s.

Each year over two million people make their way to the summit, where there is a restaurant, a souvenir shop (from which you can mail a letter bearing the Table Mountain postmark) and, along the table-top, some splendid viewing points. Wall plaques describe the short walks that lead from the cable station, and depict the mountain's nature reserve and the flora that graces the slopes during the different seasons.

Most visitors use the cable-way, a comfortable five-minute trip, and a perfectly safe one, too – there hasn't been a serious accident in the more than half a century of sturdy service. The car is in operation throughout the year (subject, of course, to good weather) from eight in the morning to ten at night in summer, eight-thirty to six in winter. Up to a year or so ago visitors had to queue for a place on board, but it's now both possible and preferable to book in advance (telephone 24-5148; the bus from town departs from Adderley Street, outside OK Bazaars.

Fitter and more adventurous souls make the ascent on foot, along one or other of the many established paths. Some of these are undemanding enough, others are strenuous, some (unless you're an experienced climber) downright dangerous. All should be approached with respect: it's only too easy to get lost, which could prove disastrous if the weather turns nasty – as it can and does do on occasion, suddenly and without much warning. Arm yourself with a good map and guide book (available in city bookshops); choose a route that is within your physical capacity; don't stray from the path, and if it's your first trip, arrange to make it in the company of someone who knows the terrain. (These are elementary precautions, but the mountain nevertheless regularly exacts its toll of human life.)

Also worth exploring are the distinctive formations to either side of Table Mountain: Lion's Head on the west (that's to say, on your right as you look up from the city) and Devil's Peak on the east. The former and its attendant ridge, which ends in the 'rump' of Signal Hill, vaguely resembles a lion *couchant*, up whose 669-metre-high head one can climb with the aid, on the more challenging stretches, of chain ladders; there are superb views from the top – of Table Mountain and the city, of the sea and Robben Island, and of the Twelve Apostles to the south. As pleasant, and a lot less arduous, is the drive up to Signal Hill, from where there are also fine views.

Devil's Peak, to your left, is notable for the three small forts the colonial British built on its steep slopes. The ascent to the summit, about 1 000 metres above sea level, should only be attempted by experienced climbers.

THE CENTRAL AREA

Cape Town is one of the few South African cities that can best be explored on foot. The central area, as we've mentioned, is small, and a good deal of what there is to see is within comfortable strolling distance of the city centre. Worth getting hold of is part or all of a series of booklets entitled *Cape Town Historical Walks*, published by the City Council and available, at a token price, from Captour's visitor's bureau.

Just to the north of the city centre, and a good place from which to start, is the area known as:

The Foreshore Not too long ago the 145-hectare expanse of level ground between city and dockland lay beneath the waters of Table Bay, making an appearance comparatively recently – during construction of the Duncan Dock in the 1930s and 1940s. The huge quantities of sand dredged up were dumped on the landward side of the harbour, creating a brand new expanse of real estate which now supports some of Cape Town's grander buildings, including the Civic Centre and the splendid Nico Malan theatre complex next door.

Slicing through the Foreshore is the Heerengracht ('gentleman's canal'), a broad, rather stately thoroughfare with a central island strip graced by lawns and palms, fountains, ornamental pools and statuary. Among the latter are the war memorial and monuments to Jan van Riebeeck (the work of Scottish sculptor John Tweed; it was presented to the city, in 1899, by Cecil Rhodes) and of his wife Maria de la Queillerie. Fountain and statues mark the old Roggebaai bayshore.

Some way to the east of the Heerengracht, and on an even earlier coastline, is the country's oldest occupied building – the impressively massive pentagonal fortress known as:

The Castle of Good Hope Built as a replacement for Van Riebeeck's original and highly unsatisfactory earthwork-and-timber fort, the Castle was completed in 1676, its ramparts and five bastions guarding a single large courtyard designed to give the citizens of Cape Town refuge from attack (in the event, none ever came). Later, the courtyard was divided in two by a defensive crosswall, or 'Kat', which in due course was used to support the 'Kat balcony', an elegantly balustraded feature fronting the spacious reception room. The latter was to become the centrepiece of the Cape governor's official residence and focal point of the town's aristocratic social life. Of note, too, is the Castle's entrance, its carved coats of arms (those of the six chamber cities of the Dutch East India Company, the VOC monogram and the crest of the Netherlands) and its belltower. The bell, also the country's oldest, is still rung on occasion.

The Castle, part of which serves as military headquarters, now functions also as a museum and tourist showpiece. On view inside are the principal paintings from the noted William Fehr collection and fine displays of furniture, carpets, porcelain and *objets d'art*; under way is a reconstruction of the original moat and bridge and of an early house. A military, and a 'restoration museum' (artefacts found during building operations) are also planned.

Adderley Street, a southward extension of the Heerengracht (see page 9) and Cape Town's principal thoroughfare, was named by a grateful citizenry after the mid-19th century British parliamentarian Charles Bowyer Adderley, who strenuously opposed a Colonial Office proposal to establish an Australian-type convict settlement at the Cape. At its lower end is the futuristic five-star Cape Sun hotel (see page 27) and the Golden Acre, a glittering complex of department stores, speciality shops, restaurants, coffee houses, cinemas and offices and part of an even more extensive concourse that runs beneath Adderley and adjoining streets. This is thought to have been the site of the Dutch settlement's first fort, of which nothing now remains. A small reservoir, dating back to the 1660s, was, however, uncovered during excavations for the modern foundations of the centre, and is now attractively displayed behind glass. Among the points linked by the concourse are the Captour and Satour information offices, the railway station, the coach terminal and two large parking garages.

On the left as you walk towards the mountain is the famed flower-market (exquisite blooms at next-to-nothing prices and an atmosphere of raucous good humour) and, farther up, the Groote Kerk, an imposing Dutch Reformed church building consecrated in 1841, though the soaring steeple belongs to its predecessor, completed in 1704. Features of note are the superb pulpit and its pedestal of carved lions (the work of the celebrated sculptor Anton Anreith and the wood-carver Jan Jacob Graaff), the timbered roofing and the old gravestones, some of which serve as paving slabs, others as wall insets.

In Upper Adderley Street is the Cultural History Museum, originally the Dutch East India Company's slave lodge (and brothel), where you'll find an intriguing selection of archaeological relics (Egyptian, Greek, Roman), and displays of furniture, glassware, weaponry, musical instruments, postal items, coins and notes and much more. While you're there, take a look at the pediment on the rear facade: carved by the ubiquitous and impish Anreith, it features a caricature of the Royal coat-of-arms, with the Unicorn showing marked distaste for an old and degenerate British lion.

St George's (Anglican) Cathedral in Wale Street, near its junction with Adderley, has served as a prominent venue for protest against injustice (and has heard some fine sermons by Nobel laureate Desmond Tutu). It's a pleasant, if generally undistinguished, 'new Gothic' edifice, though the stained glass – the rose window, the Lord Mountbatten memorial window and some work by Gabriel Lore of Chartres – has merit. And the choir sing like angels.

West of Adderley Perhaps the most appealing of the city's plazas is Greenmarket Square, a shade-dappled, cobbled, colourful, cheerful area usually filled to overflowing with street-traders' stalls festooned with handcrafts, costume jewellery, clothing, leatherwork, serendipitious bric-a-brac. Hidden among the junk is the occasional bargain.

Two of the square's more graceful buildings are the Metropolitan Methodist Church and the Old Town House, a mid-18th century Cape Baroque structure once used by the Burgher Senate (the early city council) and the Burgher Watch (the first police force); now a gallery housing some fine old Dutch and Flemish masters. The Inn on the Square runs along the western side and one can spend a pleasant hour on its sociable terrace surveying the sunlit throng (see page 32).

Among the more inviting thoroughfares in the general vicinity are:
❐ Church Street, well known for its bookstores and antique market.
❐ St George's Mall, until recently an unremarkable, traffic-congested city street but now attractively brick-paved, reserved for the exclusive use of pedestrians and venue for various open-air events of the festive kind. The excellent St Georges Hotel (see page 45) is at the bottom end; shops and arcades run all the way up either side; kiosks and umbrella-shaded bistros occupy the central pavement area.
❐ Long Street, once the heart of Cape Town, bisects the central area (one-way traffic from north to south). It's now a lot less characterful but lively enough, no-

table for its antique and well-stocked second-hand book shops (Clarke's is renowned) and, especially at the top end, its charmingly filigreed Victorian facades. Among the area's more notable buildings are the Blue Lodge; the Sendinggestig, built in 1804 and eventually to become the mother church of Dutch Reformed missionary activity (it's open to the public from Monday to Friday); Carnival Court and the nearby No. 203; and the Dorp Street and Palm Tree mosques (the latter is the city's only pristine 18th-century house). These mosques bear witness to the prominence of Cape Town's Muslim community, traditionally associated with the area farther to the west and known as:

❒ Bo-Kaap (which translates as 'above-Cape' and is sometimes, quite incorrectly, called the Malay Quarter), a suburb of charmingly picturesque little flat-roofed houses set on the lower slopes of Signal Hill. Many of Cape Town's Muslims are descended from slaves, and from a number of high-born political exiles, brought in from the Indonesian islands and other eastern parts during the 18th century. There was little intermarriage with other groups, and this devout community is still very much integrated, though it hasn't confined itself to the Bo-Kaap area. It maintains its cultural traditions (including the trance-like Khalifa, or sword dance, though some religious leaders now disapprove of the ritual) and its members regularly make their pilgrimages, not only to Mecca but to the local kramats – the tombs of holy men. The oldest and most important of these shrines is that of Sheik Yusuf (near Faure, 39 kilometres to the south-east of Cape Town), one of five such places on or near the Peninsula (there's one on Robben Island) which, together, form a 'holy circle'.

The Bo-Kaap museum, a house in Wale Street (No. 71), furnished to depict the lifestyle of a typical 19th century Cape Islamic family, is worth a visit. Running along the northern (seaward) side of Bo-Kaap is:

❒ Strand Street, once one of the city's most elegant thoroughfares but now rather nondescript. It does, though, have its points of interest, among them the Lutheran Church with its splendid pulpit and, next door, Martin Melck House, the early parsonage, now quite beautifully restored. Its secluded walled garden is a joy. Just down the road, on the opposite side, is Koopmans-De Wet House, a classic example of late-18th century Cape domestic architecture. Originally built it 1701, it was enlarged several times in subsequent decades, eventually incorporating a facade designed by the celebrated French architect Louis Thibault. Later still it became the home of Marie Koopmans-De Wet (1838-1906), a noted patron of the arts, philanthropist, socialite and passionate Afrikaner nationalist. It's now a national monument housing an exquisite collection of Cape and European furniture, ceramics (Delft) and *objets d'art*.

THE GARDENS

Cape Town's oldest residential area, and site of the vegetable patch planted by Van Riebeeck's settler party in 1652, lies just to the north of the city centre. The origi-

CAPE TOWN: CITY AND SUBURBS

nal and exclusively functional garden has, of course, changed beyond recognition: it is now a lovely six-hectare expanse of manicured lawn, colourful flowerbeds and stately trees – in fact, fully 8 000 species of flower, shrub, tree and other plant, most of them exotic, can be seen here. The large conservatory at its upper (mountain) end is known for its splendid palms and orchids; nearby is the bell that controlled the working day's of the 300 slaves who once cared for the grounds, and an attractive aviary and tea garden (the food and service are a bit too casual, but the setting is exquisite). To stroll along oak-shaded Government Avenue, the main throughway, is a delight indeed; prominent here are the endearingly tame grey squirrels, descendants of animals introduced from America by Cecil Rhodes.

The garden, a full 18 hectares at one time, was progressively reduced in extent over the decades with the encroachment of a number of handsome buildings.

On the east side are the Houses of Parliament, built in 1884 and enlarged several times since, most notably in the 1980s to accommodate the controversial three-chamber constitutional system. Of interest are the parliamentary library (200 000 books, including the fine 50 000-volume Mendelssohn collection of Africana) and the museum, whose Gallery Hall houses works of art and relics of the Cape and Union parliaments. Next door is Tuynhuys, an attractive Colonial Regency-style house that serves as the state president's town residence, behind which is Stal Plein, an open space containing an impressive equestrian statue of General Louis Botha (the Union of South Africa's first premier). Here, too, you'll find the Anton Anreith gateway to the Lodge de Goede Hoop (the country's first Masonic lodge) and the Flame of Remembrance.

Just off Government Avenue is the South African National Gallery, which holds some 6 500 works, including many by 19th and 20th century South African artists and a number of fine gift collections. An especially eye-catching feature is the nearby statue of General Jan Smuts, an unusual, and powerful, representation by the British sculptor Sydney Harpley. Farther along Government Avenue are the Great and Old Synagogues, the former an impressively domed and twin-towered building, the latter housing the historical and ceremonial treasures of the Jewish Museum.

The garden's northern perimeter is distinguished by the classical facade of the South African Library, one of the world's first free libraries and repository of a massive collection of Africana and reference works. The building houses the noted Grey Collection, among whose prized items are medieval manuscripts and valuable early printed books (including a first folio Shakespeare, a 15th century copy of Dante's *Divine Comedy*, and a 10th century manuscript copy of the four Gospels – the oldest book in South Africa).

On the western side, bounded by Victoria Street, is the South African Museum, which features excellent displays of natural history, geology, ethnology, archaeology and printing. Of special interest are the plaster casts of San (Bushmen) people, the San rock-art exhibits, and dioramas of the fossil-rich Karoo and the reptiles that lived there 200 000 years ago. Next door, and part of the museum complex, is the Planetarium, venue for fascinating shows featuring terrestrial landscapes as well as celestial subjects. The projectors are able to reproduce the night over Cape Town at any stage during a 26 000-year period (13 000 years either side of the present).

THE NEW WATERFRONT
At one time the Victoria and Alfred basins, the oldest parts of the present harbour, were very much part of Capetonian daily life but, with land reclamation (see page 9), motorway construction and the declining volume of maritime traffic, the links were broken. The charming old pier, the leisure beach and the seafront palms disappeared, to be replaced by a wasteland of functional buildings, fences, a tank-farm and a raised highway that stands as a monument to poor planning and worse taste.

But city and sea are being brought together again, joined in happy reunion by the imaginative and highly ambitious Victoria and Alfred Waterfront (VAW) scheme, a multi-million rand venture that draws its inspiration from highly successful harbour redevelopment schemes in San Francisco, Vancouver, Sydney and elsewhere.

The more interesting and colourful of the old buildings are being converted, and a lot of new ones built, to serve as hotels, restaurants, cinemas, theatres, nightspots, markets, speciality stores,

recreation and entertainment centres. Focal point will be the Pier Head complex of 80 or more shops, eleven cinemas, sixteen restaurants, a wine centre, a flea- and a fish-and-produce market, and parking for 2 500 cars. Other planned features include a new jetty, a yacht basin, an upmarket marina, open quaysides, promenades, public squares, a walkway and perhaps also a waterway to the city, a steam railway station for special excursions and a world-class oceanarium.

In short, the waterfront will become a tourist mecca – but not exclusively so: it will also function as a lived-in, worked-in area. Fishing boats will still use the basin; houses and offices are to be built. The UCT Graduate School of Business will take over the old Breakwater Prison site. The prison's facade and courtyard will be retained; for the rest, the R30-million complex will have a 302-bedroom residential section, seven lecture theatres, fifty seminar rooms, a high-tech library and computer centre, restaurant, cafeteria and bar.

Much of this is still in the future – the entire scheme will involve an investment of some R3 000 million and take ten years to complete – but things are happening quickly down at the docks. The process started in 1990, modestly enough, with a three-star hotel (the old North Quay warehouse with a new personality: see page 47); the Bertie's Landing tavern and restaurant, and the commissioning of the maritime museum and its 4 000 square metres of display area. Two of the museum's historic ships can be seen in the Alfred basin; the Dock Road Theatre, jazz club, Mitchell's Brewery and a number of restaurants and pubs are now flourishing. For sightseers, there's the Waterfront historical walk, the Penny Ferry, and excursions laid on by Court Helicopters, Waterfront Charters, Le Tigre Charters and Sealink. For the most up-to-date information, call in at the Captour visitors' centre or telephone 418-2369.

THE RIVIERA
Cape Town's 'Riviera' extends along the Peninsula's western seaboard from Green Point south to Clifton and Camps Bay – an eight-kilometre stretch of coastline characterized by rocky indentations, beautiful expanses of white sand and by charming little coves around which cluster some of the city's most fashionable residential areas. Behind them, looming over suburb and sea, are the imposing, often cloud-wreathed heights of Lion's Head and the first of the Twelve Apostles, extensions of the Table Mountain massif.

This is a prime holiday area, popular among leisure-bent Capetonians as well as out-of-town vacationers. The Atlantic waters here are cold – too cold, really, for comfortable bathing, but the backing mountains provide shelter from the prevailing south-easterly winds and sun-worshippers are drawn in their thousands to this section of the coast. It's the nearest Cape Town has to the traditional seaside 'playground' (though generally speaking it remains surprisingly uncommercial, despite its potential to rival, say, Durban's Golden Mile).

Green Point itself is a quiet enough place, a residential suburb of apartment blocks rising above scatters of Victorian and Edwardian houses; it's notable principally for its historic lighthouse (the oldest in the country: it dates from 1824), for its golf course and its fine athletics stadium. The Cape Medical Museum (at New Somerset Hospital) and the Fort Wynyard Naval Museum (in Fort Wynyard Road, just off Portsmouth Road) are worth a visit.

Close by is Sea Point, a vibrant, cosmopolitan, densely populated suburb of luxurious apartment- and time-share blocks, hotels, delis, discos, a 'culinary mile' of restaurants, round-the-clock nightlife and an elegant, palm-fringed beachfront. In fact the shoreline here is ruggedly rocky; there's very little in the way of actual beach, but a splendid open-air pool, the largest seawater one in the southern hemisphere, beckons the swimmer. Sea Point's sociable promenade is much favoured by evening strollers. At the far (southern) end of Beach Road is the President Hotel, one of the country's most attractive (see page 42): drinks on the hotel terrace, which overlooks the ocean, can fill a very pleasant hour.

Nine kilometres out to sea and clearly visible from Beach Road is Robben Island ('robben', a Dutch word, means 'seals'), used by the very early settlers as a source of building slate and as a natural cattle-enclosure – though the latter enterprise proved unsuccessful: four pairs of rabbits, introduced at about the same time, bred prolifically and their huge progeny destroyed the vegetation. In 1658 Jan van Riebeeck consigned convicts to the island; later, lunatics, lepers and various political 'undesirables' were incarcerated there. In recent times it has been used as a maximum-security 'political' prison, its most famous inmate being Nelson Mandela. But by 1991 the cells had been emptied, and there was lively debate about the island's future – the suggestions ranged from the tactless (a resort-casino complex) to the eminently sensible, and Robben Island is likely to be developed as a nature reserve, museum and dignified memorial.

Along the coast from Sea Point is Clifton, renowned for its magnificent beaches (four of them) and, a kilometre or so farther on, Camps Bay. Both places have sturdily resisted commercial over-exploitation, attracting the quieter, wealthier kind of resident, and some quite stunning houses have been built into the cliffs on both sides of the coast road. Camps Bay has a large tidal pool, a pleasant beach, some nice shops, the new and imaginatively conceived hotel called The Bay (see page 23), and the excellent Blues restaurant next door. Kloof Road, which leads up the mountainside, will take you to The Round House, an early 19th century shooting lodge that has, in recent years, served excellent meals, and The Glen, a picnic area with fine views of the bay and the sea beyond.

THE SOUTHERN SUBURBS

The line of rail runs from the city's central railway station at the bottom end of Adderley Street eastwards and then loops south, around the lower slopes of Table Mountain through suburbs that – some of them – started life in the first decades of Dutch settlement as rural outposts. Rondebosch was the site of the colony's first wheat-growing experiment, launched in 1656 near a distinctively circular grove of trees (the area was known as *'t Ronde Doorn Bosjen* at the time). Newlands, next door, functioned as a logging camp and farm before the turn of the 17th century; becoming a sought-after residential retreat among wealthier Capetonians after Simon van der Stel built a country house there in 1700. Wynberg, farther along the line, was founded in the later 1600s as the vineyard-graced farm Oude Wijnberg.

The nearest of these suburbs is Zonnebloem, a largely deserted, grass-covered area better known by the colloquial and historic name of:

District Six Until 1966, a vibrant haven to some 55 000 'coloured' people, District Six became the focus of national and international attention when the government declared it to be a 'white' area under the apartheid laws and began moving its residents to Mitchell's Plain, some 30 km away, and to other townships on the desolate Cape Flats. The suburb was demolished; only the places of worship – one or two churches and mosques – escaped the bulldozers. It was argued, by officialdom, that the removals were part of a slum-clearance programme, and indeed the place was overcrowded, unsanitary and crime-ridden, but it was also described at the time as 'the soul of Cape Town'. It had vitality, colour, charm and, above all, a powerful sense of community.

District Six is prime residential real estate, yet the developers did not move in. For over two decades it remained, for the most part, a wasteland, mute reminder of a tragic exercise in what the apologists of apartheid called 'social engineering'. Its future has recently been the subject of a great deal of debate, but pretty well everyone agrees that the land must be returned to, and be developed by, the original community – the people who once lived there.

Observatory, some way down the track, was the site selected in 1821 – by the Cape Astronomer Royal, the Rev. Fearon Fallows – for the Royal Observatory, now the South African National Observatory. Fallows' choice was roundly condemned by his successors because the hillock on which the building stood was infested with snakes, hippos wallowed in the marshes of the nearby Liesbeeck River and leopards were frequent visitors to the garden. The area is now fully developed, of course, and densely populated.

The observatory sets South African standard time, and also sends the electrical impulse that fires the noonday gun on Signal Hill. Of broader import is its function as headquarters of a network of installations that include the advanced complex established near Sutherland in the clear-skied Karoo. The national observatory works within a wide field of research (and has chalked up an impressive number of astronomical firsts), but of special interest to its scientists are the so-called variable stars, whose nature helps determine the distance of the Magellanic Clouds. The calculation of this distance, an enormously complicated exercise, will help establish the size, and therefore the age, of the universe itself.

The Astronomical Society of Southern Africa conducts tours of the observatory on the second Saturday of each month (telephone 47-0025).

Rhodes's legacy The noted Groote Schuur Estate, bequeathed to the nation by diamond magnate, politician and empire-builder Cecil Rhodes on his death in 1902, sprawls across the mountainside beneath Devil's Peak, straddling parts of the suburbs of Observatory, Mowbray, Rosebank and Rondebosch. Of its several components, the mansion – also named Groote Schuur ('Great Barn') – is the most historic: it was originally a 17th century granary, later converted into a house, which burned down and was then reconstructed for Rhodes by his friend and 'personal architect' Herbert Baker. Originally intended to serve as the prime minister's residence, it's now occupied by the state president. The architectural style is grand yet simple; the interior is distinguished by exquisite tapestries and by a fine collection of old English and Cape silver.

Nearby is Westbrooke, an elegant country house built in Edwardian times and today used as a state guest house, and The Woolsack, which once did duty as Rudyard Kipling's summer home but is now part of the campus of the University of Cape Town.

The attractively ivy-covered buildings of the university, together with its medical school – the students are trained at Groote Schuur hospital where, in 1967, Professor Chris Barnard's cardiac team performed the world's first human heart transplant operation – are also part of the estate. Higher up the mountainside stands the Rhodes memorial, a grandly Imperialistic 'temple' built in neo-Classical style and incorporating two impressive pieces of statuary: G.F. Watts's 'Physical Energy' and a bust of Rhodes, beneath which is inscribed part of Kipling's moving tribute to a man who, whatever his faults – and they were many – was undeniably a powerful force in the shaping of the subcontinent during the latter part of the 19th century.

Other prominent elements of the Groote Schuur property include the paddocks, where antelope and a number of exotic species graze (among them Chinese deer and Himalayan mountain goats); Mostert's Mill (on De Waal Drive, the main throughway), a traditional Dutch windmill and one of Cape Town's best-known landmarks, and the Baxter Theatre complex, an integral part of the university (see page 19).

Newlands One of the larger and more fashionable of the southern suburbs, Newlands, 6 km from the city centre, is noted, among other things, for its exceptionally high rainfall (over 1 500 mm a year), for its leafy avenues, for the lovely house that once belonged to socialite, social commentator and letter-writer Lady Anne Barnard and which is now the Vineyard Hotel (see page 48), and for its famed rugby and cricket grounds, venues for provincial and (in normal years) international matches.

At the entrance to the rugby stadium is the Josephine Mill, built in 1822, named after the Queen of Sweden and powered by the waters of the Liesbeeck River. The building and its huge waterwheel have been carefully restored; the latter is in good working condition; visitors are entertained by milling and blacksmithing demonstrations. The mill's first floor serves as the Newlands Rugby Museum, largest of its kind in the world: it houses exhibits and mementos dating back to 1891, when South Africa first entered the international rugby arena.

The main road from the university through Newlands – starting as De Waal Drive it changes in succession to Rhodes Drive and Union Avenue – is a scenic delight: there are graceful trees everywhere along the route and on the hillsides that rise grandly above, and the verges and centre islands support a profusion of flowering plants. To your right, driving away from the city, is the deep-green magic of Newlands forest, a popular place among picnickers, walkers and joggers.

If you turn right at the intersection of Rhodes and Union and follow the road for a kilometres or so, you'll see the entrance to:

Kirstenbosch, one of the most respected of botanical gardens, world-renowned for its beauty.

Kirstenbosch was founded in 1913 to preserve and propagate South Africa's magnificent floral heritage, and today serves as the headquarters of the National Botanical Gardens network. Here, on a 528-hectare expanse of well-watered land (yet another of Rhodes's bequests), some 9 000 of the country's 18 500 species of indigenous flowering plant are cultivated, among them the proteas and ericas of the Cape Floral Kingdom's unique fynbos vegetation; pelargoniums (the stock from which geraniums have been bred); disas and bulbs; mesembryanthemums (or 'vygies'); succulents, ferns and primeval cycads.

The displays are largely confined to some 40 hectares of intensively cultivated ground, in a series of informal gardens graced by natural features, rockeries and terraces. Part of Jan van Riebeeck's hedge of wild almond, planted in 1660 to enclose the early settlement's cattle, can still be seen on the estate. Of modest historical interest, too, is the charming little sunken pool, lined with Batavian brick and shaped like a bird, that is known as Lady Anne Barnard's bath (though incorrectly so: it was built by a Colonel Christopher Bird, some time in the 19th century). In an ampitheatre on the slopes above are the cycad plantings, one of the first collections to be developed; nearby is the Compton Herbarium, repository for about 250 000 plant specimens.

Kirstenbosch is a place for all seasons, though it's probably at its best during the months of September and October, when the spring annuals and many of the proteas are in glorious bloom. For visitors, there are inviting walks along the many pathways, guided tours, an information office, a shop that sells seeds and souvenirs, and a tea-room.

CITY AMENITIES

Until recently Cape Town has, in tourist terms, functioned largely as a one-season destination, packed with upcountry holidaymakers during December and early January and relatively quiet for the rest of the year. The pattern, though, is changing – the charms of the Peninsula in winter (the 'green season') and in the mellow months of autumn are becoming more widely known, the cruise ships are returning, the city is gaining a reputation as a leading conference centre, and a growing number of international travellers are including the place on their itineraries. In short, the local tourist industry is entering a new, more demanding, more cosmopolitan era – and, by and large, it is well equipped to meet the challenge.

Theatre and music The city's principal performing arts venue is the splendid Nico Malan theatre complex on the Foreshore, next to the Civic Centre. Opera and drama, oratorio and ballet and a sprinkling of lighter fare – operetta and modern musicals – are staged in the three auditoriums: the opera house (1 200 seats), the main theatre (550 seats) and the Arena theatre (120 seats). Most of the shows are presented by the Cape Performing Arts Board (Capab), which has a resident orchestra. There's an excellent restaurant on the premises (Blakes, which offers cabaret as well as good food); undercover parking is available to patrons; bookings through Computicket.

Some way out of town, in the southern suburb of Rosebank, is the Baxter Theatre, part of the University of Cape Town and a lively venue for mainly popular, sometimes local drama, for music and for film festivals. The complex comprises a 657-seat theatre, a 100-seat studio/workshop and a 640-seat concert hall; lunchtime concerts, performed each Wednesday during term-time by the university's music students, is a feature, and there's a restaurant and bar *in situ*. Productions of the more experimental kind feature at the Little Theatre and the Arena, both of which are on the UCT's Hiddingh Hall campus in Orange Street, Gardens. Among Cape Town's other, smaller theatres are the Herschel in Claremont, the Masque in Muizenberg (excellent amateur shows) and, most notably, the privately run and very enterprising Theatre on the Bay at Camps Bay, which has a 400-seat auditorium and a nice pub. Maynardville, in Wynberg, is a charming open-air venue for the annual (early autumn) Capab production of Shakespeare.

The Cape Town Symphony Orchestra (CTSO) gives regular performances (on Thursdays and Sundays) at the City Hall; the programmes are varied to cater for most tastes in classical and light-classical music. The CTSO, once a municipal enterprise, is now privately funded.

For lovers of jazz, rock, reggae, gothic, independent, dance and other types of popular music there's The Base in Shortmarket Street, the Fire Escape in Buitengracht Street, the Cat Club and Idols in Loop Street, Tattlers in Sea Point and Abigail's in Rondebosch. Other nightspots and some restaurants feature cabaret and dinner-dancing; discos abound. One cannot be more specific here about the local live-music scene: it's constantly changing, and those who want to keep up are advised to consult the advertisement and entertainment sections of the daily press.

Wining and dining The City and Peninsula have a great deal to offer the lover of fine food and ambient atmosphere – far too much, really, for the subject to be adequately summarised in these few pages. The range extends through the entire culinary spectrum from unpretentious, value-for-money steak-houses through unique little eateries offering ethnic specialities, to the local aristocrats of *haute cuisine*.

Among the latter are some half-dozen that carry the blazon of the Confrèrie de la Chaîne des Rôtisseurs (the international society of gourmets), including Champers (Deer Park Drive, city), Tastevin (Cape Sun Hotel, city), Top of the Ritz (Ritz Protea, Sea Point), Rosenfontein (Observatory), Truffles (Heathfield) and The Vineyard (Vineyard Hotel, Newlands). Other restaurants with comparable credentials are the Buitenverwachting wine estate in Constantia, Floris Smit Huijs in the city, Leinster Hall in Oranjezicht, The Bay in Camps Bay and the nearby Blues restaurant.

These represent a small sample of what's on offer: there simply isn't the space here to cover the ground properly. However, there are some informatively opinionated volumes on the bookstore shelves, including Peter Devereux's excellent *Good Food Guide*. Captour produces an annual *Restaurant Guide*.

City and suburbs are unusually well served by English-style pubs, and by beer-cellars with a vaguely Bavarian feel – sociable places that serve good, solid lunches of pies and ploughman's platters, oxtail, linefish and chips at very reasonable prices. Among the more inviting are the Crow Bar, the Fireman's Arms and the Wine Barrel, all on the northern edge of city centre; the Perseverance Tavern in Buitenkant Street, the Stag's Head in Roeland Street, Seagulls in Green Point, Forries (the Forester's Arms) in Newlands, and a growing cluster of watering holes in and around the new dockside development (see page 14), including the Ferryman's, Bertie's Landing, Quay Four and the recently renovated Pump House.

However, there are scores of other drinking venues to choose from, each with its own character and devoted clientele. Visitors with a healthy thirst and time to explore the possibilities would do well to invest in a copy of Mike Shay's *The Good Pub Guide of the South West Cape*: it covers around 170 establishments of one kind and another.

Shopping around The city's main retail area is the huge Golden Acre and Strand Concourse network around and beneath Adderley and Strand streets (it's apparently the largest underground shopping centre in the southern hemisphere); St Georges pedestrian mall, which runs parallel to Adderley (Stuttaford's Town Square is a must); the Old Mutual Centre in nearby Exchange Place and, on the city's southern perimeter, the modern Gardens centre complex.

Some of the best bargains within the standard range of retail goods, though, are to be found farther out, in the so-called northern suburbs – at Pick 'n Pay's Hypermarket in Brackenfell and the OK Hyperama in Parow, massive emporiums that take multi-stocking, bulk-buying and price-paring to their extremes. Alternatively, go straight to the manufacturers (*Pam Black's A-Z of Factory Shops*, available from leading bookshops, is a useful guide).

Speciality shopping: three of the bigger concentrations are the Golden Acre complex, Claremont's upmarket Cavendish Square and adjacent Link network (about 150 specialized stores together with restaurants and bistros, exhibition, demonstration and concert venues) and the all-purpose Tyger Valley centre in the northern suburbs.

Antiques: plenty of outlets are scattered around the city and suburbs; Long and Church streets are especially well endowed.

Arts, crafts and curios: again, a very wide choice. Among the more centrally situated shops are Kottler's (Adderley Street and at the Mount Nelson Hotel), the Sun Art Gallery (Cape Sun Hotel), Images of Africa (Shortmarket Street), the African Market (Pearly House, Heerengracht), the Cape Gallery (Strand Street) and the Sheep Shop, a worthwhile job-creation project on Somerset Road, on the way to Green Point.

Again, these are just a few out of many, and browsers with the time and inclination to do the rounds properly are invited to follow the recently established Arts and Crafts Route of the Peninsula and Winelands. There is also an Antiques Route. Maps of and information about both are available from Captour.

Open-air markets are an increasingly visible feature of the Cape Town shopping scene. Permanent venues include Greenmarket Square, the railway station in lower Adderley Street, and the Grand Parade; the first two offer a lot of junky bric-a-brac, some good buys and very occasional bargains; the third tends towards clothing and textiles.

Intermittent markets are held at a number of other venues, mostly over weekends and public holidays, some of them under the auspices of the Cape Crafters' Association. Biggest of the dozen or so are those at Green Point, outside the stadium (all-purpose); the Medieval Craft Fair at Constantia; the sprawl of handcrafted wares at the Old Alphen winery, also in Constantia, and the craft market at Wynberg. In 1991 the Victoria and Alfred Waterfront began hosting a Sunday Fair at the Dock Road venue and the Explorers' Market in a large warehouse. The former, modelled on the highly successful London Sunday fairs, features antiques and specialized collectables, the latter a high proportion of imported (and often chic and unusual) crafts and manufactured goods.

❐ WHERE TO STAY

AMBASSADOR BY THE SEA
Bantry Bay

This seafront hotel is superbly positioned: its top floor is at street level, the five other cliff-face floors descend to the rocks and foaming brine of the ocean far below. Looking out from the thigh-high open windows of the dining room and cocktail lounge isn't for vertigo sufferers; for others, the vista and the sensation – the salty, slightly fishy, wonderfully evocative scent of the sea that drifts in – are memorable. In fact all the rooms, public and private, have spectacular views.

A good, all-round, value-for-money establishment set in an unusually well-sheltered part of this often windy coast. The hotel restaurant is known for its splendid seafood. Bantry Bay is a small, affluent, rather exclusive and very attractive ocean suburb that lies between crowded and cosmopolitan Sea Point on the one side and the fashionable beaches of Clifton on the other.

Accommodation There are 69 double rooms and semi-suites in the main hotel and seven apartments in the buildings on the other side. Guests who are staying more than a week tend to go for the apartments. Not all the rooms are sea facing, but it's certainly worth the extra cash to get one: the view is as dramatic as that from the public rooms above, perhaps even more so since you're that much closer to the sometimes turbulent and always watchable waters of the Atlantic.

The rooms are of standard quality, comfortable, well appointed, done out in modern style in soft blends of green, peach, pink and mauve. Each is equipped with coffee machine, TV (with M-Net and video channel), and each has its private bathroom.

The apartments are two- and three-bedroomed; self-catering, equipped with high-tech appliances and utensils. All are sea facing, with sliding doors leading onto balconies.

Food, Drink and Service Waves restaurant has a fine seafood menu that features 'sole flown in from Mossel Bay, mussels from the West Coast, crayfish plucked from the cold Benguela current, fresh oysters from Knysna'. We were persuaded to sample three new creations: sole Mata Hari (very skilfully filleted, and stuffed with avocado and smoked salmon); roast fillet of beef Varenne (with a blue cheese and basic cream sauce) and profiteroles *aux Cassis* (filled with cream, Cassis liqueur and nuts). In a word; delicious.

The On the Rocks ladies' bar offers live music and is usually crowded at cocktail hour with after-workers and holidaymakers who enjoy watching the sun set over the sea.

Service: the Ambassador prides itself on being 'big enough to meet all your needs, and small enough to make it matter'; service is brisk and efficient.

Amenities The freshwater pool and its pool deck are pleasantly sociable venues. Bantry Bay is within easy strolling distance of Sea Point and its kaleidoscope variety of restaurants and shops.

Conferences: The conference and banqueting room (secretarial and travel assistance available) can accommodate groups of 60 to 70 people. The hotel has ample parking – an otherwise scarce commodity in the Bantry Bay area.

AMBASSADOR in brief
*How to get there: The hotel is on Victoria Road, the main seafront route, in Bantry Bay. Tariff (See Authors' Note on page 4): F **Official rating**: ★★★ Conference facilities: Available for up to 70 delegates. **Liquor licence**: Full. **Children**: Welcome. **Reservations**: PO Box 83, Sea Point, 8060, Cape; telephone: (021) 439-6170; fax: (021) 439-6336; telex: 5-20721.*

THE BAY HOTEL

Camps Bay

An idyllic hotel in an idyllic setting. The architects decreed: 'Let there be light', and there was light – everywhere, reflected off the whiteness of the walls, streaming in the wide windows. Across the road, the pale sand of the Camps Bay beach, fringed with palm trees, and the sea; a balmy backdrop, vivid clarity. On a sunny, windless day it's perfection – five stars and then some.

The luxurious décor, with splashes of peach, pink and turquoise, reminded us of the pale blue of a shallow sea in sunlight and the delicate pink inside of a conch shell. The effect is stunning – pristine, wide white-walled foyer and corridors, marble-tiled floors, high ceilings, large windows and an artful mixture of modern architecture, modular furniture and Victorian wicker armchairs, sofas and tables. Flawless.

The Bay is a relatively new hotel – it opened its hospitable doors in 1990 – but it has already earned the highest of competitive honours and a reputation second to none.

Accommodation 70 units, all with *en suite* bathrooms, ranging from 'Classic', 'Luxury' and 'Premier' rooms through suites to a super-luxurious penthouse. All have imposing views, either of the beach and blue waters of the Atlantic shores, Table Mountain or the craggy, towering Twelve Apostles that loom over Camps Bay. All rooms are split level: 'Classic' units have the bedroom suite above a small lounge area, beyond which are sliding doors leading into a

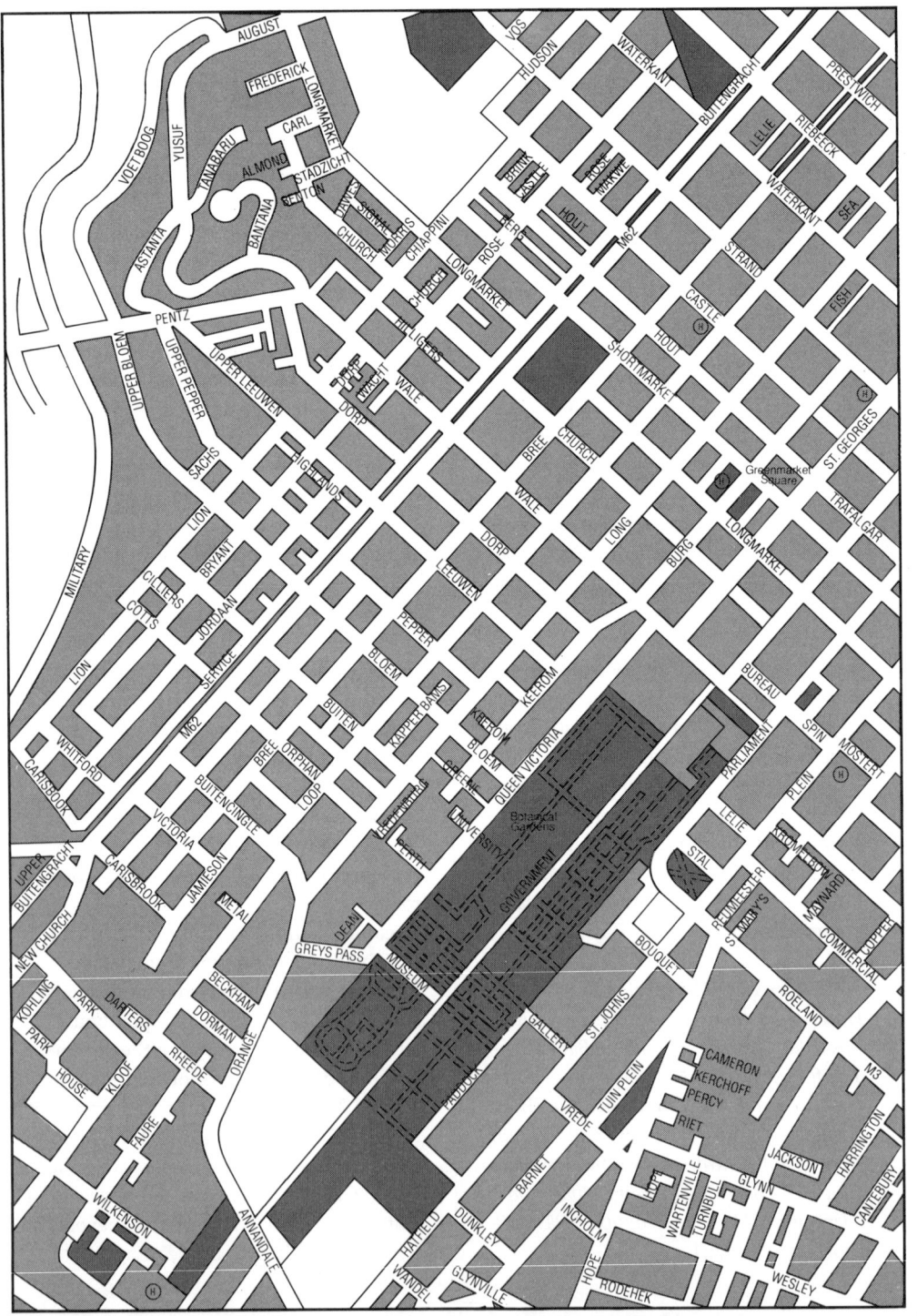

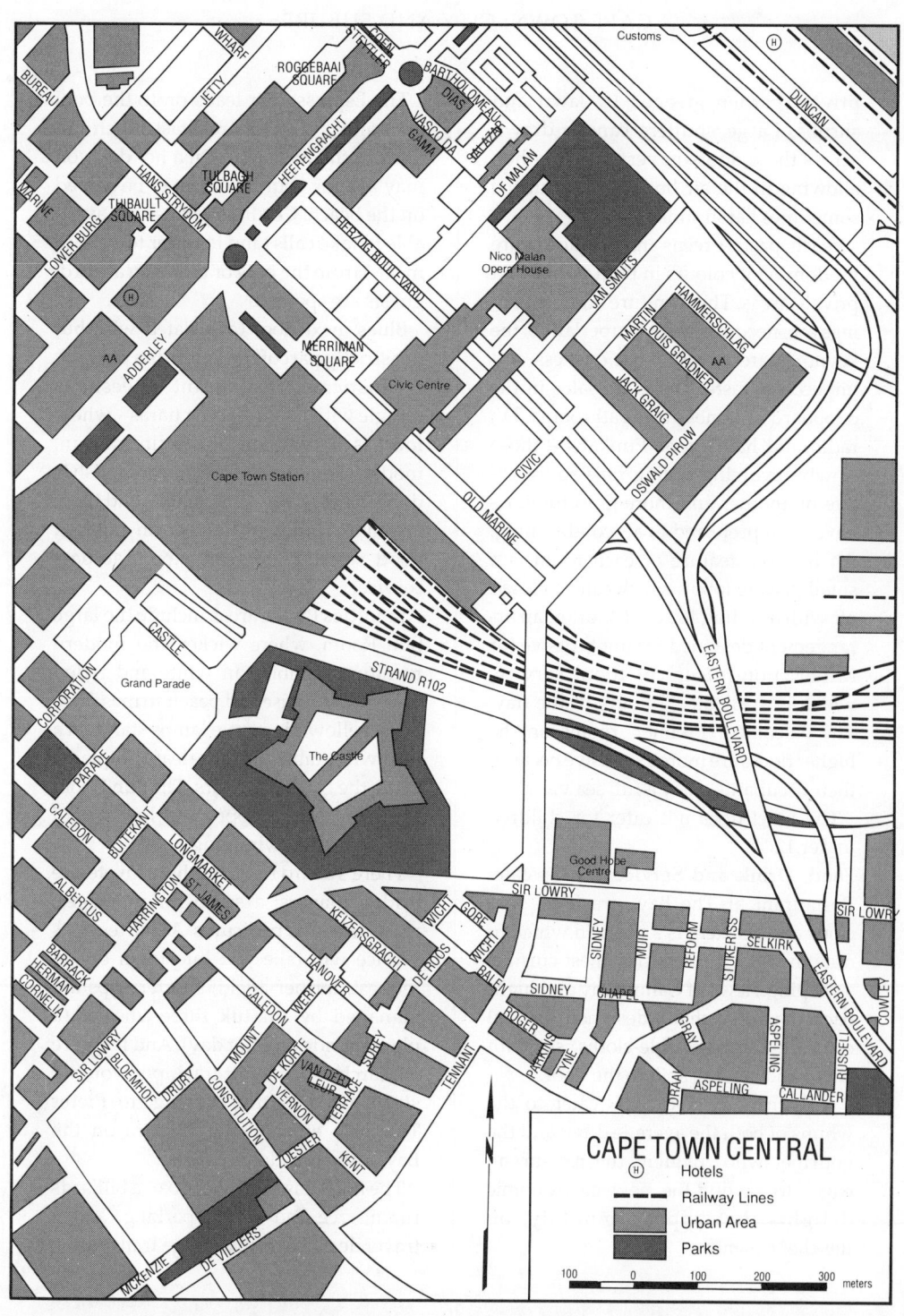

private garden greened by lawn and shrubs. Large shutters can be drawn across these doors in very hot weather, allowing in the air but keeping out the sometimes harsh sunlight.

Peach, pastel greens and turquoises are predominant colours in both public and private areas. The furniture and furnishings are, needless to say, superlative; the keynotes are luxury, spaciousness and impeccable taste. There are safes in the cupboards, phones in the bathrooms, TV, radio and hairdryers. Punkahs – those slowly-revolving ceiling fans so evocative of another and more graceful era – have been preferred to air conditioning. An unusual feature of each room is a small private lobby which can be closed off with a sliding louvred shutter: an arrangement designed for unobtrusive (or rather, non-intrusive) room service, which is available 24-hours of the day. The balconied 'Premier' rooms on the higher floors are more expensive because their occupants enjoy a full sea view.

The hotel does not cater for children under 12.

Food, Drink and Service The upstairs Restaurant at The Bay, gracious, spacious and relaxed, is a place in which to dine in style: it offers the finest cuisine, sweeping views of Camps Bay and high-backed wicker chairs designed for real comfort. Damask table-cloths, set with silver and crystal, spill to the floor.

A team of twelve chefs cater to the whims of both the average diner and the gourmet who frequent the restaurant, eager to savour the new gastronomic delights that appear, monthly, on the chef's menu.

The Espresso Bar leads on to the pool area, and is open for breakfast, lunch and late afternoon snacks. On a hot day you may ask for your breakfast to be served on the beach. Cordless phones are available to take calls (and to order towels, or meals) from the pool or beach. In a word, guests are spoiled.

Blues, next door (associated with but not strictly part of the hotel), is a casually sophisticated restaurant – teeshirts mingle with theatre-going tiaras – where food is a pastiche of Mediterranean, modern American and Cajun; crayfish is done in every way imaginable, and there are many kinds of linefish on offer. A good selection of wines too. Faultless service.

Amenities Public areas include the large Sun Room, where wicker and modern furniture combine in white and faded yellow, turquoise and peach stripes. Two large yellow pineapple lamps stand on a long white table and large leafy potplants bring the garden indoors. The Sun Room leads out to the upper and lower pool decks and the swimming pool.

There's a card room for those inveterate bridge players; a salon for massages, manicures and pedicures. A courtesy bus service will take you into town or, on request, farther afield; shorter trips are managed by tuk-tuk three-wheeler (a pleasant ride on a hot day). And if you're in search of some cultural input, you can stroll, on a balmy evening, to Pieter Toerien's enterprising Theatre on the Bay, just a few doors down.

The hotel has a gift shop, bar, a billiards room, free and ample parking, and a travel desk that will arrange transport.

Conferences and functions are spectacularly staged in the Rotunda, a lavish octagonal Victorian ballroom built in 1904 and restored as part of the hotel, in coral and grey, with a vast domed ceiling. A full 300 can be seated at a banquet with dancing, 350 without. Next door is a small 14-seat boardroom.

The main room of the Rotunda has a stage with an electric screen (the area is used for launches, presentations followed by cocktails, and for balls and weddings).

THE BAY in brief
How to get there: Take Beach Road through Sea Point and follow the coast along Victoria Drive. The hotel is in Camps Bay, set back from the seafront. *Tariff (See Authors' Note on page 4):* F *Official rating:* Grading pending. *Banqueting facilities:* Available for up to 350. *Conference facilities:* A hall for 600 by arrangement with the Theatre on the Bay, or small groups (up to 14). *Liquor licence:* Full. *Children:* Children under 12 cannot be accommodated. *Reservations:* PO Box 32021, Camps Bay 8040, Cape Town; telephone: (021) 438-44 44; fax: (021) 438-4455.

THE CAPE SUN
City Centre

One of Cape Town's newest, tallest and most sophisticated hotels, an imposingly futuristic 32-storey city-centre building from whose summit – and from whose six exterior scenic lifts – there are absolutely stunning views of mountain, city, waterfront, bay and beyond.

Five-star quality in all areas but most especially when it comes to cuisine.

The décor is imaginative, pleasing to the senses in a glittery kind of way: pink marble floors, hugely high and golden-chandeliered ceilings, mirrors and lots of yellowwood and stinkwood in the spacious public areas.

Some of these elements (notably the rare woods) are carried through to the guest rooms.

The Cape Sun is one of the few hotels in the region that provides what the international traveller of the nineties is used to; what he demands, and what he expects to get.

Accommodation A total of 362 units, each with large windows and those wonderful views we've mentioned. Twenty are luxury suites, four of them very luxurious indeed (penthouses comprising four inter-leading rooms, enormous lounge, dining area and kitchen, main bathroom with jacuzzi, guest toilet; elegantly understated decor). The standard rooms are also spacious, nicely furnished and appointed, decorated in combinations of turquoise and cream or orange and cream: each has its own lounge area, private bathroom, fridge, bar, telephone, radio, television and individually controlled air conditioning and heating units.

Food, Drink and Service Three excellent restaurants, aristocrat among which is the Tastevin, which displays the blazon of the Chaîne des Rôtisseurs. Very much for the discerning diner; *haute cuisine* in opulent, dignified surrounds; the seafood is special.

One can also eat, drink and generally relax in the roomily comfortable and visually impressive Palm Court Lounge.

Piano backing complements the stylish surroundings; a Cake Table is offered from 15h00.

The Noon Gun bar is popular for pub lunches. Service: superlative.

Amenities The Health Club on the top floor has a sauna, gym, plunge-pool and, once again, those splendid views.

The Cape Sun is at the corner of St Georges and Strand streets, and is connected to the glitzy warren of under- and above-ground malls that make up the vast Golden Acre complex and its neighbouring concourses (see page 21); speciality shops, banks, travel and tourism agencies, hairdressing salons, cinemas, eateries, all are within pleasant strolling distance.

Tours of Cape Town, the Peninsula, the winelands and surrounding areas may be arranged through the hotel. Parking facilities, and limousine and car valet services, are available.

Conferences: Banqueting and conference facilities cover more than 1 000 square metres of floor space; the eight rooms range from 30 square metres to 583 square metres. Full AV, secretarial and other aids are provided.

CAPE SUN in brief

How to get there: The hotel is in the central city area, at the corner of Strand and St Georges streets. *Tariff* (See Authors' Note on page 4): F **Official rating:** ★★★★ **Conference facilities** Available for up to 750 delegates (see text). **Liquor licence** Full. **Children** Welcome. *Reservations:* PO Box 4532, Cape Town 8000; telephone: (021) 23-8844; fax: (021) 23-8875; telex: 5-22453 SA. Central reservations: toll-free 0-800-117711.

CAPE SWISS HOTEL

Gardens

A modern, very comfortable, three-star establishment of cosmopolitan character: its management is Swiss (and predictably most professional); German, French, Italian and Swiss visitors are prominent on the guest-list. Five languages are spoken among the staff; the overall atmosphere is Continental. The hotel is in the Gardens area of Cape Town, a few minutes away from both the city centre and the popular Table Mountain cableway.

Accommodation. A total of 40 modern, air conditioned, nicely furnished standard *en suite* rooms and four suites, each with TV (with M-Net), telephone, radio alarm clock, tea and coffee machine

Food, Drink and Service The Stübli à la carte restaurant has a reputation for excellent Continental cuisine. Swiss specialities include Geschnetzeltes and Rösti (sliced veal schnitzel flamed with brandy and served in a creamy mushroom sauce with *real* rösti).

Drinks are enjoyed in the cosy, most pleasant Old Cape cocktail bar. Service is prompt and courteous.

Amenities Undercover parking is provided; the hotel is conveniently situated for access to the city, the waterfront, Clifton and, as mentioned, the Table Mountain cableway.

Conferences: facilities are available for groups of up to 100 (cinema seating).

CAPE SWISS in brief

How to get there: The hotel is on the corner of Camp and Kloof streets. Follow the signs to the cableway to Kloof Street. Turn left, the Hotel is opposite Jan van Riebeeck High School, on the southern edge of the city. *Tariff* (See Authors' Note on page 4): C **Official rating**: ★★★ *Conference facilities:* For up to 100 delegates. **Liquor licence:** Full. **Children:** Welcome. **Reservations:** Corner Camp and Kloof streets, Gardens, Cape Town 8001; telephone: (021) 23-8190; fax: (021) 26-1795; telex: 5-2435 SA.

THE CAPETONIAN

The Foreshore

All-round excellence is probably the phrase that best sums up the Capetonian. It's on the Foreshore, overlooking the harbour area – in fact, it has been built on the site of the old Cape Town pier – but within easy strolling distance of the city centre (and of the Nico Malan theatre complex, station, air-bus link, cinemas, the Golden Acre shopping centre and the historic Castle).

This is a large, dignified, four-star hotel that offers its guests the full range of amenities, business-like efficiency, real comfort and the most courteous of service: here (in contrast with too many other, less professional Cape hostelries) the customer really does come first.

Accommodation Generally luxurious; 26 double rooms, 82 twins, 51 suites, 10 penthouses. All are pleasantly appointed and decorated; each has its private bathroom (with hairdryer), air conditioning, TV (with M-net), radio and telephone. 24-hour room service.

Food, Drink and service Top quality à la carte cuisine is enjoyed in the polished-wood, candlelit Galley, a restaurant renowned for its seafood and such special favourites as tomato bredie. The wine list is well chosen. We enjoyed the Bosun's choice, a concoction of fish, mussels and shrimps, all encased in puff pastry. Less formal fare is available in Fiorinos restaurant. The buffet breakfasts are rather special.

Drinks: in the elegant cocktail bar. Service is impeccable throughout.

Amenities In the adjacent Cape Town Health and Racquet Club is a gymnasium, aerobics, sauna and a heated Olympic-size swimming pool. Just down the road is the Royal Cape Yacht club and the local bowling club. Other sports (and recreation generally): the hotel will advise you, and help you arrange your leisure programme.

Conferences are serviced by five rooms, seating from 20 delegates in schoolroom style up to 100 in cinema format. They're fully equipped with PA, video cassette systems and so on.

Children are welcome (baby-sitting services are available), but pets cannot be accommodated. The hotel has two special rooms available for paraplegic guests.

Highly recommended.

CAPETONIAN in brief
How to get there: The hotel is on the Foreshore's Heerengracht thoroughfare, just north of the city centre. **Tariff** (See Authors' Note on page 4): F **Official rating:** ★★★★ *Conference facilities:* Up to 100 delegates. **Liquor licence:** Full. **Children:** Welcome. **Reservations:** Pier Place, Heerengracht, Cape Town 8001; telephone: (021) 21-1150; fax: (021) 25-2215; telex: 5-20000 SA.

THE DE WAAL SUN

Gardens

We stayed here over Christmas and were treated to truly sumptuous fare – traditional turkey, beef, lamb and gammon, Cape Malay specialities. Normally, though, it's more laid-back; elegant in its way, and it provides the kind of comfort and professionalism that one associates with the Southern Sun group. The location is excellent: on the attractive edge of the city and perhaps quieter than the more central establishments. Close by are the lovely Gardens (see page 12); Table Mountain provides a magnificent backdrop. The Gardens shopping centre is just up the road.

Accommodation There are three suites and 127 rooms with well co-ordinated décor: differently patterned fabrics are combined in a matching colour range to very good effect. Each room has a private bathroom, radio, telephone, TV (second channel & video), and air conditioning. Facilities include 24-hour room service, laundry, dry cleaning and valet and baby-sitting services.

Food, drink and service The De Waal is renowned for its Oyster Bar restaurant, an ideal venue for a pub lunch. It features live (and late) entertainment on most evenings.

Traditional Cape fare (and the appropriate décor) can be enjoyed in Ouma's Kitchen (à la carte and carvery).

Drinks: the wine list features some excellent vintages, each evocatively described. The De Waal Sun has two cocktail bars.

Service is prompt and efficient.

Amenities There is ample parking in the area and transport to and from bus and rail terminals, and access for the handicapped. A shady swimming pool *in situ*; squash, tennis and more are nearby. The city centre is within walking distance (a most pleasant stroll through the Gardens).

DE WAAL SUN in brief

How to get there: The hotel is in Mill Street, on the southern perimeter of the city. **Tariff** (See Authors' Note on page 4): F **Official rating:** ★★★★ **Conference facilities:** Two function rooms; facilities for up to 150 delegates. **Liquor licence:** Full. **Children:** Welcome. **Reservations:** PO Box 2793, Cape Town 8000; telephone: (021) 45-1311; fax: (021) 461-6648; telex: 5-20653 SA. Central reservations: telephone: Johannesburg (011) 783-5333; Durban (031) 32-3419; Port Elizabeth, Bloemfontein and East London toll-free 010-0173.

THE DON

Sea Point

The old Silversands Hotel has been taken over by a business syndicate (it's managed by the Protea Hotels Group), thoroughly renovated and has emerged, like a moth from its chrysalis, clean and new and ready to take off. In fact it *has* taken off: it's already been given a three-star rating, and it has won the Mayor's Award for 'Service Excellence to Tourism'. The hotel is usually full: it's central Sea Point location appeals to both businessmen and tourists.

The place doesn't have many frills, but it is modern and spacious and it offers comfort, excellent service and reasonable rates. The contemporary foyer – in pale green and charcoal marbled finish, with modern abstracts on the walls – flows into the small Sands Restaurant, with the Sands Bar at one end and a colourfully furnished terrace beyond.

Accommodation A total of 68 standard rooms and six deluxe suites, some with separate lounges, others with sitting areas incorporated. All have private bathrooms, TV and telephone, and are nicely decorated in contemporary fabrics in a variety of patterns (we saw navy and maroon with splashes of orange and pale blue). Bathrooms have attractive navy-patterned tiles.

Some of the rooms are mountain-facing; others look over the promenade and the rocky beach beyond.

Food, drink and service We've already mentioned the award for service excellence; the Don also received one of the best Satour ratings for service in December 1990. Tariffs include bed and breakfast in the à la carte Sands Restaurant which, for the main meals, specializes in a variety of genuine, unpretentious South African and Italian dishes. We had a choice of kingklip, cottage pie, roasts, steak and bobotie, lasagna or canneloni.

Amenities French, German, Italian, Afrikaans and English are spoken at reception – a boon to overseas visitors. Daily tours are organized – to Cape Point, Table Mountain, the winelands and so forth (through Hilton Ross). Proximity to Sea Point's promenade shops, restaurants and nightlife is a big plus.

Conferences: facilities for small executive meetings of up to 12 people.

THE DON in brief
How to get there: The hotel is in Marais Road, Sea Point. *Tariff (See Authors' Note on page 4):* D *Official rating:* ★★★ *Conference facilities:* For 12 delegates (see text). *Liquor licence:* Full. *Children:* Welcome. *Reservations:* PO Box 21, Sea Point, Cape Town 8001; telephone: (021) 434-9559; fax: (021) 439-6896.

GREENWAYS
Claremont

A handsome house, in the Herbert Baker style, very large, built in the 1920s by people who had both wealth and good taste. It looks out over six acres of landscaped lawn and woodland to the mountain at Bishopscourt and attracts the kind of clientele (many of the guests – visiting businessmen and holidaymakers – are regulars) that appreciate attractively spacious surrounds. The atmosphere is that of an elegant country mansion: the rooms are huge, there are a lot of discreet personal touches, fresh flowers in the entrance hall and drawing room; some notable antiques; among the fireplaces is a hand-carved Kruger Hey (a valuable piece of Africana today); the walls are wood-panelled; there are pure wool carpets in the bedrooms, Persian carpets in the reception areas – in a word, quality. The dining room boasts the first domed ceiling installed in a private Cape Town house. Jeannie MacDonald, who runs the place, is a warm, genuinely hospitable person and you're looked after very well.

Accommodation Fourteen *en suite* rooms, all of different sizes and with individual colour schemes. Each is spacious; some have separate sitting rooms and superb balconies. The old master bedroom, decorated in soft leaf-green and beige, is enormous, with a beautiful crystal chandelier and an Italian-marble fireplace. The honeymoon room looks out, from both bed and bath, on a stately tree and beyond to the mountain. One room we especially liked was gaily decorated in red floral fabric and opened onto a wooden balustraded upstairs balcony with a marvellous view. There are fresh flowers, mostly from the rose garden, everywhere. All the suites have intercoms, television (and video channel) and private telephones.

Food, drink and service Greenways is not licensed. The dining room offers an English breakfast and a table d'hôte menu for the later meals. Guests can ask for either light lunch or a four-course spread; the day we were there the talented cooks had prepared a crispy salad and courgette and lemon quiche, veal valpareso (cutlets with green and red pepper), and a lighter-than-air lemon soufflé. Dinner is invariably a four-course meal.

Amenities These include a swimming pool (beside a gazebo) and a croquet lawn. Greenways is very close to the Kirstenbosch Gardens. (see page 18).

GREENWAYS in brief
How to get there: Greenways is in Torquay Avenue, Upper Claremont. Take De Waal Drive (M3) from town, via Rhodes Drive to Claremont. Torquay Avenue is to the right, off Edinburgh Drive (Bishopscourt Hill). Visitors to the city; note that De Waal, Rhodes and Edinburgh Drives form consecutive parts of the less elegant-sounding M3.
Tariff *(See Authors' Note on page 4):* D
Official rating: *Not applicable.* **Liquor licence:** *Greenways does not have a liquor licence; guests have access to an 'honesty bar'.* **Children:** *Greenways does not cater for children under 10.* **Reservations:** *Torquay Avenue, Claremont, Cape Town 7700; telephone: (021) 761-1792. fax: (021) 761-0878.*

INN ON THE SQUARE
City Centre

A largish, lively, medium-quality, good-value three-star hotel facing onto the cobble-stoned charm of Greenmarket Square, the heart of Cape Town (see page 11). The Inn's Terrace restaurant is a popular rendezvous; patrons tend to linger, soaking in the ambience. Here we whiled away a number of pleasant hours at different times – sipping drinks, eating carrot cake, enjoying the sunshine, engrossed in the kaleidoscope of passers-by, watching locals and tourists haggling at the canopied stalls of the densely-packed fleamarket opposite, listening to the sounds of polyglot humanity and of Rastafarians intoning their rather repetitive reggae. For the rest, the Inn, which belongs to the Southern Sun group, offers the standard range of city-hotel amenities, convivial bars and restaurants, good food, solid comfort – and convenience.

Accommodation There are 170 air conditioned *en suite* bedrooms all recently and nicely refurbished, each with TV (second channel), radio and telephone.

Full room service and a baby-sitting service are offered.

Food, drink and service The hotel is well endowed with restaurants and bars. Excellent à la carte fare can be enjoyed in The Spirit of Greenmarket Square restaurant; anything from steaks to cakes in the Coffee Shop; light lunches in Square One, a ladies' bar that features live entertainment (normally a pianist) at night. Then there's Cobbles, the pub and, of course, The Terrace.

Service: prompt and courteous.

Amenities The hotel is within strolling distance of shops, banks, restaurants, cinemas, health studios, sights-to-see and everything else that central Cape Town has to offer (see pages 19 – 22).

The Inn on the Square is geared to accommodate pets. Parking: at a nearby parking garage; a car valet service is available.

Conferences: amenities for up to 25 delegates; telex, travel and secretarial facilities are provided.

INN ON THE SQUARE in brief

How to get there: The hotel is on Greenmarket Square, city centre. **Tariff** *(See Authors' Note on page 4):* E **Official rating:** ★★★ **Conference facilities:** *Available for up to 25 delegates.* **Liquor licence:** *Full.* **Children:** *Welcome.* **Reservations:** *PO Box 3775, Cape Town 8000; telephone: (021) 22-1011; fax: (021) 23-3664; telex: 5-721050 SA.*

KAROS ARTHUR'S SEAT

Sea Point

We came here expecting decaying grandeur, an old hotel reputedly in need of a facelift, and found something quite different: nearly R14 million had just been spent on creating this ultimate businessman's hotel in the heart of Sea Point. Karos Arthur's Seat has plenty of features that will appeal to holidaymakers, but the emphasis is on the corporate club – the conference market. The hotel is conveniently sited a few minutes from both sea and shops. Mountain and ocean views are rather channeled by adjoining highrise buildings, but occupants of the suites enjoy splendid vistas from cleverly designed balconies.

Arthur's Seat also excels at the functions game: we arrived at the same time as a wedding party resplendent in the 1948 Bentley and 1952 Silver Rolls that the hotel, by long tradition, provides as part of the nuptial package. The honeymoon suite is thrown in free, as are flowers on the main table and a glass of champagne for each guest.

Accommodation There are 123 *en suite* standard double rooms, beautifully appointed and freshly decorated in corals, pinks and white, each with fully stocked bar fridge, TV (with M-Net), radio and trouser-press. Also four luxurious executive and two honeymoon suites, furnished and decorated in individual style.

Food, drink and service The Pavilion Court restaurant offers good à la carte fare, a carvery and sumptuous buffet, a crayfish tank from which you select your dinner live, and a corner labelled 'From the Grill' – excellent steaks.

The Garden Terrace is a pleasant turquoise-and-white ground-floor eating and drinking area that opens out to the street.

Hatters, the cocktail bar, features background entertainment; the Whistle and

Flute is a conference bar, known for its pub lunches. A guitarist plays here in the evenings.

Amenities The wind-protected pool deck on the hotel's fourth floor is a nice place on which to relax with a drink.

Arthur's Seat is a part of the Sea Point buzz; restaurants, discos, and boutiques are all around; the seafront promenade is a few hundred metres away.

Conferences are served by two floors of the hotel, which have been gutted and redesigned to accommodate function areas and suites – altogether 13 rooms, ranging from the cozy to the huge are available. The Agulhas Room is an L-shaped function area which, when the partitions are down, can hold 1 200 standing and will seat 800 at a banquet.

KAROS ARTHUR'S SEAT in brief
How to get there: The hotel is in Arthur's Road, Sea Point, clearly visible from the Main Road through the suburb. **Tariff** *(See Authors' Note on page 4): F* **Official rating:** ★★★ *Conference Facilities 13 venues (see text).* **Liquor licence:** *Full.* **Children:** *Welcome.* **Reservations:** *Arthur's Road, Sea Point, Cape Town 8001; telephone: (021) 434-1187/3344; fax: (021) 434-9768; telex: 5-27310 SA.*

HOTEL METROPOLE
City Centre

The New Met, in Long Street in the heart of Cape Town, is a smallish, friendly hotel that opened its doors in 1896 and still has something of the more leisurely past about it. The atmosphere is vaguely Anglo-Chinese colonial: the reception area has a marble inlay floor, lacquerwork, flower-print wallpaper, deep red-leather chairs, and the theme is carried through to the corridors and rooms upstairs, where paintings and prints, carpets and quilts hint at other times and other, mainly eastern, places.

The hotel was long a favourite among the more rumbustious kind of Capetonian and among visiting ship's officers and local and up-country sportsmen. Its long terrace balcony, which overlooks Long Street, used to serve as a sort of rostrum for announcing Springbok rugby teams to the partisan crowds below. The establishment, recently and very nicely refurbished, is now a lot more sedate, though the terrace and pub are lively enough – and the seafood you're served in Wheeler's restaurant is still the best in town. The management, in the person of Alan Masters, maintains an amiably high profile.

Accommodation Some 50 rooms in all, each with private bathroom, TV (plus M-Net and video channel), air conditioning, drinks cabinet and built-in safe. The best on offer is the stylishly sumptuous Taipan executive suite, distinguished by its Chinese décor, its delicate Chinese works of art and its jacuzzi, which stands in the centre of the bedroom. For the health-conscious there's a 'massage shower' and an exercise bicycle. The executive rooms on the Mandarin Floor have silver tea-services (imported, like much else in the hotel, from Harrods), and gold-plated Victorian taps in the very nicely fitted bathrooms. The standard rooms are cosy doubles and singles in soft turquoise, lilac, peach and mauve zigzag stripes with bedspreads and curtains to match. Imaginative, tasteful and comfortable.

Food, drink and service Wheeler's restaurant, which has provided fine fare since the turn of the century, was recently and most attractively redecorated and now sports, among other things, tapestry chairs, a stained-glass skylight and an Espresso machine. The ambience remains as pleasant as it's always been. It serves a solid traditional breakfast and offers a lavish lunch and dinner menu, seafood, as mentioned, taking pride of place (the lobster bisque is rather special) though the leek pie is also well worth considering.

The Terrace, like much of the rest of the hotel, has a distinct Oriental-colonial feel – there are marble inlay tables and a genuine punkah fan, Oriental prints and bamboo blinds. It's light and open, glassed in from the weather and serves light meals (cold springbok, Portuguese sausages, Irish stew) all day at very reasonable prices.

Drinks can be savoured in the Jug and Jar, a most pleasant pub with leather chairs, cherrywood panelling and a London atmosphere.

Service is excellent throughout.

Amenities The New Met is moments away from shopping areas such as the Golden Acre, St George's Mall, Stuttafords Town Square and the flea market in Greenmarket Square. There are two parking garages close by and limited hotel parking on request. Transport to and from travel terminals is laid on.

The conference room can host up to 40 delegates, and is complemented by a smaller syndicate of rooms. A full secretarial service is available on request.

THE METROPOLE in brief
How to get there: The hotel is on the corner of Long and Castle Streets; turn left from Strand Street into Long Street (it's a one-way), the hotel is two blocks farther on your right. ***Tariff*** (See Authors' Note on page 4) *Official rating:* ★★★ **Conference facilities:** *For up to 40 delegates.* **Liquor licence:** *Full.* **Children:** *Welcome* **Reservations:** *38 Long Street, Cape Town 8001; telephone: (021) 23-6363; fax: (021) 23-6370.*

MIJLOF MANOR HOTEL
Tamboerskloof

A rambling, historic, rather handsome converted homestead graced by high-walled grounds, tiled floors, beamed ceilings and a shady veranda on two sides, situated in the middle of Tamboerskloof, a suburb which sprawls across the lower slopes of Lion's Head. The original farmhouse, renovated by Jelle and Clifford Mijlof and turned into what's billed as a 'hotel for connoisseurs', dates from 1710 (the old foundations and some of the walls have been retained).

A spacious, cool, unpretentious, attractive and pleasantly sociable place, recommended to the quieter kind of visitor.
Accommodation A total of 24 nicely decorated and furnished rooms, each with a private bathroom, some with air conditioning, and five self-catering duplexes (these have fully equipped kitchenettes). All the units have TV (with M-Net) and PABX phones. The size, configuration and décor of the rooms vary: some are

decorated in Biggie Best style; some have private courtyards or gardens, others balconies. There is also a penthouse suite comprising bedroom, dining and sitting room, jacuzzi and bathroom.

Food, drink and service The breakfast room is in the original part of the farmhouse, and has heavy teak beams and sash windows. Breakfasts (and pub lunches) are also served in the Ladies Bar and on the patio; more substantial meals in Abrahamskloof, the high-ceilinged dining room. The menu is à la carte, and offers some enticing German specialities. We had a drink in the most pleasant De Achter Hoek cocktail bar, part of the old slave quarters.

Amenities There's a swimming pool (with views of Table Mountain and Signal Hill) where sundowners are served on balmy days.

The conference venue seats 80 people, and is located in a renovated house adjoining the Hotel.

MIJLOF MANOR in brief
How to get there: The hotel is bounded by Buitengracht Street and Military and Milner roads in Tamboerskloof. Buitengracht Street crosses Wale Street at the Gardens end of Town. Once in Buitengracht, Ed's Car Hire is opposite the entrance to Military Road on your right; turn right and the Hotel is over the first stop street – number 5 on the right.
Tariff *(See Authors' Note on page 4):* C
Official rating: ★★ **Conference facilities:** *Up to 80 delegates.* **Liquor licence:** *Full.* **Children:** *Welcome.* **Reservations:** *5 Military Road, Tamboerskloof, Cape Town 8001; telephone: (021) 26-1476; fax: (021) 22-2046.*

MOUNT NELSON
Gardens

The 'Nellie' has been the epitome of discreet luxury, of an understated, aristocratic elegance that has kept it firmly in a class of its own, ever since it welcomed its first guests in 1899, a few months before the outbreak of the Anglo-Boer War.

The Mount Nelson was built in the high summer of Empire, by the Castle shipping line to compete with the old Grand Hotel (which belonged to the rival Union Steamships) for the patronage of the rich and the leisured, and no expense was spared in the attempt. Set in seven acres of parkland beneath the majesty of Table Mountain, it had a sweeping driveway fringed by palm trees, a deer park, graceful fountains and the first private swimming pool in Cape Town, 150 bedrooms, a magnificent domed dining room, Chippendale furniture in the grand salon, glittering chandeliers, oak floors and great expanses of lustrous oak panelling everywhere, 20 000 bottles of imported wines in its cellars and, according to the *Cape Times* of the day, a 'beautiful veranda running along the entire frontage, in close touch with the garden and vineries, where easy chairs tempt to a lengthy after-dinner stay in the company of a good cigar'.

Predictably, the new hotel attracted people of consequence, and when you pass through the revolving brass doors you really are following in the footsteps of the famous. Kitchener used it as his headquarters, Winston Churchill stayed there after his dramatic escape from imprisonment in Pretoria (he pronounced it a 'most excellent and well-appointed establishment'; his gorgeous American mother, who joined him for a while, thoroughly enjoyed the strawberries). Cecil Rhodes entertained lavishly in its public rooms; Rudyard Kipling, John Buchan and Conan Doyle came, to be followed over the decades by a veritable who's-who of notability. Guests of recent vintage have included politicians Henry Kissinger, Edward Heath and Harold Macmillan; civil-rights leader Coretta King; tycoons Paul Getty and Harry Oppenheimer; entertainers Oliver Reed, John Lennon, Shirley Bassey and Eartha Kitt; trend-setter Pierre Cardin; sportsmen Gary Player and Lester Piggot; authors James Michener, Wilbur Smith, Arthur Hailey, Laurens van der Post and Stuart Cloete. To name but a few.

In 1989 the Mount Nelson joined the exclusive Venice Simplon-Orient Express coterie of luxury hotels around the world, a group that includes the Hotel Cipriani in Venice, the Hotel Splendido in Portofino, Turnberry Hotel & Golf Courses in Scotland and The Lodge at Vail in Colorado. A new management team, pledged to create 'the best hotel in Africa', was assembled, and a R30-million redevelopment plan launched. The results are impressive, perhaps most visibly so in the Ballroom, remodelled under the guidance of decorator Graham Viney. Classic columns, cornices, reeded mouldings, ceiling rosettes and dado rails have been added (many of these features were gilded by Italian artist Mario Lucangioli, who worked, Michelangelo-style, from scaffolding to the ceiling); the décor is green, gold and white; the walls are padded and clad with green damask, which has been used to tent the ceiling in an adjoining function room; underfoot there's an intricate Oriental carpet, woven in Durban; above you are eight crystal chandeliers, imported from Italy. The general effect is stunning.

Accommodation The 135 rooms and 24 suites are spacious and light, supremely comfortable, elegantly furnished, individually styled. The super-luxury suites comprise bedroom and private lounge. I had a double room with sofa and armchairs in faded terra-cotta on a reddish carpet, and floral curtains and bedspread in shades of brown, green and off-white. A large vase of fresh flowers stood under the window. All the rooms have radios, telephones, air conditioning and are equipped with satellite television (plus video channel and M-Net); many overlook the garden and swimming pool and some have balconies.

Food, drink and service There are three restaurants. In the summer months the informal Oasis Terrace serves continental breakfasts, buffet lunches, afternoon teas; the oak-panelled and Grecian-columned Dining Room offers good eating in the grand tradition (table d'hôte menu; classic five-course luncheons and dinners; beautiful tableware); the à la carte Grill Room has been described as 'Cape Town's leading supper club, the doyen of upmarket restaurants'. Excellent wine list; superlative service.

The Lord Nelson bar has the feel of a London Club about it – the room is richly panelled, the chairs are of leather and Lord Nelson, 'the greatest sailor the British navy has ever known', gazes down at you from the wall. Incidentally, the bust of the admiral displayed in the hotel's foyer was carved of timber from HMS *Victory*. Drinks on the terrace of a summer evening will fill a magical hour; recommended to beer-lovers is the Cornish draught.

Amenities In the grounds are a heated swimming pool, an all-weather floodlit tennis court and a squash court. Inside there's a hairdressing salon (it has a separate men's section), beauty centre and Kottlers' Boutique, which sells curios and gifts. A courtesy bus plies to and from the city centre; transport to the Blue Train and the airport is available. From the hotel you can stroll down oak-lined Government Avenue, past the Houses of Parliament, or into the Gardens (see page 12). A slightly longer walk takes you into central Cape Town.

Conferences: the Hotel has six function rooms, the largest of which is The Ballroom – it accommodates 500 delegates or, at banquets, 250 diners. Sophisticated public-address, cinema projection and closed-circuit television facilities are available, plus a powerful lighting system that can be adapted for different displays and presentations.

MOUNT NELSON in brief
How to get there: The Mount Nelson is on Orange Street opposite the start of Government Avenue in the Gardens area; its imposing portico is a landmark. **Tariff** *(See Authors' Note on page 4):* F **Official rating:** ★★★★★ *Conference facilities: For up to 500 (see text).* **Liquor licence:** *Full.* **Children:** *Welcome.* **Reservations:** *PO Box 2608, Cape Town 8000; telephone: (021) 23-*1000; *fax: (021) 24-7472; telex: 5-27804 SA; United Kingdom reservations: UK Orient Express Hotels, telephone: (071) 928-6000.*

THE NEWLANDS SUN

Newlands

To a lot of South Africans Newlands is synonymous with rugby and cricket, and if it's the game that draws you to Cape Town then the four-star Newlands Sun is probably for you.

But the hotel also attracts the ordinary holidaymaker and – increasingly – the businessman, and its rather boisterously sporty image is fading fast. A major renovation programme launched by recently appointed GM Adam Fuller is transforming the place, steadily lifting it into the top hospitality bracket.

The Newlands Sun is a lot quieter, more sophisticated than it was (but lively enough on occasion), very comfortable, very friendly – and it's conveniently located in one of the city's most attractive suburbs. Highly recommended.

Accommodation The hotel has 70 *en suite* double and 60 'King-size' bedrooms of standard Southern Sun quality, and five suites. All air conditioned, all with TV and the other conveniences. 24-hour room service.

Food, drink and service The Coach House restaurant, until recently a mock-Tudor affair of wooden beams and a lot of copper and brass, is being radically refurbished, but that won't change its essential character: it's still a vey sociable venue and the food – English traditional at the carvery, Continental varied on order – is excellent.

Drinks in Joe's Bar (its official name is Baker Street, but nobody calls it that); which is the domain of Joe Naidoo, a well-known and well-loved character and barman supreme: he never forgets a face, a name or a favourite drink, and he's probably the country's most talented mixer of exotic cocktails.

Service is efficient, courteous and, for a largish hotel with a transitory clientele, surprisingly personalized: 'the staff,' says Adam Fuller,'are trained to recognise guests and to greet them by name.'
Amenities Avis car rental and hairdressing salon on the premises; golf, bowls, squash, tennis and swimming (in an Olympic-standard pool) are nearby. As are, of course, the cricket and rugby grounds. Claremont's fashionable shops are just up the road.

The conference centre can accommodate 250 delegates, and is also used for banquets (200 diners) and as a 350-seat theatre. Smaller function rooms are also available as required.

NEWLANDS SUN in brief
How to get there: The hotel is on Main Road, Newlands, across the road from the Ohlssons brewery. Take any main route from the city. *Tariff* (See Authors' Note on page 4): E **Official rating:** ★★★★ **Conference facilities:** Available for up to 150 delegates. **Liquor licence:** Full **Children:** Welcome; baby-sitting service available. **Reservations:** Main Road, Newlands 7700, Cape; telephone: (021) 61-1105; fax: (021)64-1241; telex: 5-20686 SA. **Central reservations:** Johannesburg, Durban, Port Elizabeth, Bloemfontein and East London toll-free: 0800-117-711.

ORANIENSTEIN GUEST HOUSE

Tamboerskloof

A charming turn-of-the-century home and something of a landmark on your way up through the winding road leading to Kloof Nek and the Table Mountain cableway.

The Oranienstein is very different from your ordinary South African city guesthouse: it has an appealingly Continental ambience, a feeling imparted by the typically pension-type style of the rooms, by the candlelit tables of its dining room, and by the background and personable natures of hosts Celeste and Harry Schauss. A very pleasant (and convenient) place in which to stay on your visit to Cape Town.

Accommodation Five suites of spacious rooms, attractively decorated and furnished in vaguely Art Nouveau style. The brass and porcelain beds were specially made for Harry Schauss. Two of the rooms have balconies. Television sets are available on request.

Food, drink and service The Café Oranienstein has high pressed-steel ceilings, a marble fireplace and marble-topped tables, and it leads out to a veranda from which there's a splendid view of the mountain. Celeste does the cooking; the food is delectably Continental (each dish was evocatively explained to us); the atmosphere informal and friendly. Set menu, though there are off-menu specialities that Celeste will tell you about. The evening we spent there was quite delightful. The terrace below is a very popular rendezvous among Capetonians with a taste for light continental meals, pastries and cakes.

Amenities Sightseeing tours and day excursions to major tourist attractions (along the wine-routes, for instance) are arranged for guests.

ORANIENSTEIN in brief

How to get there: The guest-house is on New Church Street, Tamboerskloof, near the Burnside Road intersection. **Tariff** *(See Authors' Note on page 4)* **Official rating**: *Not applicable.* **Liquor licence**: *Not licensed; take your own wine into the Café.* **Children**: *The Oranienstein is not suitable for children.* **Reservations**: *PO Box 21586, Cape Town 8000; telephone: (021) 24-8429; fax: (021) 24-8428.*

PARK AVENUE

Gardens

The old Gardens Village underwent a radical transformation and re-emerged in 1989 as the Park Avenue. Gone the village feeling, gone the Village Winehouse, enter the kind of slickly sophisticated, Continental-type hotel found in, among other places, the ethnic parts of New York. The building is gaily painted, the décor contemporary. It's a shiny-bright new place with plenty laid on, and is much favoured by the local business fraternity.

Accommodation Tariffs include bed and breakfast. There are 32 designer decorated rooms, some single, some double, some interleading (these last have a central lounge and will suit the larger family). All rooms have private bathrooms, telephones, colour TV (with a video channel and M-Net), air conditioning and plenty of cupboard space.

Food, drink and service Light and airy Piaf's restaurant and coffee shop – it has perspex domes in the ceiling – offers an excellent carvery. It also serves a lavish breakfast buffet and in-between meals, coffee and cakes.

For a stylish evening of entertainment, there's Gershwin's à la carte restaurant, where live music creates the mood, and where there's dancing as well as dining. Try the special Park Avenue ham and the Polynesian chicken.

Drinks are served both in the Gershwin's cocktail bar and on the pool terrace. The service is excellent.

Amenities The hotel has a pleasant swimming pool, and guests have free access to the Cape Town Health and Racquet club and the courts at the Orangia Tennis club. For the rest, one can explore the general area: it's on the fringe of the city, surrounded by quiet, oak-lined avenues and within walking distance of the Gardens (see page 12), shopping centres, restaurants.

Conferences: well catered for (as are banquets, weddings and other functions) in the Amadeus and Mozart Rooms and, for smaller gatherings, in the boardroom and conference suite. Maximum of 120 delegates; full secretarial and audio visual facilities available.

PARK AVENUE in brief

How to get there: *The hotel is in Union Street in the Gardens area.* **Tariff** *(See Authors' Note on page 4)*: C **Official rating**: ★★★ **Conference facilities**: *For up to 120 delegates (see text).* **Liquor licence**: *Full.*

Children: Welcome. *Reservations:* PO Box 15617, Vlaeberg 8018, Cape Town; telephone: (021) 24-1460; fax: (021) 24-1497; telex: 5-20601 SA.

THE PENINSULA

Sea Point

A splendidly sophisticated 11-storey, all-suite hotel and timeshare complex combining truly luxurious hotel living with the convenience of a self-catering holiday. Each of its 110 suites has huge picture windows and unimpeded views of the sparkling Atlantic. A place for the privileged.

Accommodation The suites, in 15 different configurations, range from one-bedroom studios (open plan with lounge and kitchenette) through luxury studio (raised sleeping area and jacuzzi), mini-suite (second bathroom) and luxury suite (extra bedroom and bathroom, big kitchen and jacuzzi), to super-luxury suite, one of which has three bedrooms, a large lounge, a dining room and three patios. All have television with M-Net and video channel, telephones, jewellery safes, hairdryers and wall heaters.

The super-luxury suite really does live up to its name. The one we looked around was spacious, most attractive, supremely comfortable. The lounge had a white-tiled floor, an elegant dining table, colourful, inviting sofas and chairs, and flowers everywhere. Our eyes went straight to the view – the nearly floor-to-ceiling windows bring the sea almost into the room. The bedroom was pleasantly decorated: mottled grey and soft coral pinks and blues; leading off was a small balcony with table and chairs and an *en suite* bathroom in pale grey and white. Here we found the spa bath (with shower) and another lovely sea view. The second bedroom (also *en suite*) was done out in peppermint and pink. The open-plan kitchen was beautifully equipped – microwave, foldout ironing board, salad spinner, white Noritake crockery. The main balcony, off the lounge, had a jacuzzi and glass walls through which you could survey Lion's Head and, on balmy summer nights, the myriad lights of Sea Point's Riviera and the stars above.

The hotel provides its guests with a limited room service.

Food, drink and service For informal eating there's the Café Bijou, just off the reception area, a light and airy place with enormous windows, mirrored ceilings, cane furniture and indoor plants. More sumptuous is John Jackson's restaurant, which offers superbly creative *haute cuisine* and an extensive wine list. John ran the Country Restaurant, the Rosenfontein in Paarl and the Valkenburg Manor House – and consistently featured in the Top Ten rankings – before starting his Peninsula enterprise.

Amenities Residents have the exclusive use of two outdoor pools (one is a heated plunge-pool), sauna and a smallish gym. The hotel is right on the beachfront, in a pleasantly wind-free part of Cape Town. The giant Pavilion outdoor pool is down the road; beyond is the promenade, parallel to which runs Main Road, a rather scruffy but nevertheless interestingly cosmopolitan thoroughfare, full of junk shops, delicatessens and eateries.

THE PENINSULA in brief
How to get there: The hotel is at the southern end of Beach Road, Sea Point. *Tariff* (See Authors' Note on page 4): F **Official rating:** Not graded. **Conference facilities:** Available for up to 120 delegates. **Liquor licence:** Not applicable. **Children:** Welcome. **Reservations:** PO Box 17188, Regent Road, Sea Point 8061, Cape Town; telephone: (021) 439-8888; fax: (021) 439-8886/7. Three Cities Hotels Limited, P.O.Box 673, LONDON SW3 6SE, United Kingdom; telephone: (071) 225-0164; fax: (071) 823-7701.

THE PRESIDENT HOTEL

Sea Point

On our visit we settled on chaises by the pool in the old garden and dozed gently in the balmy Sea Point air. The President is certainly a tranquil, most relaxing place (though lively enough in the evenings); a quick drink in the cocktail lounge, or outside on the terrace, tends to stretch to a few more while one sits back and gazes somnolently at the rocks and waters of the blue Atlantic.

This gracious, restful, supremely luxurious hotel has a proud tradition, one that goes back a full two centuries. The first building on the site was the Societeitshuijs (Society House), a long, stoeped, tree-shaded edifice erected in 1766 to serve as a secluded rest-house for senior Dutch East India Company officials and which functioned as an exclusive country club for several decades. Local and overseas visitors (among them some prominent artists) came to know it as *een genoeglijke uitspanning* (a pleasant place of relaxation) until, in 1810, it became an eating and boarding house and a beach resort popular among the higher ranks of Raj officialdom. It was then radically refurbished, used as a splendid gentleman's residence (the name was changed to Sea Point House) and then converted yet again, to become the Wentworth Hotel, rebuilt and re-opened in 1887 – the year of Victoria's Golden Jubilee – as the Queen's Hotel.

This name remained until 1967, when the place was enlarged to become the international five-star beachfront establishment it is today.

Something of the charming past is still there, most evident perhaps in the stylish décor and furnishings of the older section of the building (the more modern highrise block offers comfort of a different kind) and, less definable but real enough, in the quality of the service, which recalls another, more courteous and more caring age. The hotel is invariably booked to the hilt (a tribute to quality) but one doesn't feel crowded. The guest list is cosmopolitan, and interesting.

Accommodation This is, of course, of five-star quality. There are 28 luxury double suites (15 with balconies); 115 twin-bedded rooms and 11 singles. All rooms have bathrooms *en suite*, direct-dial phone, air conditioning/heating, and TV with M-Net and video channels. Full 24-hour room service.

Food, drink and service The main dining room is the Zeezicht Restaurant, which, in fine weather, is opened out to the spacious garden terrace. À la carte and buffet fare; the luncheon and dinner menus offer some interesting, and delicious, specialities.

Snacks and light meals can be enjoyed on the Pool Terrace. The Lady Anne, one of several comfortable cocktail bars, offers seasonal entertainment during cocktail hours.

The wine list is splendid and the wine waiters unusually informative. The Zeezicht has a resident pianist. The service is polite and prompt throughout the hotel, without being intrusive.

Amenities There is a bookshop, a fashion boutique, jewellers, a general gift shop, and a unisex hairdressing salon on the premises; services include car rental, baby-sitting, valet and same-day laundry and dry cleaning.

A popular area is the pool terrace, where towels are supplied and chaises, umbrellas and poolside chairs are laid out for guests. After your swim you can perspire in the sauna and pamper yourself with the luxury of a massage. Beyond the pool is a tennis court and bowling green. Volleyball games, sight-seeing tours and deep-sea fishing trips can be arranged. The Sea Point promenade, with its huge outdoor swimming pool and tidal pools, is within easy strolling distance.

Function facilities are exceptional: five individual rooms can be combined into one; another large venue is available for banquets, conferences and weddings. The courtyard attached to the Liesching complex is a very pleasant setting for afternoon or evening gatherings, or for conference breaks.

THE PRESIDENT in brief
How to get there: The hotel is at the southern end of Sea Point's Beach Road. **Tariff** *(See Authors' Note on page 4):* F **Official rating:** ★★★★ **Conference facilities:** Five venues, plus one large complex (up to 200 delegates). Other functions are held on the Pooldeck. **Liquor licence:** Full. **Children:** Welcome. **Reservations:** PO Box 62, Sea Point 8060, Cape Town; telephone: (021) 434-1121; fax: (021) 439-2919; telex: 5-26620 SA.

RITZ PROTEA HOTEL
Sea Point

This is the place for both the business executive and the holidaymaker who likes to be where the action is: there's no getting away from it all here, right in the middle of bustling Sea Point. The hotel, a modern, tower-like structure, draws a healthy number of overseas visitors (key staff are multilingual) as well as conference-bound businessmen. Built in 1975, it was fully refurbished on becoming part of the Protea group in 1985. Good, all-round, four-star quality.

Accommodation A total of 222 rooms, six of them suites, all with sea and/or mountain views; especially splendid vistas from the higher floors. Each has its private bathroom, TV (with video channel) and M-Net; all are air conditioned, all very comfortably and most pleasantly decorated in pastels.

Full 24-hour room service.

Food, drink and service The Top of the Ritz is a stylish revolving restaurant on the 22nd floor, from which there are stunning views of mountain, sea and city (very impressive at night). Executive chef Graham Lowes has been awarded the prestigious World Master Chefs Order of

Merit, presented internationally for culinary prowess – an accolade reinforced in 1990, when the restaurant received the blazon of the Chaîne des Rôtisseurs. On offer is classical cuisine for the conservative diner, though the menu also tempts with some imaginative innovations. All in all, a culinary treat.

The Café Biar-Ritz, on the first floor, is a sun-filled informal rendezvous, adjoining the pool terrace, that provides breakfast, lunch and speciality dinners. We enjoyed the Mongolian stirfry, but also noted a very good buffet/carvery spread and a comprehensive à la carte menu. Light meals are served here throughout the day.

The wine-list complements the excellent food. The hotel has two cocktail bars, including the Panorama, which is part of the top-floor restaurant complex. There is also a lively nightclub on the premises.

Service: prompt and courteous.

Amenities The Ritz is in downtown Sea Point, close to the trendy Clifton beaches and five minutes from the city centre and Waterfront, so it's a popular place among those who prefer the livelier kind of weekend. Pool and spa are on the first floor; the pooldeck is most pleasant place for relaxing in the sun. The seafront is just across the way; and there's a kaleidoscopic variety of restaurants in the vicinity. A bonus, for the more sports-minded guest, is the hotel's affiliation to The Point Health and Raquet Club in Green Point.

The convention complex has 11 versatile function rooms, including the impressive Business Centre. They cater for anything from 6 to 370 delegates.

RITZ PROTEA in brief
How to get there: The hotel is on Sea Point's Main Road, which runs parallel to the seafront. **Tariff** *(See Authors' Note on page 4):* E **Official rating:** ★★★ *Conference facilities: 11 venues; up to 370 delegates.* **Banqueting facilities** *The Pool Terrace serves as a venue for speciality evenings and launches, and cocktail parties.* **Liquor licence:** *Full.* **Children:** *Welcome.* **Reservations:** *Main Road, Sea Point, Cape Town 8001; telephone: (021) 439-6010; fax: (021) 434-0809; telex: 5-20682 SA; central reservations: toll free 080-011-9000.*

ROSE HOUSE
Rondebosch

Rose House, a charming three-storey Victorian residence in the southern suburbs, offers solid home-from-home hospitality, unpretentious comfort, restfulness, convenience, and value for money.

Not a cent had been spent on the turn-of-the-century house in the 80 years before Priscilla Stepan bought it and created the pleasant refuge it is today. When she took it over from the Living Hope Baptist Church it had 21 rooms and just one bathroom. 'An old home is okay, but old plumbing, no,' she decided, and installed seven new bathrooms. Months of stripping uncovered splendid oak doors and wooden window frames, fireplaces and wide Oregon-pine skirting boards, and these, together with the high pressed-steel ceilings and the original Aga stove (that burns cosily throughout the winter), have combined to evoke an earlier and rather more gracious era.

Accommodation The nine bedrooms (singles and doubles) are spacious, individually decorated, each to a theme. All have private bathrooms; some open onto upstairs' balconies with glorious mountain views. One is a garden cottage behind the house, beside a small pond. Our favourite was the Tree House: it's in the attic (reached via narrow stairs) and has nice rooftop views. There are telephones and TVs in all the rooms; laundry, shoe-cleaning, clothes-pressing and so on are part of the service.

Food, drink and service Homely and informal. A good breakfast and (on request) light evening meal are served in the farmhouse kitchen. A large, help-yourself pot of soup simmers on the Aga in winter.

Amenities Rose House is conveniently located in the attractive suburb of Rondebosch. Just to the south is Newlands and its famed sportsgrounds. There's easy access to major highways, the airport, shopping centres and to some of Cape Town's best restaurants.

ROSE HOUSE in brief
How to get there: *Rose House is in Milner Road, close to its junction with Park Road. Take De Waal Drive from central Cape Town, exit on Woolsack Drive at the University. Turn right onto the Main Road, then left at the Riverside Shopping Centre into Belmont Road. Cross the second set of traffic lights (across Camp Ground Road); you're in Park Road. Look right, before the next intersection (Milner Road). Tariff (See Authors' Note on page 4):C* **Official rating**: *Not applicable.* **Liquor licence**: *Rose House is not licenced to sell liquor.* **Children**: *Rose House does not cater for children under 13.* **Reservations**: *2 Milner Road, Rondebosch 7700, Cape; telephone: (021) 689-9127; fax: (021) 689-9126.*

ST GEORGE'S HOTEL
City Centre

A tower-like four-star hotel situated at the northern end of St George's Mall in the city centre. Ideal for the business visitor: it offers exceptionally efficient (and courteous) service, all the modern comforts, and the St George's Club Room, a pleasant place in which to hold meetings. Holidaymakers also favour it – for its all-round excellence and its central location. The St George's is part of the Southern Sun group.

Accommodation The 137 units – distinguished by their deep-pile grey carpets and the restful beiges and soft pastels of their fabrics – include two suites with their own lounge and dining areas. All rooms have bathrooms *en suite*, TV, radio, telephone, and air conditioning, and they've been designed with the busy executive in mind: they are very comfortable indeed, and there's an adequate amount of working space. Each room has its mini-bar and a coffee machine.

Food, drink and service La Brasserie has a smart Continental look (tiled floors, marble tables and a centrally positioned bar) and is a favoured luncheon venue for local businessmen. It offers à la carte fare; specials are chalked up on a blackboard; dinner-time is laid-back, the food quite excellent, tending towards French Provincial. Try the delectable calamari Ile de France.

Amenities The hotel is within easy walking distance of most of the city's amenities (shops, banks and other services), art and entertainment venues and places of interest. Golf, yachting, sightseeing and so on can be arranged through the hotel. The gymnasium next door is available for the convenience of more health-conscious guests: it offers the usual circuit and aerobics facilities, saunas, a steam bath, and indoor swimming pool.

Conferences: two boardrooms, one of which accommodates 10 delegates and the other 18. The Club Room on the sixth floor is used for finger lunches and cocktail parties (up to 40 guests).

ST GEORGE'S in brief

How to get there: The hotel is in the city centre, on the Heerengracht. **Tariff** *(See Authors' Note on page 4):* E **Official rating:** ★★★★ *Conference facilities: The hotel caters for small executive meetings and functions in the sixth floor boardrooms.* **Liquor licence:** *Full.* **Children:** *Welcome.* **Reservations:** *PO Box 5616, Cape Town 8000; telephone: (021) 419-0808; fax: (021) 419-7010; telex: 5-21533 SA. Central reservations: Johannesburg (011) 783-5333; Durban (031) 37-3341.*

THE TOWNHOUSE
City Centre

A handsome, privately-owned hotel, modern in terms of origin and amenities but with an attractive old-Cape feel about it – an impression created by the Cape cart that stands outside the entrance, by the beautiful woods of the period and the cottage furniture, by the Victorian-type resident's lounge that leads off the lobby, by the Pierneef woodcuts on display, and by the evocative décor of the dining room.

The Townhouse is one of the city's most popular hotels; among its major drawcards are the restaurant and the superb Health and Squash Club (see further on).

Accommodation Each of the 104 standard rooms has a private bathroom with separate walk-in shower, TV (with M-Net), radio, telephone, air conditioning, trouser press and tea-and coffee-making facilities. The décor is pleasantly old-fashioned, with period furniture and fittings, though the amenities are modern. My room had an unimpeded view of Table Mountain.

Food, drink and service The public areas of this hotel are charming, none more so than Die Restaurant, where a combination of patterned fabrics and wallpaper in autumn shades, authentic Cape antiques and Victorian light-fittings recall a long-gone era. A la carte and table d'hôte menus; the food is both interesting and appealing, the presentation stylish. It's well worth trying one of the (daily) chef's specials; the guinea-fowl with cider sauce was delicious.

Light meals, cakes and pastries are served in the coffee shop at the entrance.

Mostert's Hoek, next to the lobby, is a most pleasant Victorian lounge, complete with wood panelling and glass mirrors. Ties and jackets are mandatory in this area.

Amenities The hotel's Health and Squash Club is a remarkable combination of modern exercise equipment, heated swimming pool, jacuzzi, sauna, squash courts, mirrors, pot-plants, Victorian wrought iron, striped fabrics, patterned wallpaper. Unusual, but marvellously effective. The jacuzzi is under a broekie-lace gazebo enclosed by circular wrought-iron railings, all in red with a red-and-yellow striped awning overhead. At the foot of the red wrought-iron staircase is a Victorian street lamp-post.

TOWNHOUSE in brief
How to get there: *The hotel is in Corporation Street, close to the Houses of Parliament. Tariff (See Authors' Note on page 4):* C *Official rating:* ★★★ *Conference facilities: None. Children: Welcome. Reservations: PO Box 5053, Cape Town 8000; telephone: (021) 45-7050; fax: (021) 45-3891; telex 5-20890 SA.*

VICTORIA AND ALFRED HOTEL

The Waterfront

A romantic new happening on Cape Town's waterfront, in the heart of the docks and a marvellously atmospheric (and supremely comfortable) hotel.

Converted from the 1904 North Quay warehouse, this elegantly Edwardian place thrives in a kaleidoscopic, animated setting that delights the senses: here the air is full of the scents of the sea and of the working dockside; gulls wheel and mewl, tugs hoot, music plays; a fleet of ships – container vessels, tramps and trawlers – is anchored in the dark-green waters of the Alfred basin; beyond them are the high-rises of the city and the great sandstone mass of Table Mountain. All highly evocative of that very special Cape experience.

Accommodation The hotel has 68 spacious, air conditioned double rooms, pleasantly furnished in modern fashion (though there are old-style trimmings), each with a kingsize bed, bathroom *en suite* and a separate toilet and separate shower. Each room boasts a fully stocked bar fridge, TV with M-Net, and fine views from the windows of harbour and dockside, city and mountain.

Round-the-clock room service.

Food, drink and service One eats either at The Waterfront Café (Continental cuisine; the line fish is excellent) or on the rather handsome enclosed veranda, which is a thoroughly enjoyable experience. There's also a sociable cocktail bar.

Amenities The hotel is in the thick of the buzzing Waterfront world of boutiques and speciality shops, restaurants, bistros, bars, theatre, maritime museum, brewery and the rest (see page 14). A shuttle bus-service every 15 minutes takes you to and from the city. For the more energetic there are walking, cycling and jogging routes, and there's plenty for the watersports enthusiast (angling, scuba diving, powerboating and sailing), within the harbour area. The Metropolitan Golf Club is nearby.

In-house facilities include secretarial, chauffeur and travel services, telex and fax machines.

VICTORIA & ALFRED in brief
How to get there: *The hotel is on Table Bay harbour's Alfred basin quayside.* **Tariff** *(See*

CAPE TOWN: CITY AND SUBURBS

*Authors' Note on page 4):F **Official rating:** Grading pending. **Conference facilities:** Boardroom facilities for 8 people. **Liquor licence:** Full. **Children:** Welcome. **Reservations:** PO Box 16157, Vlaeberg 8018, Cape; telephone: (021) 419-6677; fax: (021) 419-8955; telex: 5-21556 SA.*

VILLA LUTZI
Oranjezicht

A quiet, very comfortable, very friendly, rather cosmopolitan little guest-house set on the lower slopes of Table Mountain. The views from the house – a substantial, high-ceilinged affair of Edwardian vintage – are splendid: you look down on city, bay and the ocean beyond; behind you is the towering majesty of the mountain. Overseas visitors, and especially holidaymakers from Germany, feature prominently in Villa Lutzi's clientele, though it also has a faithful coterie of local regulars. Your hosts, Lucia and Frank Tucker, are a courteous, kindly couple, and they look after you very well indeed.

Accommodation Each of the twelve rooms has been individually and nicely decorated; each has a private bathroom, telephone and fridge; three have balconies, two share a private patio.

Food, drink and service Breakfast is the only meal provided, but there's a pleasant barbecue area in the garden and a kitchenette in the house (microwave; tea and coffee facilities). Some excellent restaurants are to be found in the general area and, of course, in the city below.

Amenities The garden is shady, spacious, tranquil and a most pleasant place for contemplative relaxation. There's an inviting pool for the slightly more energetic. Table Mountain's cableway is nearby; central Cape Town is just down the hill.

VILLA LUTZI in brief
How to get there: The guest-house is in Rosmead Avenue in the inner (mountain) suburb of Oranjezicht. Turn up Hof Street, next to the Mount Nelson, and drive up to the Volkshospitaal, on your left. Bear right, past Buxton (left); turn left into Kensington. Rosmead Avenue is the first road to your left. *Tariff* (See Authors' Note on page 4): D **Official rating:** Not applicable. **Conference facilities:** None. **Liquor licence:** Villa Lutzi is not licensed to sell liquor. **Children:** Children under 12 are not accommodated. **Reservations:** 6 Rosmead Avenue, Oranjezicht, Cape Town 8001; telephone: (021) 23-4614 and 26-1468; fax: (021) 26-1472.

THE VINEYARD
Claremont

A *hotel extraordinaire*, an aristocrat. It was built in 1799 as a country residence for social commentator and woman-of-letters Lady Anne Barnard, who must have been entranced, as we were, by the setting. It is surrounded by acres of beautifully cared-for parkland in Newlands; from its windows there are wide-angle, uninterrupted views of Table Mountain. Indeed we were struck by how close the mountain appears to be: on a clear day almost in the grounds.

Architecture, décor and furnishings are exquisite: Cape Georgian; high ceilings, classical columns, stately staircases, tapestries, artworks, fountains, pools, masses of fresh flowers and indoor greenery, all coming together to produce visual delight. A relatively new addition to the reception lobby is a large and intricate ceramic panel (nearly 8 square metres) made in 1981 by the celebrated ceramic artist Esias Bosch – a kaleidoscope of the Cape floral kingdom: arums, proteas and fynbos; bright blue butterflies and lizards. Circular insets portray white-washed cottages in a field of flowers with Karoo hills behind, a Cape Dutch homestead with vineyards and a mountain backdrop, and seagulls over the sea with Table Mountain beyond. It's a technically and artistically superb collage of what the Cape is all about.

The Vineyard is one of the country's finest hotels, and one of the best-patronized: it runs at 99 per cent occupancy in summer, 87 per cent in winter.

Accommodation Good taste and supreme comfort are probably the words that best sum it up. There are 124 standard rooms in all – 108 of them newly and nicely decorated – and nine spacious suites, each individually furnished with, among other things, a dining table and lounge suite. My standard room had a floral quilted bedspread in blue, white and brown, with striped fabric in the same colours on the chairs; above the bed hung a pressed-flower picture. Double french doors led out to the garden; the overall effect was cottagey. All rooms are air conditioned and have *en suite* bathrooms, radio, direct-dial telephone and TV (with M-Net).

Slightly more is charged for the mountain-facing units.

Food, drink and service The restaurant bears the blazon of the prestigious Chaîne des Rôtisseurs, and serves classic dishes in what was originally the ballroom, now the loveliest of dining rooms: rather formal, a little old-fashioned, supremely elegant. Soft piano music plays while you savour the cuisine. The daily chef's specials on the wide-ranging menu (casseroles feature prominently) are worth trying; I had wild vineyard mushrooms followed by crayfish grilled with garlic, herbs and Bombay butter and, to finish, a superb cassata ice-cream. You are free to visit the well-stocked cellar before dinner to select your wine. The cellar also serves as an occasional venue for private gourmet dinners.

The Coffee Shop and Swiss Patisserie, part of the lobby area, serves home-baked Swiss and Danish pastries to the gentle tones of harp or piano; light meals are served in the Garden Courtyard. We also had tea in the sitting room that overlooks trim lawns, and drinks in the wood-panelled, leather-chaired cocktail bar.

Service: impeccable.

Amenities On the premises is a hairstylist, an antique shop and a gift shop; in the gardens a recently developed and inviting pool area. Newlands is one of the soggier but more pleasant of the southern suburbs; Claremont's upmarket shopping centres are just down the road, and there's easy access to central Cape Town and indeed to all parts of the Peninsula.

Conferences: five function rooms, three of which can each accommodate 150 delegates apiece.

THE VINEYARD in brief
How to get there: The hotel is in Protea Road, Newlands. *Tariff (See Authors' Note on page 4):F* **Official rating:** ★★★ *Conference facilities:* Five venues (see text). *Liquor licence:* Full. *Children:* The Vineyard is not suitable for young children. *Reservations:* PO Box 151, Newlands 7725, Cape; telephone: (021) 64-2107/or 64-4122; fax: (021) 683-3365; telex: 5-722954 SA.

WINCHESTER MANSIONS HOTEL
Sea Point

Gracious and spacious; a dignified, palm-fringed old hotel, quiet, right on the promenade and full of character. And much evidence of civilized good taste: where else do you find Royal Doulton in the rooms?

The hotel has been in the Harvey family since 1948, and pride in ownership is evident everywhere. We were impressed by a lot that extended just that little bit above and beyond the run-of-the-mill: a vase of fresh flowers on a white table outside the restaurant, the tapestry sofa in the foyer, silver trays with cut-glass decanters and tumblers in some of the rooms, delicate imported brass, porcelain and crystal chandeliers, antique screens, very tastefully chosen prints and oils, and trompe l'oeil on the walls. The present owner, Mrs Wainford, lives in London and personally supervises the refurbishing, sending fittings, knick-knacks and fabrics out from London. Each room has been individually appointed and decorated; the overall look has something of the old-style colonial about it (aristocratic Kenya perhaps), especially the open arched corridors with Roman balustrades facing onto a central courtyard filled with palms and bright pink umbrellas. Centrepiece of the courtyard is a gentle Victorian fountain cascading in the midst of a ring of greenery.

Manager David Day, a kindly, interested host, has his heart and soul in the running of the place. Among the guests while we were there were regulars who have been coming for years, businessmen on conferences, and a party of appreciative French tourists. Young children are not encouraged.

Accommodation There are 44 elegantly decorated rooms (the ocean-facing doubles are rather more expensive than those without a sea view), including two beautiful honeymoon suites with four-poster beds, smaller suites, and 12 self-contained executive apartments.

The executive units are spacious enough to accommodate private seminars. The one we looked in on had a glassed-in veranda with a breakfast table and sofas, a large chandeliered lounge-cum-dining room with a very charming French-looking table and chairs, an antique screen behind, classic patterned loose carpets on wooden floors, a kitchen and bedroom with a large bathroom: a very long bath. In fact all the hotel's baths are generously proportioned (the executive bath-taps are distinctive – the water pours from a dragon's mouth).

The smaller suites have bedrooms, lounges and bathrooms. Most rooms have pleasant sea views, and all have TV (with M-Net), fridge, tea set and kettle.

They're also graced by another of Mrs Wainford's little touches – fresh potpourri from London.

Food, drink and service The restaurant, Gerard's, opens onto the central courtyard, seats 45 and has a piano. The chef is French and the à la carte menu is fairly varied – anything from Karoo lamb to vegetarian dishes, pastas, poultry, seafood and good South African steaks. Well-chosen wine list.

The Orangerie Coffee Shop, which serves light lunches, delicious homemade cakes and a *real* cup of coffee, is a charming room with an uninterrupted sea view and trompe l'oeil pots containing orange trees on one wall (artist John Longman was brought out from London especially to add his touch to the public rooms). Refreshments and light meals are also served in the courtyard.

Drinks: there is no cocktail bar; the hotel has a wine and malt licence.

Amenities The swimming pool is in an enclosed courtyard, sheltered from the wind, with a skilfully-executed trompe l'oeil on one wall depicting a veranda with Roman railings, a doorway, an upstairs balcony and two palm trees.

Hairdressing salon *in situ*. There is access for the handicapped. The hotel is within easy walking distance of tennis, squash and golf facilities nearby.

WINCHESTER MANSIONS in brief

How to get there: *The hotel is on Beach Road, about half way along Sea Point's attractive seafront.* ***Tariff*** *(See Authors' Note on page 4):* D ***Official rating:*** ★★★ ***Conference facilities:*** *Two function rooms; up to 30 delegates. Executive suites are used for private seminars.* ***Liquor licence:*** *Wine and malt.* ***Children:*** *Children under 12 are not accommodated.* ***Reservations:*** *121 Beach Road, Sea Point, Cape Town, 8001; telephone: (021) 434-2351; fax: (021) 434-0251.*

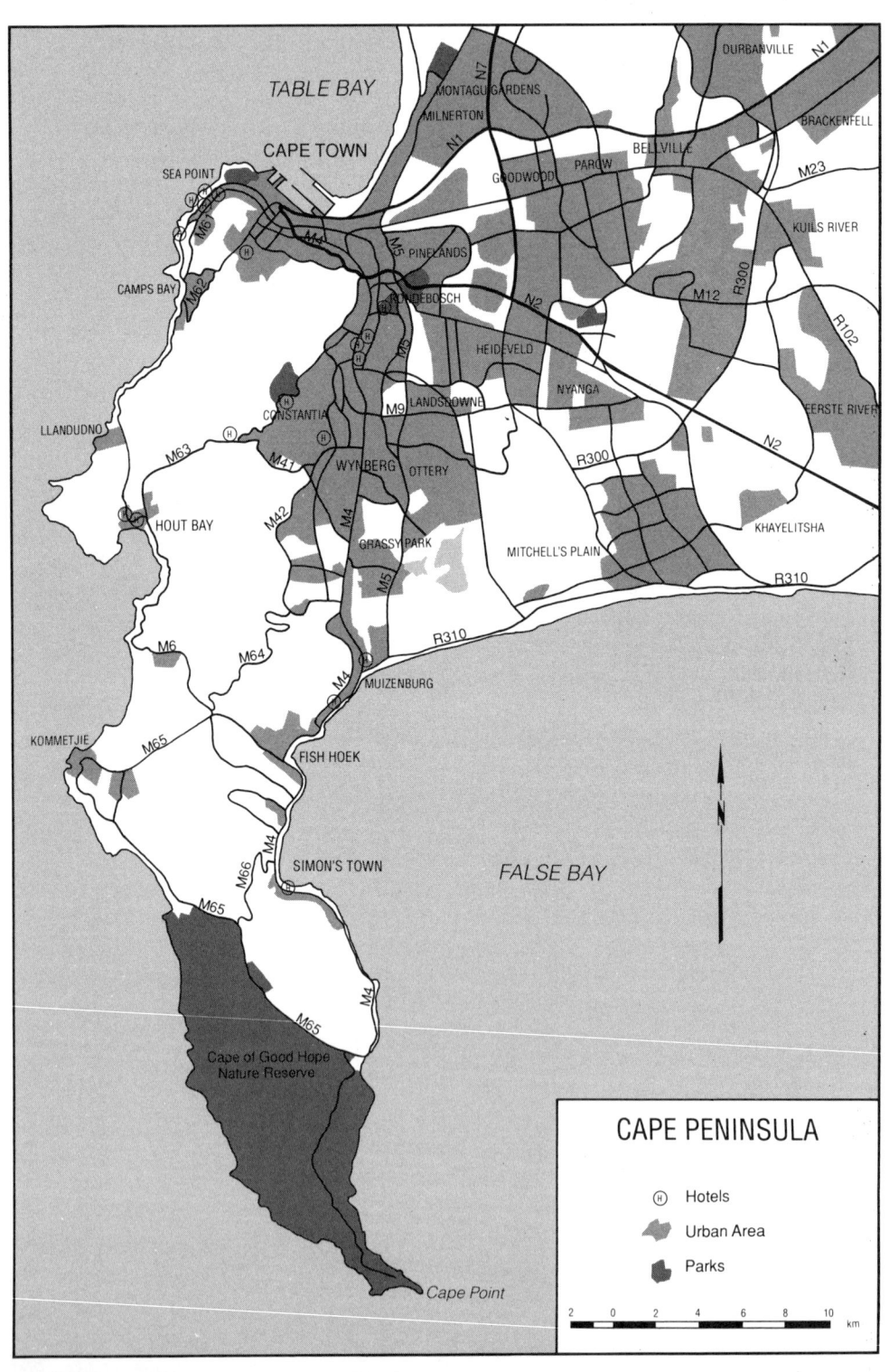

THE PENINSULA

❏ WHAT TO SEE AND DO
❏ WHERE TO STAY

◘ WHAT TO SEE AND DO

The Cape Peninsula stretches 75 kilometres from Table Bay, southwards to the Cape of Good Hope nature reserve and Cape Point. Much of the central part is taken up by a forested and strikingly beautiful highland plateau, an extension of the Table Mountain formation; its western and eastern shorelines are graced by attractive little (and some not so little) residential and resort centres that, in the warmer months, attract thousands of holidaymakers, boating enthusiasts, swimmers, surfers, divers and sunworshippers.

In geographical terms it is a modest enough area – just 620 square kilometres in extent – but one that is full of contrast. The waters off the western, or 'Atlantic', coastline are for instance markedly cooler than those that lap the eastern shores; False Bay, on the other hand, suffers the full force of the prevailing summer south-easter while the western strip remains, for the most part, pleasantly sheltered by the high mountains of the Peninsula's spine.

There are, too, startling variations in the lie of the land – high hill, deep valley and gentle plain give way to each other with dramatic suddenness – and in temperature and rainfall: it can be pouring in Newlands while Hout Bay, just over the Nek, basks serenely in the sunshine.

This diversity carries through to the plant life. The Peninsula is part of the Cape Floral Kingdom, a zone that extends over the winter-rainfall belt running along the country's south-western and southern coasts – a strip that occupies just 0,04 percent of the world's total land area, but which enjoys equal status with the great Boreal Kingdom that extends over North America and most of Europe and Asia. The Cape kingdom is immensely rich in flora: it supports around 8 600 species – compared with 15 000 in the whole of Australia, which is nearly 100 times larger in area. Of the 989 genera occurring, fully 193 are unique to a particular part of the region; as many as 120 different species have been found growing within a single 10-square metre patch.

Collectively, this floral wealth is known as 'fynbos', and for the most part comprises such tough, low-growing, small-leafed, evergreen shrubs as the lovely ericas (600 species of them), the proteas (368 species; the king protea is South Africa's national flower), the almost leafless, reedlike 'restio' and a great many bulbous and cormous plants. About 3 000 fynbos species – rather more than a third of the total – occur on the Peninsula itself.

Despite the steady encroachment of suburbia, much of the Peninsula remains uninhabited, the central and northern parts given over to protected forest, the southern to a nature reserve. And it has much to offer the leisure-bent visitor: the seaboard is graced by fine beaches, charming bays, hidden coves, attractive little fishing harbours; inland there are leafy byways to be explored, pathways that beckon, entrancing picnic spots, historic homes and vineyards, farm stalls filled with the scents of fruit and fresh produce and, everywhere, the greenness and beauty of wooded mountain slope.

THE WESTERN SEABOARD

Victoria Drive follows a virtually deserted and scenically stunning 12-kilometre stretch of coastline from the ocean-washed suburbs of Sea Point, Clifton and Camps Bay to the small, fashionably exclusive seaside village of Llandudno. To drive along this route, at any time of the day, but especially during the magical hour of sunset, is delight indeed: on your left are the towering, often cloud-wreathed heights of the Twelve Apostles; on your right cliffs that tumble far down to rocks and the blue ocean. Llandudno itself, with its fringe of bay and its backing of high mountain peak (a distinctively shaped one known as Little Lion's Head) has a particularly spectacular setting. Around the promontory to the south is Sandy Bay, a secluded stretch of beach much favoured by sunbathers of the less inhibited kind. The main coast road above Llandudno leads on to the valley of:

Hout Bay, a substantial and most pleasant harbour town nestling in a wide green valley between mountain and sea. In translation the name means 'Wood Bay', a reference to its value as a source of timber during the earliest colonial years (it boasted a sawmill before the turn of the 17th century, though it remained very much an unspoilt and practically uninhabited wilderness until about a hundred years ago). Today it is a expanding residential area that functions variously as prestigious dormitory settlement, as thriving tourist centre and as the headquarters of the Peninsula's crayfishing fleet.

Crayfish, though, aren't the only sea harvest: during June and July great quantities of snoek are caught offshore and sold on the quayside (the annual and very popular Snoek Festival is held during this period). The harbour is one of the Cape's most attractive, girded by mountains, full of sturdy fishing boats and expensive-looking yachts. The main attraction at the moment is Mariner's Wharf, an emporium, modelled on its famed namesake in San Francisco, that offers fresh fish and live lobster, nautical gifts, a bistro and an excellent restaurant. From the harbour, one can embark on a boat trip to nearby Seal Island, and there are cruises to more distant destinations. The waterfront is earmarked for tourist development (speciality and craft shops, pubs and eating houses). A five-star hotel is planned for the beachfront.

The Hout Bay museum is worth a visit, as is Kronendal, a Cape Dutch H-plan homestead (on Main Road) dating from 1800 and now a restaurant, art centre and national monument. A little way up the valley is the World of Birds, one of the largest and most imaginatively conceived bird parks in the country: the aviaries are cleverly landscaped to simulate natural habitat, and are fully accessible to the public; one walks through them while the residents (more than 3 000, belonging to 450 different species) carry on with their daily lives.

From Hout Bay, you can either drive inland, up the valley and over Constantia Nek to the historic and very lovely winelands of Constantia (see page 59), or continue southwards along the coastal route, a dramatic 10-kilometre stretch known as:

THE PENINSULA

Chapman's Peak Drive, a tortuous, scenic, 600 metre-high road cut through multi-coloured strata of granite and sandstone. The views from the lookout points and picnic sites – of Chapman's Bay below and of Hout Bay and its unusual Sentinel peak across the waters – are magnificent.

The marine drive then descends onto the flat, low, marshy plain of Noordhoek and its wide, white, eight kilometre-long beach – the western Peninsula's largest. Noordhoek's shoreline attracts hikers, horse-riders, anglers and surfers, but the sands are generally too windy for comfortable sunbathing and the sea too chilly (and the backwash too strong) for swimming. Beyond lies Kommetjie, a small seaside village clustered around a basin-shaped tidal pool. Nearby Long Beach is a noted venue for championship surfing.

Final stop-over on the western coastal route is Scarborough, a modest but attractive enough collection of cottages and holiday homes scattered over wild-looking, heath-type countryside. The local restaurant, the Camel Rock, is a charmingly informal place famed for its seafood.

From Scarborough, one turns inland to reach the entrance to the Cape of Good Hope nature reserve and, at its southern extremity, Cape Point (see page 58).

THE EASTERN SEABOARD

False Bay's warm and often wind-blown waters lap the whole of the Peninsula's eastern coastline, stretching from Cape Point northward to Table Bay and, beyond, to the Hottentots-Holland range of mountains and Cape Hangklip. The bay's name derives from the many occasions on which early navigators mistook the Point for Hangklip – an often tragic error, for the winds and the currents are perverse and, over the centuries, a great many ships came to grief on its shores. Today, though, it puts on a more benevolent face, serving as one of the country's foremost angling, surfing and boating playgrounds and as a treasure-house for marine biologists.

The bay is fringed by a 35-kilometre, almost continuous stretch of beach and, in its southern reaches, by a number of old-established seaside towns and resort villages linked by rail and by coastal road. From the city one drives out on the M4 or M5 metropolitan highways (or takes the suburban train) through Cape Town's southern suburbs (see page 16) to Muizenberg and then follows the shoreline through St James, Kalk Bay, Fish Hoek and on to historic Simon's Town and the entrance to the Cape of Good Hope nature reserve.

The Muizenberg area A hundred years ago Muizenberg took pride of place among the southern hemisphere's seaside resorts: Capetonian gentlefolk loved the place; so did the holidaying multi-millionaires of the Rand. Cecil Rhodes spent his last years nearby, in Barkley Cottage on the main road to St James (the house has been preserved, complete with personal effects and memorabilia, as a museum). Rudyard Kipling wrote evocatively of the 'white sands of Muizenberg ... spun before the gale', and indeed the beach is rather special: a wide, gently sloping expanse of fine, pale sand pounded rhythmically by long lines of breakers. The water is shallow, safe for bathing, ideal for surfing, yachting and boardsailing.

The town itself is old-fashioned, perhaps a little run-down, the atmosphere one of genteel neglect, but there's a lot of charm in its turn-of-the-century villas, boarding houses, converted fishermen's cottages and its colourful bathing huts. At the railway station end of the beach is a candy-striped pavilion that offers pools and putt-putt, boat trips and miniature train rides, a waterslide, a playground and restaurants. The station, designed by Rhodes's architect Herbert Baker, is one of the town's feature buildings, as is the nearby Posthuys, built in 1673 as an observation post and small fort and now the oldest habitable European-style domestic dwelling in the country. Down the road is The Fort', an imposing Italianesque edifice that houses the Natale Labia Museum, a branch of the National Gallery named in honour of Prince Natale Labia (1877-1936) and his wife Princess Ida Louise. On display inside are works of art and some fine furniture.

Just to the north of Muizenberg is Sandvlei, an attractive stretch of water much enjoyed by boardsailors, canoeists and yachtsmen. In the middle is Park Island, a recreational area; on the eastern shores the unusual waterfront suburb of Marina da Gama.

St James, on the coast road a short distance to the south of Muizenberg, boasts a cosy little beach and some attractive Mediterranean-type domestic architecture (white walls, wooden shutters, red roofs). Farther along is Kalk Bay, a pretty little resort and fishing harbour much visited and photographed by holidaymakers, especially in June and July, when the snoek are running (the catches are sold on the quayside). Rising behind the shoreline between Muizenberg and Kalk Bay is a modest range of hills – the Kalkbaaiberg – that are a magnet for ramblers, hikers, nature-lovers and, especially, for speleologists: the wild and rocky area has a huge profusion of caves.

Fish Hoek, farther south, is a substantial middle-class residential centre and South Africa's only 'dry' town – one cannot buy liquor within the municipal bounds (a relic of the days when thirsty British sailors from nearby Simon's Town threatened its tranquility). A fairly ordinary place, but it has a splendid beach and the sea in summer is colourful with the sails of yachts, catamarans and sailboards. Inland, in the valley that runs straight across the Peninsula to Chapman's Bay on the west coast (the valley was once beneath the sea, the land to the south an island), is the celebrated Peer's Cave, an important archaeological site (of 15 000-year-old Fish Hoek Man) whose walls are decorated with prehistoric paintings.

Simon's Town is the terminus of the suburban railway line and final port of call before entering the Cape of Good Hope nature reserve. Founded by and named after Cape governor Simon van der Stel, who recommended the bay as an anchorage in 1687, it eventually became the Royal Navy's principal South Atlantic base, the dockyards reverting to South African proprietorship in 1957, at the beginning of the Republic's era of isolation. Not surprisingly, therefore, naval history mantles the town, the nautical past most visible in the Simon's Town and Martello Tower museums, and in St Francis' church, whose interior walls are splendidly adorned with maritime scenes. Of quite a different kind are the displays of the Stempastorie, the original Dutch Reformed parsonage that now functions as a museum of national symbols.

The Cape of Good Hope The southern portion of the Peninsula is occupied by the Cape of Good Hope nature reserve, a 7 750-hectare expanse of indigenous fynbos that is magically transformed when the wild flowers bloom, briefly but gloriously, in springtime. Altogether, about 1 200 plant species have been identified within the reserve. Fauna includes bontebok (a type of antelope once threatened with extinction, but now flourishing and a variety of other buck, Cape mountain zebra, Cape fox, caracal, and four troops of rather unusual chacma baboons – they are thought to be the only primate group in the world (excluding fish-eating man) that subsists, largely, on marine foods. They are also partial to handouts, which creates something of a problem: they tend to become familiar with and dependent on visitors and, by natural progression, troublesome and even aggressive. The troop near Cape Point is adept at raiding cars. In your interest and theirs (those that become a nuisance have to be put down), lock your vehicle when you get out, and don't, please, feed the animals.

The reserve is criss-crossed by a network of roads and trail paths that lead to viewsites, picnic spots and barbecue areas; other visitor amenities include an old homestead that now functions as a restaurant; tidal pools for swimmers, and a slipway (at Buffels Bay, which also has a pleasant beach) for boating enthusiasts.

Principal attraction, though, is Cape Point, the massive prominence whose 300-metre cliffs fall sheer to the southern sea below and around which gannets and gulls wheel in noisy profusion. The purists will assure you that the Atlantic and Indian oceans meet off Cape Agulhas far to the east, but here, at the Point, the cold Benguela and the warm Agulhas currents merge to produce a far more striking effect.

There are breathtaking views from the base of the old lighthouse at the top, which one reaches either on foot (a hard slog) or by the regular shuttle bus.

The headland has its place in legend as well as geography: it is off Cape Point that the *Flying Dutchman*, the phantom ship with broken masts and tattered sails, has reportedly been sighted by generations of seafarers – including Britain's King George V, in 1880, when he was serving in the Royal Navy as a young midshipman.

THE INLAND AREAS
Much of the central portion of the Cape Peninsula – that which lies to the west of the suburban line of rail – is hilly, beautifully wooded, scenically superb.

From Kirstenbosch (see page 18), take the road south, turn right at the T-junction and continue on the embowered and winding route that leads up to Constantia Nek. About half-way along, on your right, is the entrance to Cecilia forest, an enchanting place for rambling, for picnicking, for communing with nature. Farther on, at the summit of the Nek, the route divides, the road to your right leading down to Hout Bay (see page 55), that to your left taking you through green and lovely countryside of Constantia, and to the most renowned of its homesteads:

Groot Constantia This splendid mansion, centrepiece of the famed Constantia vineyards, was originally conceived and built by the outstanding Cape governor Simon van der Stel, who spent a happy retirement there until his death in 1712. Later, in 1778, the estate passed to the Cloete family, whose patriarch, Hendrik, added a fine cellar, a two-storeyed building designed by the celebrated French architect Louis Thibault (its exquisite cherub-adorned pediment is the work of the sculptor Anton Anreith).

The farmstead burned down in 1925, but has since been taken over by the government, superlatively restored and declared a national monument.

On view inside this stateliest of homes is a fine collection of period furniture, of *objets d'art* and of delicate porcelain (Rhenish and Delft, Chinese and Japanese); outside attractions include the cellar (hourly guided tours are laid on), the adjacent museum, which tells the story of wine and wine-making through the centuries, and an oak-lined avenue leading to an ornamental pool in which the Cloetes and their distinguished guests once bathed.

Groot Constantia offers two restaurants: the Jonkershuis, which serves traditional, and superb, Cape lunches and teas, and the Tavern (buffet lunches, bench seating, Germanic atmosphere, often crowded, always fun). Many visitors, though, choose to bring a picnic basket and relax on the shady lawns.

Hendrik Cloete had impeccable taste when it came to architecture, furnishings and landscaping. He was also a winemaker without peer, developing Constantia's vineyards to produce vintages of legendary quality, sweet and rich wines that found their way to the royal tables of Europe. Unhappily his secrets did not survive the passing of the estate's vintners, but the area still yields splendid reds. They are much sought after by discerning buyers, and tend to be in short supply. Daily wine sales are held *in situ*.

Groot Constantia is one of three functioning wine farms in the valley. Somewhat less grand, but as attractive in their own way, are its two neighbours:

❐ Buitenverwachting, an historic complex of gabled house, stables, gabled and thatched cellar and slave quarters, resurrected from obscurity relatively recently and faultlessly restored to the condition the buildings enjoyed in their heyday. Buitenverwachting runs one of the Cape's best restaurants, and produces some of the best wines (the maiden vintages appeared in 1985 and in the brief years since have won international awards). Cellar tours are conducted by appointment, and there are daily tastings and sales on the premises.

❐ Klein Constantia, nearby, is an enchanting old homestead, built in 1796 and also rescued from neglect and decay to become one of the jewels of the Peninsula. It's rather more private than the other two (it has no restaurant), but the wines are consistently to be found in the top ranks – the first of the modern vintages, the 1986 Sauvignon blanc, was adjudged best white at the South African Wine Show. Again, there are cellar tours by appointment (the modern cellars have won design awards), tastings and sales.

The Tokai area, to the north-east of the Constantia valley, has suffered suburban encroachment but has its attractions, most notable of which are the Tokai forest, which extends up the slopes of Constantiaberg and whose trees are of many different and lovely varieties; the arboretum (near the Constantia Village Centre), and, just outside the forest reserve, the manor house, dating from 1795 and described by one authoritative writer as 'the most outstanding homestead in the Peninsula'. To the north of the forest is the:

Silvermine nature reserve, an unspoilt expanse of wilderness that, together with its eastward forest extension, sprawls across the waist of the Peninsula from Muizenberg and Kalk Bay in the east to Noordhoek Peak in the west. This is rugged, splendidly wooded countryside, and a magnet for the picnicker, the hiker and the rambler.

The reserve area is bisected by Ou Kaapseweg ('Old Cape Road', or the M64), one of finest of the Peninsula's scenic routes. It runs south from Westlake, traversing the Steenberg and Silvermine before descending to the Fish Hoek valley. The vistas from its sweeping curves are quite entrancing.

Rondevlei nature reserve, across the railway line to the east, is also well worth a visit: it's one of the Cape's more important wetlands, haven to some 220 waterfowl and other bird species and site of a research station. The 137-hectare reserve encompasses a shallow lake, marshland and indigenous bush, a picnic area and a small museum.

❑ WHERE TO STAY

ALPHEN HOTEL
Constantia

One of the loveliest of the Cape's hotels, a national monument set in the rolling countryside of the Constantia Valley some 20 minutes' drive from Cape Town's city centre.

The Alphen is mantled in history: in 1753 the double-storeyed (one of the country's earliest) Cape Dutch homestead was home to the Lever family, and the property changed hands many times until purchased in 1850 by the Cloete family, doyens of the 18th century wine industry, who still own it. It has functioned as a hotel since 1963, but was renowned for its hospitality long before then, numbering among its distinguished guests Governor Lord Charles Somerset (who presided over huge breakfasts in the Agterkamer before setting forth to lead the local hunt). Anglo-Boer War Generals Roberts and

Kitchener talked strategy over the port in the same room; Dr James Barry fought a duel on the south steps; literary giants Mark Twain and George Bernard Shaw dined there; Cecil Rhodes and Jan Smuts stayed over on occasion.

The ambience of aristocracy and time-honoured stateliness is still there, impressively evident in the classic façade of the building, the gracefully proportioned rooms, the high-beamed ceilings, the tall leaded-light windows, the gabled cellars and, especially, in the antique furniture, the oil paintings and *objets d'art* that are everywhere and which, together, are considered one of the country's finest private displays.

Notable are the wall paintings, recently discovered when renovators stripped away the paint of centuries; and the magnificent yellowwood and stinkwood screen between *voorkamer* and *agterkamer*. This screen was later copied for inclusion in De Tuyn Huys, the official residence of the State President.

The grounds are extensive, oak-shaded, trim and serene.

Accommodation Just 29 bedrooms, of which three are suites (one of them in the old Manor House), scattered about the sprawling complex, each individually and quite beautifully decorated and furnished, many with antique pieces. A four-poster and *chaise longue* are featured in the honeymoon suite.

Newly renovated and comfortably appointed rooms open off pleasant little courtyards, while the Victorian Dower House and the historic Manor House offer individually decorated luxury suites and rooms.

Food, drink and service Quietly sophisticated; moderately large menu; generally simple dishes; classic cuisine. We had spiced prawns with peppercorns to start and the chef's special loin of lamb for the entrée; the more adventurous could try the pan-fried ostrich steak. The menu changes every quarter. The elegant Agterkamer accommodates a little over 50 diners; the smaller, candle-lit Heerenkamer and Cullinan dining rooms provide a more intimate setting. There are fresh flowers everywhere.

The wine list is predictably excellent, and includes the notable Alphen Cabernet Sauvignon (adjudged Champion Red Cultivar Wine in 1985) and the Pinotage Blanc de Noir (South Africa's first), which won gold medals for three years running at the prestigious Stellenbosch Wine Show – fitting tributes to Alphen winemaker Marinus Bredell's commitment and skill. The private cellar holds, among others, the celebrated Chateau Alphen '73 and the Klein Constantia Chardonnay '88.

Well worth visiting is the Winery, gabled showpiece of the estate's 'great square'. Incidentally, suburbia has been steadily encroaching on the historic vineyards and Alphen vines now grace the slopes of the Helderberg, not far from the town of Somerset West.

The Boer 'n Brit bar features a roaring log fire and superb pub lunches in winter; the Mill terrace, overlooking the leisurely Diep River, is a much-favoured social venue (memorable seafood and meat braais under the oaks in summer).

Service is professional and amiable; guests' names are remembered.

Amenities Part of the old Alphen estate, a comfortable stroll from the hotel, has been given over to the Constantia Health and Racquet Club (tennis, squash, gymnasium, aerobics, heated swimming pool). The hotel itself has a smallish, attractive pool; jogging and walking along the leafy Constantia byways is popular and there is easy access to the mountain along the Diep River. On the premises is a hairdressing salon; among other services on offer are transport to and from travel terminals.

Conferences: the Long Gallery can accommodate about 40 people; the largest reception area up to 150; the private Heerenkamer dining room is available for functions; the small Cullinan room seats up to 12.

Suggested visits: to nearby Kirstenbosch Botanical Gardens (see page 18); to Groot Constantia (page 59).

THE ALPHEN in brief

How to get there: From central Cape Town, take De Waal Drive to the Blue Route; off at the Plumstead/Constantia/Hout Bay ramp, which curves back towards the highway. Left into Constantia Main Road, right at the first set of traffic lights into Alphen Drive, thence to the hotel on your left. **Tariff** *(See Authors' Note on page 4):*F **Official rating:** ★★★ **Conference facilities**: Up to 150 delegates (see text). **Banqueting facilities**: Up to 200 (room not available for conferences). **Liquor licence**: Full. **Children**: Welcome in standard rooms; children under 12 are not accommodated in the luxury rooms or suites. **Reservations**: PO Box 35, Constantia 7848, Cape; telephone: (021) 794-5011; fax: (021) 794-5710; telex: 5-26195 SA.

THE CELLARS COUNTRY HOUSE

Constantia

The Cellars, as its name suggests, started life in 1750 as a winery in the heart of the magnificent Constantia Valley, was later converted to an elegant country homestead (part of the Klaasenbosch estate) and now does duty as one of the Cape's most charming private hotels – a place for the connoisseur. It looks out on great expanses of woodland, is beautifully furnished and decorated, and it offers quiet relaxation in exquisite park-like surrounds, fine food, old-style hospitality, warmth, ease and the personal touch – and not a little historical interest. The site was in use well before the advent of the winery: a recent archaeological survey unearthed artefacts, a drainage canal and documents that date the property to around 1693.

The Cellars has recently been upgraded to four-star status. It does not cater for children under 16.

Accommodation Thirty units in total; six of them suites, each with *en suite* bathroom, well-stocked mini-bar, direct-dial phone, television and a quite splendid view. Ground-floor rooms open onto the garden terrace.

Really special are the big brass beds, the antique pieces and the stylish designer fabrics: my room had yellow walls and a yellow nightfrill on the bed, yellow cushions and blue-and-yellow patterned curtains that echoed the luxurious feel of warm sunshine that streamed through the windows. All rooms have underfloor heating.

Food, drink and service Table d'hôte and à la carte cuisine is prepared for the gourmet, in the most pleasing of environments. Tableware is of the very best, the lighting is subtle, the service unobtrusively good. The management pays homage to its fine wines, keeping them in just the right conditions and at the correct storage temperature.

Summer country-style breakfasts (and drinks in the evening) are served outside, beneath a 300-year-old oak tree. In winter, one takes one's glass of cheer in the chintzy drawing room, beside a roaring log fire.

Amenities The Cellars is a place in which to relax quietly, and to enjoy the finer things of life. It has a pleasant courtyard pool for swimmers, but there's not much else laid on in the way of formal entertainment and recreation. There's plenty to see and do in the general area, though. We enjoyed walking in the adjacent Cecilia Forest, under trees that were planted in the early years of the Dutch colony; Kirstenbosch and Groot Constantia are nearby; Cape Town (pages 6 – 51), the Peninsula (pages 52 – 60) and Winelands (pages 72 – 110) are easily accessible. 11 golf courses are within an easy drive.

THE CELLARS in brief
How to get there: The Cellars is on Hohenhort Avenue, Constantia. Take De Waal drive (M3) from the city, past UCT to the Hout Bay/Kirstenbosch turn on Rhodes' Drive in Newlands. The traffic lights are the first set past UCT. Turn right onto the M63, pass Kirstenbosch Gardens; turn right at the T-junction, to Hout Bay. A left turn, opposite Cecilia Forest takes you into Hohenhort Avenue: right at the T-junction and follow the road to The Cellars on your right. *Tariff (See Authors' Note on page 4)*: D **Official rating**: ★★★★ *Conference facilities*: A small meeting room at your disposal (12 to 14 people). *Liquor licence*: Full. *Children*: The Cellars is not suitable for children under 16. *Reservations*: Hohenhort Avenue, Constantia 7800, Cape; telephone: (021) 794-2137; fax: (021) 794-2149.

GROOT MODDERGAT
Hout Bay Road area

A marvellous old Cape Dutch homestead hidden among the oak and olive trees on a 65-acre estate between Constantia and Hout Bay. It's owned by Ineke and Fritz Palthe, who have filled it with beautifully chosen period furniture; our hostess was the cheerfully convivial Christine Templeton, a former naval officer (she ran the catering at the Simon's Town base) who looks after the guesthouse, and the guests, with loving care.

The original gabled house and its wine cellar were built in 1841 by the Boonzaaier family, who changed the name from Moddergat to Valley Grange and lived there until 1918, when they were forced to sell after the dreaded phylloxera disease destroyed their vines. The property was then bought by Wilfred Haine; olive groves were planted by the renowned Italian grower Costas (who then returned each year, from his base at Paarl, to harvest the crops; today olives still feature in Groot Moddergat's fare).

The pride of Moddergat is its yellowwood and stinkwood dining-room table, fully two metres wide and five metres long, which easily seats 24 people and which, on special occasions – notably weddings (the ceremony is held in the garden; the reception inside) – is resplendent with lace, crystal, silver, flowers and antique candelabra.

Most guests learn of the place by word of mouth, and they tend to return again and again.

Accommodation There are seven rooms, two in the main house, one in a thatched cottage across the courtyard and four, slightly more modern units, in the old slave quarters, high up on the property – a homestead with a splendid view over the olive grove to the mountains. Probably the nicest rooms are in the main house: one has a fireplace, brass bed and lovely antique dressing-table. Each of the two upstairs rooms has its own balcony; all have private bathrooms, and are equipped with kettles, telephones, clock radios, heaters for winter and fans for summer. There's TV in each of the two lounges (one in the main house, the other in the slave quarters).

Occupancy is limited to 14 guests 'to ensure friendly attention and old fashioned courtesy'.

Food, drink and service A full breakfast is served in the dining room each morning, but dinners are only offered for special functions. Guests usually go out to one of several excellent restaurants in the general area.

Amenities The Roman-style swimming pool is in a lovely garden setting overlooking Hout Bay Valley and is equipped with a cabana bar, built-in braai and telephone extension. Groot Moddergat is within easy reach of Hout Bay (see page 55), the wine estates of Constantia, the beautiful Cecilia Forest and the gardens of Kirstenbosch.

Conferences: The dining room is much in demand for board meetings and the smaller type of seminar.

GROOT MODDERGAT in brief
How to get there: The guest house is 1,8 km down the Hout Bay road from Constantia Nek (you'll see the sign on your left, opposite the rather imposing entrance to Longkloof). From Cape Town, take De Waal Drive to the Rhodes Avenue turn-off (signposted Hout Bay), turn right and continue past Kirstenbosch to the T-junction; swing right and follow the winding route up to the Nek. Alternatively, try the longer but equally scenic coastal route from Sea Point to and through Hout Bay (see pages 55 – 56). **Tariff** *(See Authors' Note on page 4):* D **Official rating**: *Not applicable.* **Conference facilities**: *Available for small seminars.* **Liquor licence**: *Unlicensed.* **Children**: *Children under 12 are not accommodated.* **Reservations**: *Main Road, Hout Bay 7800, Cape Province; telephone: (021) 790-1110; fax: (021) 790-1070.*

HOUTKAPPERSPOORT
Hout Bay

The place – a virtual village of stone and timber nestled in the deep-green magic of a Peninsula pine forest – reminded us vaguely of a North American wilderness area.

Houtkapperspoort, ('woodcutter's canyon)', was the original name of the area, which used to be a dense, almost impenetrable expanse of alien Port Jackson willow until Canadian Gordon Kling arrived there. He had the land cleared, roads and services installed and the rustic-looking resort built.

Far back in the early colonial days this lovely stretch of upland terrain was ravaged by a Cape Dutch settlement desperately in need of timber. Woodcutters and their slaves hacked away at the melkbos, wild olive and yellowwood – but happily the damage was limited: roads and vehicles were primitive; the area was remote, barely accessible, and it resisted the onslaught. The celebrated astronomer John Hershel, who arrived at the Cape in 1834, described the Hout Bay setting as 'wild and inhospitable'. Today, imaginative clearing and landscaping programmes have created a gentler woodland haven.

Houtkapperspoort and its surrounds are wonderful for walking, for riding, for communing with the quieter muses. After we had struggled up to Eagle's Nest, which towers above the cottages, we saw the waves rolling in on the beach at Muizenberg and below, on the Atlantic side, the azure blue of Hout Bay harbour in bright sunlight. Definitely worth the climb. You can walk to the top of Table Mountain, or to Kirstenbosch National Botanical Gardens (see page 18) directly from the resort.

Accommodation There are 26 self-catering (one-, two- and three-bedroomed) cottages; some freestanding and some semi-detached; most double-storeyed and offering at least one bedroom one the second floor, but three are of the bungalow-type. All are nicely furnished and carpeted (some have under-carpet heating), each with its bathroom, kitchen equipped with electric or gas stove and hob (some also have microwave ovens), fridge, crockery and cutlery, TV (with M-Net), PABX telephone, outside braai, garden furniture and individual parking. Bedding is provided and towels may be hired. There's a coin laundry. Houtkapperspoort's staff keep the rooms admirably clean.

The cottages are cleverly positioned in beautifully landscaped grounds to ensure relative privacy, with hedges and trees serving as screens.

Food, drink and service Constantia Nek restaurant is just across the road and Kronendal, Barristers and many other restaurants are nearby – in Hout Bay or Constantia – but everything is there in the cottages to prepare your own meals.

Amenities Solar-heated swimming pool, all-weather tennis court and children's play facilities *in situ*; a myriad of walking trails to be explored in the vicinity (the property borders Orangekloof and Cecilia State Forest). The Groot Constantia, Klein Constantia and Buitenverwachting wine estates are nearby (see page 59), and it's also worth spending time in Hout Bay (page 55), a charming little harbour town that has good shops, good restaurants, a pleasant stretch of beach, a museum, Mariner's Wharf and the outstanding World of Birds.

HOUTKAPPERSPOORT in brief

How to get there: From central Cape Town, take De Waal Drive past UCT, right into Rhodes Drive (Hout Bay signpost), past Kirstenbosch to the T-junction, turn right and follow the winding road up to Constantia

Nek, and bear right around the traffic circle. The entrance is about 300 metres down the hill, on your right. You can also take the longer, equally scenic drive along the coastal road to and through Hout Bay (see page 55). **Tariff** (See Authors' Note on page 4): B **Official rating**: Not applicable. **Liquor licence**: Not applicable. **Children**: Welcome. **Reservations**: Houtkapperspoort, Hout Bay Road, Constantia Nek 7800; telephone: (021) 794-5216; fax: (021) 794-2907.

LORD NELSON INN
Simon's Town

The Lord Nelson, in Simon's Town at the southern end of False Bay, recently underwent a major facelift to emerge as one of the most invitingly attractive of the Cape Peninsula's smaller hotels – an inn in the classic English tradition: cute and cottagey, cosy and comfortable, beautifully appointed and gleaming with polished wood and brass. Warmed in winter by open fires, the place has a rather contrived but very appealing nautical character.

It's an unusually hospitable hotel: guests are received warmly and looked after with genuine thoughtfulness. Highly recommended.

Accommodation Just ten rooms atop the oak-bannistered staircase, individually and very nicely decorated; colonial style, with wood finishes and soft pink carpets. Each unit has its naval-associated name: Trafalgar; Lady Emma Hamilton, Lord Nelson, HMS *Victory* and, topically, Just Nuisance (who was a well-known Great Dane dog, much beloved of British sailors stationed at Simon's Town during the Second World War). Several rooms are graced by large balconies overlooking the bay; each has its private bathroom (stocked with shampoo, bath foam and fabric washer), its telephone, TV (with M-Net), radio. Fresh flowers and a complimentary bottle of wine add the welcoming touches.

Food, drink and service In decorative terms, Horatio's, the main restaurant, is an attractive mix of nautical (rope-covered pillars and a fishnet ceiling) and cottage styles (sieves and bush saws on the walls).

Cuisine can be described as Cape regional with the emphasis, predictably, on seafood: live fish and crustaceans are kept in a tank, awaiting your choice; on chilly winter evenings the clay pizza oven warms the room. Everything is fresh: the fruit, the vegetables, the fish from nearby Kalk Bay.

We tried Knysna oysters and French vineyard snails with 'the galley's secret fluffy garlic sauce', delectable perlemoen (abalone) thinly sliced in garlic, herbs and white wine, a generous and not too costly seafood platter (crayfish, prawn, black mussel, kingklip), and pancakes and tipsy tart to end.

Breakfast comprised a selection of fresh fruit, yoghurts, fish, eggs, bacon, sausages, health bread, scones and Danish pastries.

The wine list is excellent. Lighter and most pleasant meals are served in Hardy's, the other restaurant.

There are two pubs, The Powder Monkey and Emily's Den, both of which are popular with the locals (always an encouraging sign).

Amenities Simon's Town has a lot to offer the visitor (see page 57). There are several small, sheltered and most pleasant beaches on this stretch of the coast, among them Boulders, Seaforth (which is backed by lawns and trees) and, along the bridle path, Foxy Beach. The largest expanse of sand is Glen Cairn, to the north; nearby are two tidal pools. Walking excursions on the mountain slopes behind the town – where the indigenous fynbos (heath) is in pristine condition – may be arranged; there's golf and bowls at Simon's Town Country Club. Cape Point and the nature reserve are just along the road to the south; picturesque Kalk Bay is nearby.

LORD NELSON in brief
How to get there: The hotel is in Simon's Town. Take the M5 to Muizenberg and continue along the coastal road, through Fish Hoek and into the town, past the train terminus to the Inn in the Main Road, on your right. Tariff (See Authors' Note on page 4): E **Official rating:** ★★ **Conference facilities:** *Amenities for up to 16 people. Contact the Hotel for details.* **Liquor licence:** *Full.* **Children:** *Welcome.* **Reservations:** *58 St George's Street, Simon's Town 7995, Cape; telephone: (021) 786-1386; fax: (021) 786-1009.*

MONKEY VALLEY
Noordhoek

Here, in the middle of one of South Africa's last milkwood forests, we found something that comes somewhere near Eden. White-plastered chalets and log cabins are staggered on the hillside, hidden from each other by the overhanging branches of the dense-foliaged trees in the valley below Chapman's Peak. Almost every unit – they comprise at least two bedrooms, a bathroom, and a lounge/kitchen/dining area, some of them are built on stilts – has a lofty view, framed by overhanging branches, of Noordhoek's wide, white and invariably deserted beach, which stretches for eight kilometres all the way to Kommetjie to the south.

We loved this place. It reminded us a bit of Nature's Valley near Plettenberg Bay: unspoilt, skilfully designed for maximum privacy and careful to retain almost every tree in the forest. A path through a tangle of woodland leads down to the beach. The management makes a point of stressing regeneration – of us weary mortals as well as the ecology of the area.

Monkey Valley is essentially a time-share resort, but units can be rented on a casual basis.

Accommodation Each chalet has a different name – Seagull, Octopus, Bushbaby, Pelican, Turtle Villa, Dolphin, Baboon Lodge, Albatross – and all are furnished in Cape-cottage style, each one unique. The two- and three-bedroomed units can take six and eight people respectively; the smaller ones are for couples, perhaps with a baby. Comfort, even luxury, and the view are the drawcards; we were delighted to find that there was an oven, microwave and dishwasher, telephone and colour TV with M-Net (though no radio when we were there; take your portable). Beautiful Zimbabwean earthenware crockery is supplied, an ethnic touch echoed in the woven rugs and wicker baskets. Bathing is bliss: the window reaches the edge of the bath and the view is superb.

Food, drink and service The chalets are self catering. Bring only your food and drink; the local supermarket (at Sun Valley) is five minutes away. In the same shopping centre is a restaurant, and there are a number of other eateries within easy reach – most notably at Hout Bay. While we were there, drinks were available in the makeshift pub, and the main building (taken up with offices) was to be converted into a restaurant. Braai units and wood are supplied; supper on the wooden terrace (which runs the length of the cabin), taken while the sun sinks below the sea, is magic indeed.

Amenities Experienced horse riders, which we are not, canter along the beach at dawn and dusk. The local Sunbird Riding School has only eight mounts so it's necessary to book in advance. We preferred to walk along the sands. Bird lovers can motor the 12 kilometres to Hout Bay, along the glorious Chapman's Peak Drive, to Mariner's Wharf or the World of Birds (see page 55). Shops in the general area sell art and crafts, handmade jewellery, homemade foods and farm produce.

MONKEY VALLEY in brief

*How to get there: From central Cape Town, take Beach Road through Sea Point, continue along the Victoria Drive coastal route to and through Hout Bay, over Chapman's Peak Drive towards Noordhoek, where you'll notice the Monkey Valley signs. Alternatively, take the inland route, via Constantia (see pages 58 – 60) Tariff (See Authors' Note on page 4): Chalets, D **Official rating**: Not applicable. Conference facilities: Available, contact the complex for details. **Liquor licence**: Not applicable. **Children**: Welcome. **Reservations**: PO Box 114, Noordhoek 7985, Cape; telephone: (021) 789-1391 or central reservations: toll-free 0800-12-3000; fax: Cape Town (021) 789-1143; Johannesburg (011) 484-2752.*

ROBIN GORDON HOTEL

St James

An ordinary family hotel, which will appeal to those who really do want a quiet and undemanding weekend away, without frills and fuss. There's no glitz here, and few pretensions: it rates just one star, and provides solid value for money.

The Robin Gordon is old-fashioned – genuinely so: it hasn't simply been refurbished to imitate a turn-of-the-century hostelry. It retains its authentic character: a little dark, a little cloistered in parts, but comfortable enough, and thoroughly hospitable. Physical features of note are the thick walls and high ceilings, some of pressed steel and engraved with the date 1913. And not much, bar the people who run it, has changed since then. The present Italian management has been in harness for about twenty years.

From the windows you have a magnificent sea view across False Bay, behind the hotel are the mountains; Kalk Bay fishing harbour is below the main road. Altogether a charming setting.

During the Second World War the Robin Gordon was used as a convalescent home for soldiers, a number of whom still – after five decades – come back year after year for their holidays.

Accommodation There are fifty rooms in all, some of them family units with curtained alcoves holding bunk-beds for children. Much of their original nature is still evident: old oak dressing tables (most now painted white), Art Nouveau-type octagonal tiles in the *en suite* bathrooms. And every room is different. Telephone and radios are available, but no television (you go through to the TV lounge for this). Again, superb views of the bay from the bedroom windows.

Food, drink and service The Luna Restaurant is presided over by an Italian chef who specializes in seafood fresh from Kalk Bay, and in homemade pastas. He also produces some excellent international fare. À la carte for dinner; set menu for light lunches. There's a nice pub *in situ* which serves bar lunches.

Service is courteous and friendly; the staff prides itself on addressing each guest by name.

Amenities Kalk Bay harbour is around the corner; anglers (rock, surf and deep-sea) favour the area; tidal pools offer safe swimming for children. Along the road is a row of antique shops that beckon the browser; the St James suburban railway station (frequent trains to and from the city) is within easy walking distance. Golf and other sporting amenities are either nearby or easily accessible.

ROBIN GORDON in brief

How to get there: The hotel is on the seafront at St James, 26 km from Cape Town. Take the M4 or M5 roads from the city and follow the signs to Muizenberg. St James is just beyond. A regular train service connects St James with Cape Town. **Tariff** *(See Authors' Note on page 4): B* **Official rating:** ★ *Conference facilities: None.* **Liquor licence:** *Full.* **Children:** *Welcome.* **Reservations**: *St James, 7945, Cape Province; telephone: (021) 88-1141/2/3/4.*

SHRIMPTON MANOR

Muizenberg

Shrimpton Manor is South Africa's Fawlty Towers, or so says your host (and maître d'hôtel, entertainer and friend) Tony Fischoff. In fact Tony does himself and the hotel an injustice: it certainly does have its eccentricities, but they're stylish ones, reflections of his own whimsical nature and distinctive management approach.

He is a man with a flair for the unusual, a passion for fuchsias, roses, novelty stickers and bow ties (a great many of them, ranging from a diamanté cat's face to a monstrous polka-dot affair that reaches almost to his waist), and, when it comes to running hotels, the ultimate professional. The same guests return year after year, which says a great deal.

The Manor is a smallish, cream-coloured edifice tucked away in one of Muizenberg's back streets. On the outside, the building is bright with coloured awnings and window-boxes filled with flowers; inside, there are pink velvet chairs, tasseled curtains in rich fabrics, an old-fashioned gate-lift and an air of Edwardian grace and propriety. It's very much a family place; we were looked after beautifully, made to feel at home – and we thoroughly enjoyed our stay.

Accommodation Twenty-one rooms of three different types: singles (*en suite* shower room), doubles (larger, with twin beds or double beds; shower or bath) and deluxes (separate lounge; fully appointed bathroom). All have television, radio, direct-dial phone, early morning tea and coffee service, a basket of 'essentials' (aspirin and so on), and complimentary newspaper deliveries, complete with personalized decals. Décor and furnishings are fussy but delightful; frills and knick-knacks are everywhere. Most of the rooms have pleasant views.

Food, drink and service This is Hilary Fischoff's preserve, and she handles it with flair. Shrimpton's caters (in her husband's words) for 'young lovers and old romantics' and does so stylishly.

The extensive menu pays homage to the seasons; the seafood is truly special, richly sauced and imaginatively presented.

For a starter, try the Eastern Medley, a delectably decadent mix of seafoods cooked in a creamy curry sauce scented with *garam masala*; a main course *par excellence* is the seafood and ravioli ragout or the roast duckling.

Décor complements the elegance of the food. The main restaurant is The Crystal Room: pinkish colours, impressive chandeliers and a cosy log fire; the adjoining China Room is a more intimate patio area overlooking pool and garden.

Amenities The hotel has a swimming pool and a nicely developing garden. Close by are other restaurants, and shops, banks, a golf course, bowling greens, the local library, features of sightseeing interest and fine beaches (see page 56). Cape Town, the Peninsula and all they have to offer are easily accessible.

SHRIMPTON MANOR in brief
How to get there: The hotel is in Alexander Road, just off Atlantic Beach Road, in the centre of Muizenberg. From Cape Town, take the M1, follow the signs to Muizenberg. Turn left into Atlantic Beach Road; the second road to the left is Alexander Road. *Tariff* (See Authors' Note on page 4): D **Official rating:** ★★ *Conference facilities:* Up to 15 delegates. *Liquor licence:* Unlicensed. *Children:* Shrimpton Manor is not suitable for children. *Reservations:* Alexander Road, Muizenberg 7951, Cape Town; telefax: (021) 788-1128.

SILVERMIST MOUNTAIN RETREAT
Constantia

A lovely, hilly hideaway at Constantia Nek, above Hout Bay and Constantia, tucked away among the trees, and high enough for you to watch the evening mist trail up the Longkloof Valley and to gaze over at Cecilia Forest, at the southern slopes of Table Mountain, the Twelve Apostles and the Vlakkenberg. Here, serenity reigns supreme.

Accommodation Silvermist comprises clusters of self-contained, fully serviced, comfortable cottages in various designs ranging from the spacious Vlakkenberg and Constantia suites, which have verandas, to the smaller Colonial Annex (notable for its large fireplace) and Ridge Cottage, which is split level. Each unit has two double bedrooms, a kitchen, dining and living room; all enjoy splendid views across their wide verandas, the green lawns and the pool level below to the mountains beyond.

Food, drink and service The cottages are very well equipped for cooking; domestic help keeps them clean and tidy.

Amenities The black Roman-style swimming pool, high on the hillside, has a pool-house with sofas and a bar fridge. Guests can hold barbecues here, although the cottages have their own braai facilities, well-protected from the prevailing wind.

Silvermist has its own mountain walk: it leads up the slope and across to the top of Chapman's Peak, a five-hour hike – one can, of course, settle for a shorter stretch. The countryside is very beautiful. A leisurely stroll through the Cecilia Forest takes you to Kirstenbosch. The Constantia wine estates are just down the hill on one side; Hout Bay and its Mariner's Wharf on the other.

SILVERMIST in brief

How to get there: Silvermist is 18 km from central Cape Town. Take De Waal Drive and its extension, turn right at the Hout Bay sign, past Kirstenbosch, right again at the T-junction and follow the winding route to the top of Constantia Nek. The retreat is 200 metres down the road to Hout Bay. **Tariff** *(See Authors' Note on page 4): Per unit, check.* **Official rating**: *Not applicable.* **Liquor licence**: *None; bring you own drinks.* **Children**: *Welcome.* **Reservations**: *Silvermist Constantia Nek Mountain Retreat, Constantia Nek, 7800; telephone: (021) 794-7601; fax: (021) 794-7602.*

THE WINELANDS

- ❏ WHAT TO SEE AND DO
- ❏ WHERE TO STAY

THE CAPE WINELANDS

❐ WHAT TO SEE AND DO

The splendid hills and the green valleys to the north and north-east of the Peninsula were the first of the country areas to be occupied by the early white colonists: prompted by the need to feed an expanding Cape Town, they began moving into the traditional Khoisan lands of the interior during the 1660s. Stellenbosch, on the upper reaches of the Eerste ('first') River, was founded as an agricultural centre in 1679, a venture that, in terms of food production, proved so successful that the farmers soon turned their energies and surplus resources to the growing of vines.

Thereafter, valley after valley was settled, villages laid out, the rolling foothills around Stellenbosch and, later, Franschhoek and Paarl and the rich alluvial soils of the Breede River valley turned over to pasture, to wheat, and to grapes. In 1688 a small group of French Huguenots, skilled people, some of them versed in the sciences of viticulture and wine-making, arrived to lend impetus to an industry that was already well established.

And as the farms prospered, so their owners extended their sturdy little homes, adding wings and cellars, stables and coach-houses, slaves' quarters and *jonkershuise* (houses built for the eldest sons); laid courtyards encircled by whitewashed walls; steepened the pitch of the roofs to allow for a gabled loft. By the final decade of the 17th century a distinctive architectural form was beginning to emerge – a style that owed something to medieval Holland, to the France of the Huguenots and to the islands of Indonesia, but which developed in unique fashion to become known, and admired, as Cape Dutch.

The winelands are graced by an impressive number of lovely Cape Dutch country houses. Some are modest in proportion, others truly grand, most are beautiful – and accessible to the sightseeing visitor by way of the various wine routes.

THE SPIRIT OF THE VINE

There are few more pleasant ways of exploring the south-western Cape hinterland than to follow one or another of the wine-routes. For many Capetonians, and for visitors, they provide a splendid excuse to get out into the countryside for a day's or a weekend's casual sightseeing.

An hour or two spent at an estate or farm is a pleasant experience indeed. Most of the cellars offer tastings and tours; some run excellent restaurants; at others you'll find a farm stall selling local specialities – produce, fruit, home preserves, distinctive cheeses. Many of the homesteads, as we've mentioned, are both historic and handsome; a few of them have museums *in situ*. The growers are proud of their vineyards and of their wines, and the welcome they extend to you goes well beyond a simple quest for sales and profit. As their guest, you learn something of the subtleties and secrets of the wine-making process, inspect the bottling and labelling machinery and the wooden casks tiered in the coolness of a wine- and wood-scented cellar; sample the vintages at your leisure, perhaps buy a bottle or two, take lunch on the terrace and then go on to the next farm. Nothing

THE CAPE WINELANDS

is hurried: there is time to absorb, to assess, compare, savour, enjoy. Those who are more serious about wine can add to the stock of their favourite labels, explore new areas, discover new tastes, maybe pick up a bargain caseload on the way.

Bear in mind, though, that you'll be able to cover only a small fraction of the ground during a day's excursion. There are literally hundreds of estates, farms and wineries and they produce, between them, over 2 000 different labels. A visit to four or, at the very most, five different venues along a route is probably the most you can expect to manage on a single outing.

So far, nine routes have been created, though four of them lie outside the traditional wine areas of the Boland. First to make its appearance was that of:

Stellenbosch Modelled on the famed *Routes de Vin* of France and Germany's *Weinstrassen*, the route was established in the early 1970s to take in 17 private cellars and five co-operative wineries, all located on four major roads within a 12-kilometre radius of the town. Among the more prominent are Spier (two excellent restaurants), Saxenburg (restaurant; museum), Avontuur (the farm boasts some lovely thoroughbred horses), Blaauwklippen (a charming gabled house, built in 1789; a stall selling traditional 'Cape Malay' preserves and relishes); Delaire (at the top of the Helshoogte Pass, from which there are stunning views); Hartenberg (an excellent vintner's lunch) and Delheim, on the high slopes of the Simonsberg and described as 'a touristic jewel and photographer's paradise'.

Paarl's route is rather smaller, but as aristocratic. Nederburg, though not technically part of the route, is perhaps the best-known of all the Paarl estates: its origins and reputation for fine wines go back to 1792; the H-shaped, gabled and quite entrancing homestead, set in a wide countryside mantled by vines, has been lovingly preserved. Nederburg's Wine Auction, held in April, is perhaps the premier event (and social gathering) on the local calendar: merchants, collectors, investors, private buyers and others with good (or at least plausible) reasons for being there come from afar to enjoy the sales, the tastings, the fashion shows, the food and the carnival atmosphere. Other notable venues are Backsberg (very attractive tasting parlour, self-guided tours, closed-circuit television demonstrations, and a small wine museum); Villiera (their tapas-style lunch on the terrace is a delight); Rhebokskloof (traditional Cape restaurant; 45-minute estate tours in a 4x4); Fairview (superb goat's milk cheeses), and De Leeuwen Jacht (lovely building, and lovely views).

The Vignerons de Franschhoek is a rather exclusive association, formed to promote the wines of the scenically superb Franschhoek region and as a commemorative tribute to the early Huguenots. The wines are made centrally, on a co-operative basis, and not all its members open their establishments to the public. Perhaps it shouldn't really be classed as a 'route', but some fine cellars grace the valley, best known of which are probably Bellingham (which boasts a natural ampitheatre, venue for occasional musical and other performances) and, above all, Boschendal, a beautifully restored Cape Flemish-style manor house famed for its buffet lunches, its museum displays (including Ming porcelain) and its splendid vineyards. Among other notable homesteads of the region are La Provence and Haute Provence, whose owners are also talented potters (their work is on show, and on sale). Vignerons de Franschhoek wines can be sampled at the Franschhoek Vineyards Co-operative in town. Two of the estates (Pierre Donne and La Provence) have stalls next door; Die Binnehof, a most attractive tasting shop, is nearby.

The Worcester and Robertson wine routes are rather more rural, perhaps less sophisticated but inviting nevertheless: along them, one enjoys country hospitality at its warmest. About a quarter of the national grape harvest is produced in this north-eastern region; Worcester's route takes in three estates and 22 co-operatives – the area is celebrated for white wines that vary from dry to the lusciously sweet muscadels and hanepoots. The Robertson Wine Trust comprises nine estates and eleven co-operatives; the KWV concentrate plant in town is geared to process an annual 200 000 hektolitres of grape-juice.

STELLENBOSCH

The town, set in the green and fertile valley of the Eerste River and overlooked by the Papegaaiberg ('parrot mountain'), is the second oldest, and one of the most historic, of South Africa's white settlements. It has grown gracefully and with dignity over the centuries, distinction conferred by the avenues of oak trees planted by the early townsfolk, by the public buildings and churches and sturdy, thatched-roofed houses they erected. Today, oak trees still embower the thoroughfares, and much else of the past remains. The legacy is perhaps seen at its best along Dorp Street, which has the longest row of historic buildings in the country, and Die Braak, the village green once used for parades and festivals, feasting and country games. Specific points of tourist interest include:

❐ The Village Museum in Ryneveld Street, a collection of splendid houses dating from a number of eras, all carefully restored and furnished in period style, the gardens planted with the types of tree, shrub and flower that would have beautified the original homes.

❐ Among the historically significant buildings are the Schreuderhuis (1709), the gabled Blettermanhuis (1760 – 1890), Grosvenor House (1800 – 1830) and the house of O.M. Bergh (1840 – 1870).

❐ Die Braak, round which cluster the VOC-Kruithuis (Dutch East India Company powderhouse, 1777), now a national monument housing a small military museum; the old Burgerhuis (1797), and the attractively thatched Anglican Church of St Mary (1852).

❐ D'Ouwe Werf, in Church Street: a lovely little hotel (see page 89) that started life as a boarding house as far back as 1710.

❐ Oom Samie se Winkel, an early shop that's been rebuilt in period style and is crammed with a fascinating array of

THE CAPE WINELANDS

traditional (Afrikaner) home-made preserves, bric-a-brac, curios and excellent wines of origin. Local colour at its most colourful.

❏ The University: a celebrated institution that started out as the Stellenbosch Gymnasium and then, in 1881, became the Stellenbosch College before gaining its present status in 1918. The campus, which is integrated with the town, has some fine buildings, an art gallery (at the corner of Dorp and Bird Streets), and a botanical garden noted for its indigenous succulents, orchids, ferns, cycads and bonsai.

❏ The world of wine is, predictably, well represented in and around town. Well worth visiting is Libertas Parva, a gabled mansion that houses the massive vats, the Cape furniture and brassware of the Stellenryck wine museum and, upstairs, the celebrated Rembrandt van Rijn art gallery.

Wine past and present is also on view at the Bergkelder, hollowed out of the mountain and containing vats of quite enormous dimensions (tours and tastings offered) and at the Oude Meester brandy museum on Old Strand Road. On the southern fringes of town (opposite Stellenbosch Farmers' Winery) is the Oude Libertas Centre, which contains an impressive winery (tours by appointment) and whose ampitheatre provides a lovely summertime venue for open-air Sunday music and drama.

OUTSIDE STELLENBOSCH

Among the recommended tourist venues in the general area is the Van Ryn brandy cellar, near Vlottenberg on the R310 to Cape Town and one of the country's largest distilleries (tours, audio-visual presentations, cooperage demonstrations, musical evenings and a 'brandy breakfast': a train journey from Cape Town enlivened by brandy cocktails and sustained by a solid brunch).

For those with an interest in fine crafts, there's the Jean Craig pottery on the Devon Valley Road. This offers a wide range of products; one stands in a central viewing area to watch the throwing, glazing and other processes.

Animals are on show at the Wiesenhof Wildpark north of Stellenbosch (they roam freely; the park has a small lake, picnic and braai sites and other facilities for family outings); much the same at Safariland game park, and at the Tygerberg Zoo, also north of town.

To the east lies the Jonkershoek valley, a scenically splendid area. The Eerste River rises here; ravines, lovely hills and spectacular peaks. Within the valley are the Lanzerac and Oude Nektar estates, both of which beckon the visitor; the Jonkershoek state forest, the Fisheries research station and its hatcheries, and the Assegaaibosch nature reserve, a stretch of montane fynbos that serves as sanctuary for rare proteas (there's also a small wildflower garden *in situ*), for viewing small buck and for some interesting bird species. Farther to the east is the much larger (23 000-hectare) Hottentots-Holland nature reserve, an attractive expanse of rugged cliff, tumbling river, deep valley and green woodland.

Another scenic delight is the Helshoogte pass, a steep route (the gradient is 1:10 in places) that both challenges the motorist and rewards him with stunning views – of the Simonsberg and the Wemmershoek mountains – before leading him down to the beautiful Drakenstein valley and to:

FRANSCHHOEK

The small town, whose name in translation means 'French Glen', was founded in 1688 on land granted to a party of French Huguenot refugees who had fled a Europe torn apart by religious strife. Though they were a proud people, and fiercely independent of mind, they were not allowed to form a separate community in the Cape hinterland – they were mixed in with the resident Dutch and German freeburghers – and within a few decades little remained of their cultural heritage: French was no longer spoken; assimilation was complete. The Huguenots did, though, have a strong influence on the development of the adolescent wine industry, and, as we've seen, on the gracious rural architecture of the period: many of the stately homes still bear names that reflect their Gallic origins – La Motte, La Bris, La Provence, Haute Provence, Les Chênes, Moutonne-Excelsior and others.

Franschhoek is a pleasant little centre that serves the region's fruit and wine farmers; of note in the town itself is the large but delicately graceful Huguenot Memorial and the next-door Huguenot Museum complex. To the west stretches the lovely Groot Drakenstein valley, overlooked by the mountains of that name and home to vineyards and also to a great many fruit orchards (the area was in fact the birthplace of the country's thriving deciduous fruit export industry). Within the valley is The Dutch Mill (De Hollandsche Molen), a popular recreational resort. To the south is the Franschhoek pass, one of the so-called 'Four Passes' of the region and a scenically stunning route over the high hills and down into the Riviersonderend basin. The road, which early settlers knew as the Olifantspad ('elephant's path') follows the original track made by animals migrating over the mountains.

SOMERSET WEST

An attractive and fast-growing residential town (many of its residents commute to and from work in Cape Town and Stellenbosch), set between the grandeur of the Hottentots-Holland mountains and the waters of False Bay, and adjacent to the seaside municipality of the Strand. Of interest to visitors is the local and quite excellent Country Craft Market, the historic Dutch Reformed church, the Ou Pastorie and, on the edge of town, the 400-hectare Helderberg nature reserve. From the massive dome of the Helderberg peak, home to the black eagle and peregrine falcon, there are spectacular views of the sea and the surrounding mountains, vineyards and farmlands.

Principal attractions of the Helderberg reserve are the lovely scenery, the indigenous plant life (notably the thickets of proteas and, in one charming patch of natural forest, the yellowwoods, stinkwoods and rooi-els) and the delightful array of birds, some rare and others unique to the region. The reserve is also sanctuary to a variety of buck species. For visitors, there are pleasantly undemand-

THE CAPE WINELANDS

ing rambles, some strenuous walks (including the mountain road and the path to Disa Gorge), an oak-shaded picnic area, a tearoom, a herbarium, lily ponds and a duck pond.

The main highway running eastwards from Somerset West rises precipitously to the summit of Sir Lowry's pass (superb views of the mountains, the sea and the coastal plain below) to take the traveller to the bountiful apple orchards of Elgin and Grabouw, in the region known as the Overberg (see page 127). The coastal road east leads to Gordon's Bay, a fishing village, small-craft harbour and popular holiday resort. In the warm summer months Capetonian weekenders flock to the bay to sail, fish and bathe; Bikini Beach is sheltered from the wind and is much favoured by sunbathers. There are some lovely walks and scenic drives in the area.

PAARL

The name derives from the three giant boulders of the buttress that towers over the Berg River: they caught the eye of an early Dutch explorer, reminding him of a 'diamandt-ende perel berg' (diamond and pearl hill) when viewed in the early morning, with the sunlit dew glistening on mica-studded rock surfaces. The image persisted, conferring a name on the enchanting valley beneath – the Pêrelvallei – and then on the town that was founded there in 1720 as a wagon-building and farming centre.

Paarl is the largest of the western Cape's inland towns, one of the more attractive (its suburban gardens are a joy; the surrounding countryside famed for its scenery) and one of the longest – its oak- and jacaranda-lined main street runs a full 10 kilometres from end to end. The place is also noted for its fine buildings, its close association with the wine industry, and its prominence in the fascinating story of the Afrikaans Language Movement.

Of special interest to sight-seeing visitors is the Wagonmakers Museum (fascinating displays of a once-flourishing trade); the Oude Pastorie (originally the parsonage, now a museum of Cape Dutch furniture, silverware, copperware and relics of early settler culture); the Strooidakkerk ('thatched church'; an architectural gem); the Holy Trinity (Anglican) church in Main street; the old Zion Church in Church Street, and the Taalmonument (language monument) on the slopes of Paarl Mountain. The monument is a splendid structure of three linked columns, soaring spire and fountain, each element symbolizing a debt owed by the language – to the western world, to Africa, and to Cape people of eastern origin.

La Concorde, an impressive neo-classical building on Main Street, serves as the headquarters of the KWV (Ko-operatieve Wijnbouwers Vereniging), the world's largest wine co-operative. The KWV organization's massive wine and brandy cellar in Kohler Street is open to the public; on offer are tours, tastings and lectures. The co-operative also owns Laborie, a lovely old manor house and model wine estate set on the slopes of Paarl mountain: tours by arrangement; traditional Cape fare can be enjoyed in the restaurant.

The mountain, accessible to the motorist via a circular and scenically attractive road (it's well worth stopping in at the Mill Stream wild flower garden on the way), is the centrepiece of the Paarlberg nature reserve, a pleasant expanse of countryside graced by protea and other fynbos species, by aloes and wild olives and by groves of natural forest. Paths criss-cross the area; there are picnic/braai spots, and anglers fish for the unusually large black bass that inhabit the several dams. La Bonheur crocodile farm, in the southern Paarl area, is worth visiting for the thousand and more of these giant reptiles it contains, and for the leatherwork goods that can be bought at the gift shop.

WELLINGTON

This rather ordinary looking but most welcoming little town lies just to the north of Paarl (the two centres are almost conjoined) in a pleasant valley through which the Berg River flows. When the area was first settled by white farmers, in the later 1680s, it was regarded as the very extremity of 'civilization' and accordingly named Limiet Vallei; much later, after the discovery of Kimberley's massive diamond deposits far to the north, the local transport industry began to flourish and the general area was renamed Wagenmakers Vallei. The town itself was formally laid out in 1840 on the farm Champagne, assuming its modern name in honour of England's 'Iron Duke', the victor of Waterloo.

Wellington is the centre of South Africa's dried-fruit industry, and of a prosperous wine-producing region (its vineyards are part of the Paarl wine route: see page 74). Notable features of the town are:

❒ The Old Blockhouse, most southerly of the nearly 8 000 small forts commissioned by General Kitchener to contain the elusive Boer guerilla commandos during the South African War (1899 – 1902).

❒ The buildings of the Huguenot College, of which Samuel Hall is probably the most impressive.

❒ Victoria Park's splendid roses; the jacaranda trees that bloom so beautifully in springtime, and the lovely suburban gardens.

❒ Twistniet, the original homestead of Champagne, and a number of fine Cape Dutch manor houses in the general vicinity, among them Versailles and, in the Bovlei area, Groenfontein, Liliefontein and Welvanpas, the one-time home of the Retief family, of later Voortrekker fame.

For scenic splendour, few of the Cape's passes can rival Bain's Kloof. Thirty kilometres in length, it accommodates the R303 highway north-eastward from Wellington, and it treats the motorist to some quite magnificent views – towards Paarl to the south and the distant Swartland to the west. There's an inviting picnic spot at the summit, after which one descends over the northern slopes of the mountain range, through a deep ravine, to a land of river and waterfall, to the Wolvenskloof ('hyena's pass'), a rugged patch of countryside renowned for its wild flowers and dramatic rock formations, and finally into the Breede River valley (see later). The Wolvenskloof offers some superb hikes; the circular walk starts from the Bainskloof forestry station on the pass.

The Breede (or Bree) River rises in the high Ceres basin, gathers momentum through the narrow and spectacular Michell's pass, plunges down between the Witsenberg and Elandskloofberg ranges and then meanders south-eastwards through a green and pleasant countryside of orchards and vineyards and into the Robertson area. To the north of the Breede's headwaters is:

TULBAGH

This little town, set in the basin of the Little Berg River, began life as a farming outpost during the first years of the 18th century, later growing – around the Old Church, built in 1743 – into a charmingly tranquil country settlement graced by some lovely public buildings and private homes. Many of these were destroyed by the earthquake that shook the Ceres/Tulbagh area in September 1969 (it measured a surprising 6,5 on the Richter scale), but the damage was repaired and the buildings meticulously restored to their pristine condition. Those along Church Street, a full 32 of them, now comprise the largest single group of national monuments in the country.

One of the buildings to survive the quake was the Old Drostdy (the office and residence of the landdrost, or magistrate) in Van der Stel Street, a splendid edifice designed by the noted French architect Louis Thibault. The Drostdy now serves as a museum (early Cape domestic displays), as an art gallery, and as the headquarters of a leading wine company (visitors sip a hospitable glass of Drostyhof while they view works by local artists; the wine cellar offers daily tours).

Among the other buildings to emerge unscathed and which are accessible to the public are Monbijou, in Church Street, also designed by Thibault (antiques and works of art are on display; tours by appointment); The Victorian House (period furniture and décor), and the Old Church Museum (Victorian furniture; paintings by the prolific and much underrated Thomas Baines). The four are component parts of the Oude Kerk Volksmuseum.

THE CERES AREA

Ceres was named after the Roman goddess of agriculture, and most appropriately so too: the mountain-fringed basin in which the town nestles is one of South Africa's most bountiful fruit-growing regions, yielding splendid harvests of apples and pears, peaches and nectarines (and, for good measure, vast quantities of potatoes as well). The local fruit-packing enterprise is the southern hemisphere's largest. For the rest, there are trout in the upland streams; skiers are drawn to the snow-capped hills in wintertime; the highland air is crisp and clean, invigorating cool even in summer, and the Dwars River which ambles through town invites visitors to relax, to fish, swim, enjoy the picnic and beauty spots along its banks. In short, a prime holiday weekend area.

When in Ceres, do make a point of visiting the Transport Riders' Museum: on show is a fascinating array of wagons,

THE CAPE WINELANDS

carts, and of the equipment and utensils that these ruggedly independent early traders took with them on their houses-on-wheels. Outside town is the Ceres nature reserve, established to conserve the montane fynbos of the area. Some of the floral species you can see along the self-guided walks are rare. On view, too, are some interesting San (Bushman) rock paintings.

To the north is the charming little centre of Prince Alfred Hamlet; to the south-west the town of Wolseley, attractively set at the entrance to Michell's pass, a cleft in the lofty and otherwise impenetrable mountains through which a fine highway was built in 1848 by Andrew Geddes Bain, southern Africa's foremost 19th-century road engineer (he was also an explorer and geologist of note). Until the 1870s, when the road over the Hex River pass was completed (see below), this was the principal route linking Cape Town with the plains of the Karoo and the highveld beyond.

Even more spectacular are the Hex River mountains and valley to the east. The sandstone range runs north-east to south-west, rising in parts to 1 800 metres and more above sea level (highest peak is the 2 251-metre Matroosberg), and the cliffs and ravines of the area are a magnet for climbers, the wintertime slopes for skiers. The valley below is wide, immensely fertile, sustaining nearly 200 farms that, between them, produce most of the late-maturing grapes that the country produces for export. The valley, through which the main N1 north-south highway passes, is a visual delight throughout the year, but especially so in autumn and early winter, when the summer greens turn to a lovely patchwork of browns and golds. The north-south railway line cuts through the heights above, and passengers enjoy the most breathtaking of vistas.

KAROO DIGRESSION

Beyond the Hex River pass, now negotiable through the recently completed Huguenot tunnel (though the old, tortuous, rather nerve-wracking but scenically wonderful road is still open), the countryside becomes drier, starker, increasingly featureless.

This is the southern edge of the Great Karoo, an immense and apparently empty land that covers more than 400 000 square kilometres of the Cape province and some of the Orange Free State – a region of low rainfall, clear and bone-dry air, blistering days and, in winter, freezing nights, and of a haunting beauty all its own.

Travel a hundred kilometres beyond the pass and you'll come to the perfectly preserved, wholly charming little cluster of 19th century buildings known as Matjiesfontein.

The village began life in the 1880s when James Logan, a railwayman with a liking for wide spaces and crisp, dry air (he suffered from bronchial problems), invested what little money he had saved in the land that surrounded the railway siding, planted trees, sank boreholes to provide passing trains with the water they needed, and then opened a refreshment room for their passengers. Soon enough Matjiesfontein became known among the rich, famous and fashionable as

THE CAPE WINELANDS

something of a health resort, and to accommodate them Logan built a splendid hotel, naming it the Lord Milner in honour of the British High Commissioner (see page 95).

The village, meticulously preserved by hotelier David Rawdon and wholly Victorian in character, still caters for the discerning weekender, and for those with a penchant for nostalgia. Among the legacies of the cherished past that Logan, the 'Laird of Matjiesfontein', would have recognized are the lampposts he imported from England, the post office, trading store and coffee shop, and the cottage where author Olive Schreiner lived for a while (and where she completed her acclaimed *Thoughts on South Africa*). The tiny museum is crammed to its low eaves with fascinating trivia.

Back south again, over the mountains to the Hex River valley. At the valley's southern entrance is:

WORCESTER

The Breede River valley's largest town and a flourishing commercial, industrial and farming centre, founded in 1822 and named by Cape governor Lord Charles Somerset after his brother, the Marquis of Worcester. The new town developed around its magnificent drostdy, which also doubled as the Governor's occasional residence and 'shooting box' and which is now considered to be the finest Regency building in the country.

Chief among Worcester's tourist attractions is probably the Boland open-air museum (located just outside town), a permanent exposition of the life and times of the pioneering Dutch farmer.

Specific features here include replicas of early cottages and huts, tobacco shed, milk room, horse mill, butchery, domestic kitchen, ovens, kiln; demonstrations of blacksmithing, wheat-milling, tobacco-rolling, bread-baking, candle-making and so forth, and seasonal programs that focus on threshing, weaving, sheep-shearing, brandy-distilling. A busy and fascinating place. Attached to the museum is the Kleinplasie, a fine old (1800) homestead whose outbuildings serve a country market where local wine-producers display (and invite you to taste) their wares, and where stallholders sell preserves, cheeses, honey, confectionery and other good country fare. The Kleinplasie farmhouse itself is given over to a pleasant taproom and restaurant.

While in town, try to visit the three components of the Worcester museum: Beck House (Baring Street; late 19th century furnishings); Hugo Naudé House (Russel Street; on display are works by this celebrated South African artist), and the Afrikaner Museum (Church Street; exhibits include a fully equipped turn-of-the-century doctor's surgery).

The Worcester area lies on the western fringes of the Little Karoo, in a transitional zone, best observed in the Karoo National Botanic Garden just north of town. Here the flora of what is called the Karoo broken veld – mainly succulents together with some tree species – has been conserved within a proclaimed area of some 150 hectares, ten hectares of which are under cultivation, the plants logically grouped according to type, climate and region. Special displays are devoted to some floral collections – bulbous species, succulents, carrion flowers and so forth. All beautifully done; the International Organization for Succulents ranks the reserve as one of the world's five authentic succulent gardens.

ROBERTSON

A largish, attractive town set against the high Langeberg some 45 kilometres south-east of Worcester, in a region renowned for its rich alluvial soils, its apricots, peaches and emerald-green lucerne; for its muscadel grapes (Robertson is known as the 'muscadel capital' of South Africa; one of local the estates produces the outstanding Mont Blois Superior muscadel label); for its sherries, jeripigos (fortified, high-sugar, high-alcohol wines) and brandies. The local KWV distillery is thought to be the largest in the world, boasting about 130 stills.

The countryside around Robertson is also distinguished by the number and quality of its thoroughbred stud farms – 14 in all within a 30-kilometre radius of town. Between them, they sustain some 700 broodmares and produce a great many racing champions.

Suggested ports of call for visitors: the KWV Branewynsdraai taproom and restaurant (traditional Cape fare); Robertson museum (various displays, including a fine collection of lace); the Silwerstrand resort, on the banks of the Breede just outside town (watersports, golf, restaurant); the Normandy farm stall a short distance along the Ashton road (crafts, local produce, restaurant, wine-tasting, stud-farm tours); Shielam farm, near town (where around 3 000 varieties of cactus and succulent are cultivated); Plaas-Farm, just over 20 kilometres away (ostriches; the drive out is especially pleasant), Vrolijkheid, on the McGregor road (a predator research station that also, interestingly, trains canines to hunt jackal).

Well to the south of Robertson is the somewhat isolated, very charming little centre of:

MCGREGOR

Named after the Rev. Andrew McGregor, a Scotsman and a leading figure within local Dutch Reformed Church circles during the last four decades of the 19th century, the town is notable for its enchanting blend of visual impressions: the buildings and whitewashed, black-thatched homes are almost pristine Cape Dutch, the general atmosphere that of an English village, the whole earning an authoritative accolade as 'the best-preserved and most complete example of mid-nineteenth century townscape in the Cape'. The church is surrounded by a garden of flowers.

To the east of Robertson, and on the very edge of the Little Karoo and also in a region of flourishing fruit farms and vineyards, is:

MONTAGU

An attractive town, and an historic one. Though founded less than a century and a half ago (in 1851), it boasts fully 23 buildings proclaimed as national monuments, 14 of them in Long Street alone. The countryside to the north is known as the Koo, a lovely region of rugged hills, of wild flowers and splendid orchards of peach, apricot, apple and pear. The road

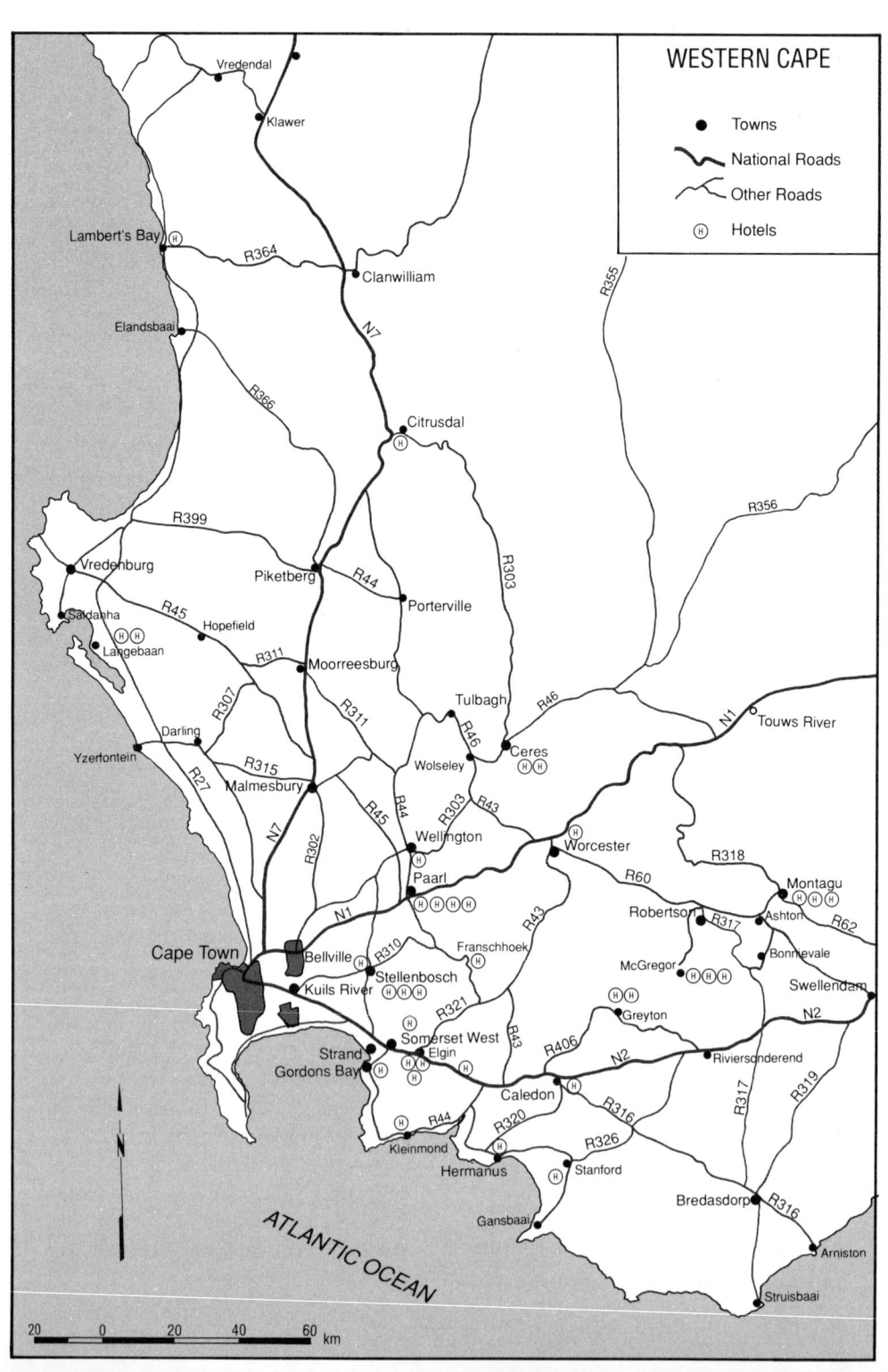

leading south, from Montagu to the small town of Ashton (notable for its huge fruit cannery, and for the thoroughbred horses and the roses of the area) leads through the scenically diverse and beautiful Cogmans Kloof. Here, at the entrance to the Keurkloof ravine, there's a wattle-shaded camping ground with picnic and barbecue sites, at the entrance to the Keurkloof ravine; and one enjoys wonderful views of the distinctively hued mountains from the small Anglo-Boer War fort (built by the British) from the ridge known as Kalkoenkrans.

Montagu has been renowned for more than two centuries for its warm (43 °C) mineral springs, located in the Badkloof just to the north of town and accessible either by road or by a shaded footpath named Lover's Walk.

The springs and the nearby nature reserve (see below) were badly damaged by the floods of 1981 but have been pleasantly redeveloped to serve as the centrepiece of a holiday resort (cottages; time-share apartments and a good hotel: see page 86). There is another hot spring, on the farm Baden, some 4 kilometres distant.

The Montagu mountain nature reserve, which fringes the town and takes in part of Cogmans Kloof (see above), is a 1 200-hectare wilderness area proclaimed to protect the aloes, succulents, fynbos and other floral species of the Langeberg's northern parts. This is magnificent highland country, greatly favoured by nature lovers, ramblers and hikers; the established trails range from 12 to 15,6 kilometres, the latter leading to Blou Punt, from where five towns can be seen.

Among the features of interest within Montagu itself are its wildflower gardens (the Centenary nature reserve, on the southern edge of town), which has the country's largest collection of *mesembryanthemums* ('vygies'); and the museum, located in what was once the mission church, which houses local (Little Karoo) displays, including a gruesome relic of a long-ago murder, and collections of natural herbs (these are for sale). Joubert House, oldest of Montagu's dwellings, is part of the complex.

❐ WHERE TO STAY

ARUMWOOD LODGE
Somerset West

Here, one is a house guest; not for a moment does it feel like a hotel. Arumwood nestles in a valley of the Hottentots-Holland Mountains, small and welcoming, an old home beautifully converted by owners Annemarie and Guy Liebenberg. It has just six guest-rooms. The Lodge is set in glorious parkland under huge trees; there's a crystal-clear pebble-filled brook at the bottom of the garden. The atmosphere is very 'English country-house'; English visitors and stressed businessmen (and honeymooners) feature prominently in its clientele.

Guests are received and entertained in the red-and-green and off-white drawing-room. Here there's a trolley of decanters and crystal glasses, and fresh flowers: a cosy, intimate room for relaxation and, in winter, cosy chats by the fireside.

THE CAPE WINELANDS

Accommodation Each room and suite is individually and tastefully decorated; there's a basket of fruit on the table, chocolates on the pillow, the personal touch everywhere. The Honeymoon Suite has been done out in cream and the palest of pinks; it contains a quite beautifully draped- and canopied-fourposter bed.

Food, drink and service The dining room is intimate, graced by attractive antique furniture and knick-knacks; service is very personal.

The food is excellent; guests receive a complimentary bottle of wine with their dinner each evening, and enjoy a solid English breakfast each morning. Picnic hampers are provided if you want to take luncheon by the brook.

Amenities Arumwood is a place of gentle pursuits: for contemplative trout-fishing in the brook (actually, the Lourensford River), for birdwatching, for communing with nature in the nearby Helderberg reserve (see page 77), for rambles in the lovely countryside, for hiking in the mountains. Golfers may make use of nearby golf-courses; sunbathers have the lawn-fringed swimming pool to enjoy.

ARUMWOOD in brief

How to get there: Arumwood is in Somerset West (take the N2 from Cape Town), off Lourensford Road. **Tariff** *(See Authors' Note on page 4):* D **Official rating:** *Not applicable.* **Conference facilities:** *None.* **Liquor licence:** *Unlicensed.* **Children:** *Children under 13 are not accommodated.* **Reservations:** *Lourensford Road, Somerset West 7130; telephone: (024) 51-1970; fax: (024) 2-5037.*

AVALON SPRINGS HOTEL
Montagu

Montagu's old, genteel and rather tired Montague Baths Hotel was washed away by the floods of 1981, to be replaced by a modern, cosmopolitan establishment that officially rates three stars but in some ways has a five-star feel about it. The warm and healthful mineral waters around which the hotel has been built well up at the foot of a sheer, towering cliff face that is floodlit at night. To wallow in the 43 °C waters under a clear and brilliantly starred night sky is a memorable experience.

Accommodation There are 12 hotel rooms and 29 timeshare suites. The rooms are nicely appointed with cane furniture and huge beds, decorated in shades of beige and brown; each has large picture windows (overlooking the springs) and an impressive, marble-finished, much-mirrored private bathroom. Other comforts include air conditioning, remote TV (with second channel), radio, telephone and a stocked bar.

Food, drink and service Avalon Springs has three à la carte restaurants. Cogman's is stylish; da Vinci's is more relaxed; Le Bistro, on the fifth floor, offers a superb view, as does the bay-windowed John Montagu cocktail bar.

Amenities These, of course, centre around the hot springs, and are extensive enough to please the keenest of health addicts. They include one indoor warm-water mineral pool, and one cold-water plunge; poolside bar, three outside mineral pools, a gym, health spa, sauna, steam bath and three jacuzzis (one of them a largish communal affair in the gym). A masseur is on call between eight in the morning and six at night. Early morning is a fine time to enjoy the outdoor pools: you lie in the warm water watching the sun rise through wreaths of mist. Good for the body, and for the soul.

The hotel has putt-putt, a trampoline and a braai area; there are tennis and squash courts next door, at the Montagu Springs resort (see page 99), and some nice rambles in the area, notably through the kloof along what is known as Lover's Walk. Golfers, cyclists, horse-riders and watersportsmen can all do their thing in and around the small town. Also on offer is a protea-viewing tractor trip.

Conference and function facilities are available for up to 100 people.

AVALON SPRINGS in brief
How to get there: From Cape Town, take the N1 highway to Worcester, the R60 east to Robertson and the R62 to Montagu. The hotel is at the end of Uitvlucht Street just to the west of the town. **Tariff** *(See Authors' Note on page 4):* C **Official rating:** ★★★ **Conference facilities:** *Available for up to 100 delegates.* **Liquor licence:** *Full.* **Children:** *Welcome.* **Reservations:** *PO Box 110, Montagu 6720, Cape; telephone: (0234) 4-1150; fax: (0234) 4-1906.*

CUMBERLAND HOTEL
Worcester

A modern, sophisticated and highly regarded big-city-type hotel in the commercial heart of the lovely Breede River Valley. The Cumberland, recently remodelled and enlarged and now part of the Protea group, offers an outstanding range of guest amenities, and caters (most professionally) for representatives and other businessmen; also for an increasing number of holidaymakers.

Accommodation Very comfortable, functional. The 36 standard rooms are in the old wing, the 23 deluxe rooms in the new section, all nicely decorated in soft browns, beiges and greens. The recently built, very modern units have light-wood finishes. All have private bathrooms, air conditioning, telephone, TV (with video but, as yet, no M-Net).

Food, drink and service The Cumberland has two restaurants and four cocktail bars. The Barlinka is an intimate, subtly-lit venue offering an à la carte menu; the less formal Cabernet Gallery coffee shop, located alongside the pool courtyard, is light and airy and specializes in carvery fare and light meals. The food generally is well up to Protea's culinary standards.

The Cabernet Bar, which runs down one side of the courtyard, has pale wicker tables and chairs, and a pale-wood bar counter. The Kramer bar is a more cosy place, done out in dark wood and striking black-and-white tiling.

Service is prompt and courteous.

Amenities The new Leisure Centre incorporates a swimming pool, gymnasium with spa bath and sauna, a glass-backed squash court and a tennis court. The complex is integrated with the coffee shop and the Cabernet bar area to form a most impressive whole. There's yachting and angling at nearby Brandvlei dam; bowls and a Gary Player-designed golf course also close.

THE CAPE WINELANDS

A little farther afield, in the foothills of the Brandwag mountains, is the Karoo National Botanic Garden (see page 82); the Kleinplasie open-air farm museum is just outside town. And, of course, there's the exquisite Breede River Valley waiting to be explored.

Conferences: The modern function rooms are used for conferences, seminars, banquets. The Cabernet I and II rooms each cater for 150 people and can be combined to accommodate 300. The smaller Pinotage I and II rooms can each accommodate 40; the Shiraz Room 50 delegates.

THE CUMBERLAND in brief
How to get there: The hotel is in Stockenstrom Street, Worcester. Take the N1 past Paarl, exit on the R43 to Worcester. Follow the signs in the town. Tariff (See Authors' Note on page 4): C **Official rating:** ★★★ *Conference facilities: Available for up to 300 delegates (see text).* **Liquor licence:** *Full.* **Children:** *Welcome.* **Reservations:** *PO Box 8, Worcester 6850, Cape; telephone: (0231) 7-2641; fax: (0231) 7-0211.*

DEVON VALLEY PROTEA
Stellenbosch

One of the smaller Protea hotels, enchantingly set in the fertile horseshoe of the Devon Valley eight kilometres from Stellenbosch. The hotel, which has its own vineyards, is close to some of the country's finest wineries.

Dark wood, steep-pitched roofs and small-paned, white-trimmed windows combine to create the impression of a Black Forest country inn; the grounds, graced by beautifully mature trees, look over splendid winelands and to the Hottentots-Holland mountains in the blue-hazed distance.

This is friendly, sociable, tranquil, moderately priced and a very well run family hotel, and is thoroughly recommended.

Accommodation Just 35 units: four single and 31 double or twin, some of which are classed as 'superior' (among other things, they have Jetmaster fireplaces). Décor generally is Cape cottage-style: colours are pastel, fabrics patterned; wooden French windows lead out to garden or pool. All the rooms are light and airy; each has a private bathroom, telephone, TV (with video channel), radio.

Food, drink and service We were invited to 'take a little wine for thy stomach's sake', which we did most enjoyably with our 'Devon Fare' in the airconditioned dining room, which offers both table d'hôte and à la carte menus – good, plain country food (the devilled kidneys with bacon went down a treat) backed by an excellent cellar of local wines. Light meals are served on the terrace.

There are dances on special occasions; Paul's Pub is a convivial early-evening haunt.

Amenities Two swimming pools and a whirlpool spa; mini-tennis, quoits and volley-ball at the hotel, golf and horse-riding nearby.

Walking in the environs of the hotel is a delight; the hotel arranges tours of the Stellenbosch wine-route; not too far to the south-east is the False Bay coast (swimming, surfing, boating, fishing,

THE CAPE WINELANDS

lazing in the sun: (see page 78). The Strand and Gordon's Bay seaside resorts are 25 minutes' drive away; Cape Town is 35 minutes away easily reached via the N2 highway.

Conferences: The Olive Room can accommodate 70 people.

DEVON VALLEY in brief
How to get there: The hotel lies in the valley to the south-west of Stellenbosch; on entering the town from the south (R310), turn left into Devon Valley Road and follow the signs.
Tariff (See Authors' Note on page 4): C
Official rating: ★★ *Conference facilities:* For up to 70 delegates. *Liquor licence: Full.*
Children: Welcome. Reservations: Devon Valley Road, Stellenbosch 7600, Cape; telephone: (02231) 92-012; fax: telephone, then ask for fax; telex: 5-22558 SA.

D'OUWE WERF
Stellenbosch

The name means 'old yard', and it's said to be the country's oldest existing inn. The site – on quiet Church Street in the older part of Stellenbosch – was originally occupied by the settlement's first church, which burned to the ground in 1710, to be replaced (though not until 1802) by the Wiums Hotel, a charming, single-storeyed, gabled hostelry that enjoyed a fine reputation among Victorian travellers. After a second fire, the place was rebuilt in larger and statelier guise, with a second storey, a lovely Georgian façade, two staircases and beautifully proportioned, raftered rooms. Later still (a little over a decade ago), it was taken over by Gert Lubbe, the present owner, who has lovingly renovated and finished it to match the elegance and time-honoured charm of this most historic of towns.

To stay at D'Ouwe Werf is an experience to be savoured, and remembered.

Accommodation Sumptuous is the word. A good proportion of the 25 rooms are furnished with fine antiques (including canopied four-poster beds) and rich fabrics, the rest – the standard units – in meticulously contrived period style; all have luxurious private bathrooms, some with gold-plated fittings. All have telephones, radios and air conditioning. My bedroom was graced by a small balcony overlooking terrace and swimming pool. In another part of the property there's a cottage which has it's own lounge and terrace and five bedrooms with extra-large *en suite* bathrooms – ideal for large-family and group occupation. In summer, concerts are sometimes held on the terrace.

Food, drink and service Traditional Cape country fare is served in the Koffiehuis, a quite entrancing little restaurant with an outside area shaded by vine-covered pergolas. The ambience is marvellous. Delicious homemade cakes (all the baking is done on the premises) and good coffee are served here throughout the day; among the more substantial delectables on the menu are grilled lamb sosaties, smoked pork ribs, oxtail stew, bobotie and rice, and smoked river-salmon. The salads and sandwiches, pâtés and quiches are superb. As a starter, try the smoked pepper mackerel. Sunday lunches (in two sittings) are very popular among both locals and visitors.

Wine list: excellent (the Meerlust reds are magnificent, though not always available). Service is informal, courteous and efficient.

Amenities The hotel has a swimming pool (drinks are served on the pleasant terrace). Stellenbosch and all it has to offer (see page 75) is on your doorstep. Tours of the wine-route can be arranged through reception. Gert Lubbe has drawn up a seven-day programme covering the route, museums and walks – a well thought-out plan that enables you to see all the major and many of the minor places of interest without feeling rushed. It's well worth spending ten minutes at reception browsing through leaflets that offer information on restaurants, galleries, shops, wine farms and so on. A helicopter service is available for sightseeing trips farther afield.

D'OUWE WERF in brief

How to get there: D'Ouwe Werf is in Church Street, Stellenbosch. Take the N1 or N2 from Cape Town, the road to Stellenbosch is clearly signposted. *Tariff (See Authors' Note on page 4):* E **Official rating:** ★★★ *Conference facilities:* Unavailable. **Liquor licence:** Full. **Children:** Children under 14 are not accommodated in season. *Reservations:* 30 Church Street, Stellenbosch 7600, Cape; telephone: (02231) 7-4608/7-4618; fax: (02231) 7-4626.

GOEDEMOED COUNTRY INN

Near Paarl

A fine old Cape homestead set among the lovely hills and vineyards of the Paarl area; the centrepiece of a small estate graced by shade trees, smooth green lawns and beds of roses. Very appealing. Goedemoed has been on the tourist map since 1988, when Anneke and John Phillips (whose families have been part of the Paarl scene for five generations) turned their home of twenty-six years into an elegantly comfortable haven for visitors. The enterprise, though, hasn't been an aggressively commercial one: the place still has the feel of a well-loved, well-used, well-cared-for private house; guests are received and looked after as friends. The L-shaped, antique-filled lounge is still very much a family room where everyone gathers to chat in the evening and to sip a convivial glass of wine (which comes with the compliments of your host and hostess).

Accommodation There are eight very pleasant rooms: four in the main house, four in a separate wing. Each has a private bathroom, radio-alarm clock, hair-dryer, heater, air conditioner, direct-dial telephone and plenty of tea, coffee and rusks. Each room is different; mine was decorated in soft pastel shades, very feminine, with pretty cushions on the beds and an easy chair; an inside room features a canopy bed and lots of frills. Rooms in the wing are decorated in jewel colours accentuated with black.

Food, drink and service A full country breakfast is enjoyed in a dining room distinguished by gleaming brass, a grandfather clock and some fine yellowwood and stinkwood pieces. Afternoon tea is served on the lawn. For the rest, guests explore the culinary delights of the area: there are five fine restaurants within five minutes' drive, and one within seven minutes' walking distance. Your hosts will give you the run-down on their relative merits and specialities.

Amenities There's a lovely lawn-surrounded pool, and a private patio and barbecue area. All that the winelands have to offer (see pages 73 – 75) is within comfortable driving distance.

Conferences: Goedemoed caters for small gatherings; Anneke will serve lunch and dinner, but equipment must be provided by the organizers.

GOEDEMOED in brief
How to get there: The Inn is on Cecilia Street, Paarl. Take the N1 from Cape Town, Exit 17 into Paarl, follow Main Street for several blocks, (past the KWV headquarters on your right), turn right into Berg River Boulevard and right again into Cecilia. You'll see the entrance to Goedemoed on your left. Tariff (See Authors' Note on page 4): C Official rating: Not applicable. Conference facilities: Available for small groups (see text). Liquor licence: Unlicensed; guests are invited to share a glass or two of wine with their hosts. Children: Goedemoed is not really suitable for children. Reservations: PO Box 331, Paarl 7620, Cape; telephone: (02211) 61-1020; after-hours (02211) 2-6613; fax: (02211) 2-5430.

THE HERBERG GUEST HOUSE

Ceres

People come to Ceres in winter to see the snow and to ski on the Matroosberg; they visit in spring for the wild flowers, in summer for green hills and orchards heavy with fruit, and throughout the year for relaxation amid scenic splendour. A lot of them stay at the Herberg. The air is fresh and clean; the surrounding mountains stunningly beautiful.

The Herberg is a first-class, professionally-run private guest house that serves as a comfortable (and, when we were there, remarkably inexpensive) base from which to enjoy one of the most attractive parts of the Cape hinterland.

Accommodation There are 20 family, double and single rooms inside the main building (some with and some without private bathrooms), and seven pleasant chalets in the grounds, each named after a sign of the zodiac, nicely spaced out on the very large lawned area. All have radios, telephones and heater/fans (but no TV; for this you may go through to the lounge).

Food, drink and service The Koffiekan restaurant and coffee shop – spacious, light and bright – serves breakfast, and snacks throughout the day. Lunch and dinner are enjoyed in the grillroom next door. Good value.

Amenities The Herberg has a king-sized swimming pool in an enclosed area, shady gardens in which to relax, secluded braai spots; a tennis court. The Snuffelmark antique shop is next door; the golf-course just a chip away. Trout waters nearby beckon the keen angler.

THE HERBERG in brief
How to get there: The guest house is in Main Street, Ceres. Take the N1 past Paarl, then the R43 to Wellington. Turn right onto the R303, over the spectacular Bain's Kloof, down into Ceres. Tariff (See Authors' Note on page 4): B Official rating: Not applicable.

Conference facilities: Not available. *Liquor licence:* Limited; wine and beers are served in the grillroom. *Children:* Welcome. *Reservations:* Either 125 Voortrekker Street or P.O.Box 491, Ceres 6835; telephone: (0233)2-2325. fax: (0233) 2-2336.

HIGH RUSTENBERG HYDRO
Ida's Valley, Stellenbosch

When we gave ourselves into the care of High Rustenberg, in the most attractive Ida's Valley outside Stellenbosch, we expected, and got, an invigorating mix of Spartan living, purification and pampering.

We were starved, pummeled, kneaded, stroked, steamed, sprayed with jets of water by both masseurs and machines; anointed with aromatic oils, soothed and stimulated, and only allowed to drink hot or cold water with lemon juice – no tea or coffee.

Smoking was allowed, but only in the privacy of our rooms.

We feasted on three fresh fruits daily and went to exercise and aquacise in the pool where, in Jani Allen's words, one is 'sprayed with a jet of icy water while clinging to the bathrails like a rose-beetle on a rhubarb leaf'.

For all that, a marvellously non-stressful atmosphere of good cheer prevails at this renowned health resort; each guest/client/patient/victim is individually assessed and monitored by doctors and nurses.

The results are excellent: we left feeling serene, alert, vital, recharged and glowing with health, just as it promises in the brochure.

We must stress, though, that this isn't the place for a quick and careless weekend break: one really needs to spend at least seven, preferably ten, days of controlled living and eating to extract maximum benefit from the regimen.

Accommodation Rooms are comfortable, well appointed, graded from superior to standard; in the main building, single, all with *en suite* bathrooms. The single rooms in the garden annexes have one bathroom between two units; all have telephone, TV (with a video channel), M-Net, radio, air conditioning or fans, and central heating for the winter months. Some rooms have balconies from which, on a clear day, you can see False Bay and Table Mountain, 60 kilometres distant.

Food, drink and service The service is, obviously, continuous and excellent; the food severely limited to fresh fruits three times daily at first – in order to rest the system and begin ridding it of toxins, followed later by more luscious fruits and salads to help to stimulate the metabolism. Close attention is paid to presentation: tomatoes, avocado, lettuce, carrots, pawpaw, beans and cucumber are sliced and artistically arranged with cottage cheese on the plate.

Amenities These include an indoor and an outdoor swimming pool, a well-equipped gymnasium and recreation centre (for, among other things, evening entertainment), and facilities for massage, hydrotherapy, sauna, Kneipp therapy, baths, yoga, progressive relaxation classes, water aerobics, circuit training and light exercise. Also a shop, and skin and bodycare clinic.

THE CAPE WINELANDS

High Rustenberg is surrounded by orchards, forests and mountains, and we enjoyed taking in the scenery while strolling in the grounds. One can also make forays into the surrounding countryside (the wineries, though, are forbidden territory).

HIGH RUSTENBERG in brief
How to get there: Take the N2 (airport) road from Cape Town; take the exit for, and follow the signs to, Stellenbosch; continue into the town (you're now on the Adam Tas road; Stellenbosch station is on your left). Pass two traffic lights, over Bird Street; turn right, at the third light, towards Helshoogte/Franschhoek – first left is Lelie Avenue: continue to the Hydro gates. *Tariff* (See Authors' Note on page 4): Dependent on treatment. *Official rating:* Not applicable. *Liquor licence:* Not applicable; no liquor may be consumed at High Rustenberg. *Children:* The Hydro does not cater for children. *Reservations:* PO Box 2052, Stellenbosch 7660; telephone: (02231) 9-8600; fax: (02231) 5163.

THE LANZERAC

Stellenbosch

Set among vineyards and gardens at the entrance to the Jonkershoek Valley, mellowed by the centuries, delighting the eye with its graceful lines – this is the Lanzerac, a queen among country hotels.

The estate was founded just over 300 years ago, in 1689, though the homestead changed ownership (it belonged to a family of freed slaves for a while) and its nature greatly over the following decades. The Cape Dutch homestead we know today dates from around 1830.

For all its tranquil surrounds, the Lanzerac is a rather busy hotel (it is immensely popular among Capetonian weekenders), encompassing three restaurants, a cake-and-coffee garden, lively bar facilities, an art gallery, and helipad. None of this detracts from the charm of the place: the beauty is of a lasting kind, drawn from the countryside around, from the shady maturity of the grounds, from the splendid architecture of the main house and its satellite buildings, and from the time-honoured elegance of the rooms inside.

Accommodation A total of 37 rooms – doubles, family, suites – are on offer, all *en suite*, all with with bar fridge, TV (all channels), radio, phone, hairdryer; most are air conditioned.

Each of the rooms is individually and most attractively decorated and furnished, many with fine old Cape antique pieces. The Marie Rawdon suite has its own courtyard; the honeymoon suite is a delectable peaches-and-cream affair.

The hotel provides guests with an 18-hour room service.

Food, drink and service As mentioned, three restaurants, all very different in character. Die Maleise Kombuis in the old wine cellar serves authentic Malay cuisine, prepared by Malay chefs in the true Malay tradition. More formal is the main dining room (breakfast, traditional Cape buffet/carvery lunch, and dinner). In the third eatery one can savour plowman-type cheese lunches. Coffee, tea and homemade cakes are served in a pleasant garden setting.

There are several cocktail bars. The wine list, predictably, is excellent.

Amenities The grounds are lusciously green, magnificently treed and shrubbed, and you're free to stroll around the lovely vineyards. There is a small, courtyard-enclosed swimming pool in which to cool off.

On display in Lanzerac's art gallery are works by the popular landscape and representational artist Tinus de Jongh (1885 – 1942), and his son Gabriel de Jongh.

For businessmen, there are conference facilities and a secretarial service.

LANZERAC in brief

How to get there: Leave Cape Town on the N2, turn onto the Stellenbosch/ Vlottenberg road and pass through the town. Take the Jonkershoek road out of Stellenbosch through the suburb of Unie Park, turn right after 3 km and follow the signs. **Tariff** *(See Authors' Note on page 4):* E **Official rating: ★★★ Conference facilities:** *For up to 30 delegates.* **Liquor licence:** *Full.* **Children:** *Welcome.* **Reservations:** *PO Box 4, Stellenbosch 7600, Cape; telephone: (02231) 7-1132; fax: (02231) 7-2310; telex: 5-20395 SA.*

THE LORD CHARLES HOTEL

Somerset West

The brochure reminded us that John Ruskin once said, 'Quality is never an accident, it is always the result of intelligent effort'. A great deal of intelligent effort has gone into the pursuit of excellence at the (deservedly) five-star Lord Charles, on the fringes of Somerset West. You get the feel of the hotel as you come up its wide sweep of driveway to the white-pillared, multi-flagged *porte-cochere*. It's a large and elegantly opulent place, the quality most immediately evident in the expanses of marble, the high ceilings, the beechwood trims, the cascades of plantings, the lovely flower arrangements, the impeccable service. State of the art, as they say.

Accommodation A total of 196 units, all luxurious, beautifully appointed. The standard rooms have private bathrooms (shower as well as bath) and the usual conveniences – telephone, TV (plus M-Net and video channel), bar-fridge (stocked on request), telephone, air conditioning, heating, hairdryer; décor is modern, serenely restful (pastels and light-wood furniture). The 24 deluxe rooms have kingsize beds in place of twin; the eight suites are spacious and sumptuous – each comprises a lounge and guest toilet, private balcony, two bedrooms and two bathrooms, and each enjoys a fine view over False Bay. Twelve of the rooms are for non-smokers; four have been specially appointed for disabled guests. Full 24-hour room service is provided.

Food, drink and service The larger of the two restaurants is the Garden Terrace, a sunlit and cheerful place at breakfast and lunchtime, subtly illuminated and rather more formal in the evening. Despite its size (it holds 200) the room has an intimate atmosphere. Superb à la carte menu, lavish carvery, and a wine list that won the Diner's Club award for two consecutive years (no mean achievement considering the Lord Charles has been in business only since 1988).

The Courtyard restaurant, part of the green and pleasant atrium complex, features an ivory-white grand piano and is

a delightfully informal venue for light meals, pastries and cakes. Planters, the colonial-style cocktail bar, also looks into the atrium.
Amenities The Lord Charles has a swimming pool and adjoining terrace area, three tennis courts, a volleyball court, *petanque* pitch and trimpark. Nearby is a trout-stocked dam (the hotel will provide rod, tackle and picnic hamper). On the premises is a boutique, hairdressing salon, a health and skin-care salon and a library; travel facilities include a petrol filling station, a currency exchange, car rental and courtesy bus and helicopter services.

Somerset West has excellent shops and restaurants; sportspeople in the area may choose from horse-riding, bowls, golf, or established walks and trails. The Helderberg nature reserve is well worth a visit (see page 77). The Strand, the town's seaboard twin, offers beaches and the full range of watersports; deep-sea fishing excursions may be arranged through the hotel. Stellenbosch and the wine-routes (see pages 73 – 75) are a few minutes' drive away.

Conferences: the hotel is able to accommodate 800 delegates in six venues, one of which, the Somerset Suite, has a 450 cinema-format capacity (350 schoolroom-) and it can be divided into three smaller areas. The conference and function wing is separate from the main hotel building; it has its own bar, stage and portable dance floor; is equipped with overhead projectors, video, PA system, slide projectors, laser pointer, and offers telex, fax, photocopying, PC and secretarial services.

LORD CHARLES in brief
How to get there: The hotel is on the corner of Stellenbosch and Fauré roads, on the Cape Town side of Somerset West. From Cape Town, take the N2 highway past D. F. Malan airport to Somerset West, before which you can turn onto the Stellenbosch Road. *Tariff* (See Authors' Note on page 4): F **Official rating:** ★★★★★ *Conference facilities:* Six venues, catering for a total of 800 delegates (see text). **Liquor licence:** Full. **Children:** Welcome. **Reservations:** PO Box 5151, Helderberg 7135; telephone: (024) 51-2970; fax: (024) 55-1107; telex: 5-21595 SA.

THE LORD MILNER
Matjiesfontein

This stately, proudly-turreted and deservedly celebrated country hotel (it has filled top positions in the competitive rankings) is the centrepiece of the Matjiesfontein 'living museum' complex, an enchanting legacy of the late-Victorian era that we cover briefly on page 81.

Set in the dry harshness of the Great Karoo, just off the N1 highway 250 kilometres from Cape Town, it was built during the high summer of Empire, shortly before outbreak of the Anglo-Boer War, and named after arch-Imperialist Sir Alfred (elevated to Lord) Milner, governor of the Cape at the time. It later fell into decline but re-emerged from the dog-years in 1970, magically restored to its pristine splendour by hotelier David Rawdon. The place, now a national monument, is brimful of fine period furniture, paintings, ornamentation, bric-a-brac; much of it displayed in the now seldom-used public rooms – the writing room, first and second parlours, the library and the music room, which houses among other things a 'square' Broadwood piano dating from about 1850 and an early 19th century harp made by the noted London firm of Sebastian Erard.

When you arrive at the Lord Milner you pass though a time warp to enter another, more leisurly world, one inhabited by such eminent Victorians as Cecil Rhodes and Olive Schreiner, Lord Randolph Churchill and the Duke of Hamilton – and by Jimmy Logan, the much-loved 'Laird of Matjiesfontein'. Their ghosts, it's said, and those of many others, still walk the hotel's creaking boards: if you're awake and about in the empty hours after midnight you can hear their footsteps, their genial laughter, the clink of their glasses and the click of their billiard cues.

Accommodation Most of the 36 guest rooms are upstairs in the main hotel (the staircase is a rather grand three-way affair), others are scattered around the grounds and village in various smaller buildings – annexes, old police cottages, the lodging house (once Logan's Masonic Lodge, oldest of Matjiesfontein's edifices) and so on, each with its unique character and its story to tell. The Honeymoon Suite is glorious: among other things it has a canopy over the bed and a double bath. Old-fashioned comfort is the keynote: each room has its private bathroom; décor and furnishings are eclectic. Radio, telephone but, appropriate to the nature of the place, no television.

The Karoo can be bitterly cold in winter, though the rooms are quite warm enough; some parts of the hotel have underfloor heating. On the drawing board are plans to extend the accommodation to about 70 units.

Food, drink and service Good, solid country fare enjoyed in a hall-like dining room whose linoleum (of 'Elephant Quality') was laid down more than nine decades ago. The ceiling is supported by a splendid lacquered cast-iron pillar; time is recorded by an ornate Victorian bracket clock. A bugle call summons you to meals – children under twelve dine separately – and guests are asked not to be too casual in their dress (jackets and ties are obligatory at dinner). Extensive table d'hôte menu; the desserts are especially delicious. Service is courteous and obliging.

The Laird's Arms is a pleasantly sociable venue for pre-dinner drinks.

Amenities The grounds are spacious, botanically interesting, green from the waters of the fringing Baviaan's River – all in all, an oasis in the wilderness (a very apt cliché in this instance). There's a tennis court and a large swimming pool (filled from underground water; not too clear but very clean). Sunday church services are held in a tiny chapel that borders the grounds; across the road is a gold-rush type railway dining car used for fun occasions.

Hotel and village comprise a unit. We wandered down the main (and only) street at leisure and enjoyed the history; afterwards we went for walks through the Karoo scrub and didn't see a living soul. Most guests arrive at Matjiefontein by car; some by train, a few by private aircraft (there's a landing strip).

LORD MILNER in brief

How to get there: The hotel is just off, and visible from, the N1 national highway, 250 km from Cape Town. *Tariff* (See Authors' Note on page 4): B **Official rating:** ★★ *Conference facilities:* Not available. *Liquor licence: Full. Children: Welcome;* families with children under 12 stay in the Boarding House. *Reservations:* Logan Street, P.O. Matjiesfontein 6901; telephone: (02372), ask for 5203. fax: (02372) 5802.

McGREGOR COUNTRY COTTAGES

McGregor

'We discovered you almost by accident and now wish accidents like this would happen more often,' wrote a guest who stumbled serendipitously upon this delightful place. Another couple booked for two nights and stayed two weeks.

The complex comprises a Buitekombuis, adjoining the main house – the winter venue for meals and for cheerful evening gatherings around a large wood-burning stove – and seven thatched and whitewashed self-contained cottages, each one an original but modernized *volkshuis*, the whole set in a newly-planted orchard of apricot trees. Owners Barry and Margie Philip are old hands at entertaining guests (they owned the Constantia Nek restaurant for nearly twenty years): Margie cooks (she is also, incidentally, most knowledgeable about wines); Barry looks after the bar and, together, they are the very best of hosts.

Accommodation Each of the cottages has its rather charming name, and its own character: Peppertree has a bed-sitting room, kitchenette, bath, shower and toilet; Mulberry a bedroom with a Queen Anne stove, living room, kitchen, shower, toilet; Pear Tree an open plan bedsitter/kitchen, shower, bath, two handbasins and two toilets; Almond Tree two bedrooms, a small lobby and lounge, kitchen, bath, shower and toilet. The Vines comprises three units – Chardonnay, which has a bedroom, living room with fireplace, shower, bath and toilet and shared kitchen and braai with Cabernet and Shiraz. The latter two have an interleading bathroom and shared kitchen – The Vines complex is hired out as a large unit for four to six people. Lady Grey has two bedrooms, a living room with fireplace, bath and toilet; Prince has a lounge/dining room, two bedrooms, kitchen, bath and shower. All the cottages have their own braai facilities.

Food, drink and service Meals for groups of ten or more; Margie cooks her traditional country fare on a wood stove in the Buitekombuis/pub, chatting to guests while she does so – a marvellously sociable arrangement. You help yourself from stove or dresser and eat at long Oregon pine tables or, in summer, outside on the shady patio. Breakfast is a solid affair of bacon, eggs, sausages, muffins, homemade bread, jams and preserves.

Margie will prepare a cold lunch and a hot dinner (perhaps a roast with all the trimmings or, on balmy evenings, a barbecue spread).

For something different in the way of cuisine, there's the splendid dining room of the nearby Old Mill House Lodge (see page 103).

THE CAPE WINELANDS

Amenities There's an attractive swimming pool, and an attractive pool area called the Oasis (a most pleasant place to retire to with a good book).

Children enjoy visiting the next-door farm, which has ostriches, horses, geese and chickens. Established hiking trails in the area include the four-and-a-half-hour Boesmanskloof, which leads past pools and waterfalls and an abundance of wild flowers to Greyton, 16 kilometres away, and the new Rooikat Ring Trail (16 kilometres, an hour away; splendid views).

A bird hide nearby overlooks a large dam where buck and waterfowl can be seen in a delightfully tranquil setting. Burger's Tractor and Trailer will take you on a delightful trip to the top of the Langeberg; there are 22 wine estates within 20 minutes drive: individual tours can be arranged. Angling, golf, tennis, squash and bowls are within a few minutes of your cottage; mountain bikes can be hired in the village.

Conferences: small seminars can be accommodated.

McGREGOR COUNTRY COTTAGES in brief

How to get there: Shortest route from Cape Town is via the N1 national highway to Worcester and the R60 to Robertson. McGregor is just 10 minutes' drive to the south of Robertson. **Tariff** *(See Authors' Note on page 4):* C **Official rating:** *Not applicable.* **Conference facilities:** *Available for small groups; contact the Cottages for details.* **Liquor licence:** *Unlicensed.* **Children:** *Welcome.* **Pets:** *Welcome.* **Reservations:** *PO Box 53, McGregor 6708; telephone: (02353) 816; fax: (02353) 840.*

MIMOSA LODGE

Montagu

This is a very special place, an aristocrat among lodges. It graces a quiet street in the sleepy town of Montagu, a double-storeyed Edwardian building with long, wide verandas looking out to the mountains that fringe the Little Karoo. Inside, there are high-ceilinged rooms and period furnishings, and the kind of elegant comfort that belongs more to a well-loved and cared for family home than to a guest-house.

And, in fact, a home is just what Mimosa is. It's owned and run by Adin and Sharon Greaves, who receive and look after you precisely as if you were an old and esteemed friend (a fellow-guest confirmed this impression, remarking that being there was 'like staying with someone you know very well'). Adin is a big man with a big personality, a catholic range of interests and a deep affection for this rather lovely part of the country, and he will go to endless trouble to make sure you enjoy yourself. He and Sharon are also chefs *extraordinaire*, effortlessly conjuring up meals of quite heroic proportions and of cordon bleu quality.

Accommodation Just ten rooms, each different from the others, all eclectically but beautifully furnished in period style. Mine was the Hideaway (its door opened out onto stoep and street), which had large and shuttered sash windows, invitingly comfortable furniture, books for Africa, masses of fluffy towels in the bathroom, and a rather faded, velvety look about it. An old-fashioned and most pleasant room, made more so by such small and thoughtful touches as the sewing kits and the little medicine ensembles that Sharon puts together. Most of the rooms lead out to veranda areas (ideal for a summer-afternoon cup of tea or a sundowner); all have *en suite* bathrooms.

Food, drink and service The cuisine, as mentioned, is for both the gourmet and the gourmand. We began in the convivial barbecue area with a huge bowl of prawns, skilpad (a South African traditional dish), three kinds of homemade bread, and complimentary glasses of the sweet, palatable Muscadel of the region.

Then inside for the main meal – three different soups in one plate (tomato, butternut and parsley) followed by a fruit cocktail (a *real* cocktail, with a kick: one had to guess which liqueur went into it). Next, a tuna roast with olive sauce, or a rare roast fillet of baby beef, each accompanied by fresh and imaginatively presented vegetables (the creamed broccoli, for instance, came in puffed pastry) – a difficult choice. To end: either a delectable confection of meringue, Tia Maria cream, kiwi fruit and grapes, or Sharon's renowned tipsy tart.

The evening finished up *savoir-vivre* with conversation and coffee in the frilled, flounced and tasselled Edwardian drawing room; Adin acted as master of ceremonies, demonstrating some of his remarkable antique 'machines'; and a thoroughly good time was had by all.

The Lodge is not licensed. Guests are encouraged to bring their own wine selections, which are properly presented; Adin and Sharon freely recommend the local wines from Weltevrede and Van Loveren estates.

Amenities The lodge has a pool, set in lovely garden surrounds; nearby are the famed mineral springs (see page 85). Your hosts will take you around Montagu; organize rambles, walks, hikes, mountain-bike excursions and angling expeditions, and also visits to wine estates, stud farms and the renowned tractor-trip to the top of the Langeberg (a must). They will also make up a splendidly sustaining picnic hamper to see you through your day.

MIMOSA LODGE in brief
How to get there: The Lodge is on Church Street, Montagu. From Cape Town, take the N1 highway to Worcester, the R60 east to Robertson and the R62 to Montagu. Follow the signs to the Lodge. **Tariff** *(See Authors' Note on page 4): C* **Offical rating:** *Not applicable.* **Conference facilities:** *None.* **Liquor licence:** *Unlicensed.* **Children:** *Mimosa Lodge is not suitable for children.* **Reservations:** *PO Box 323, Montagu 6720, Cape; telephone: (0234) 4-2351, fax: (0234) 4-1408.*

MONTAGU SPRINGS
Montagu

This is a largish resort complex, set in landscaped parkland, bisected by the Keisie River and adjacent to Montagu's famed mineral spring (and to the Avalon Springs Hotel; see page 86). The 119 pleasant and even luxurious chalets, cottages and villas are privately owned but available for hire. Some lovely trees and shrubs grace the grounds; ducks, geese and swans float, waddle and wander at will; guests have access to the hotel's mineral waters, and the resort's amiably

THE CAPE WINELANDS

energetic staff make quite sure that everybody has a good time.

A most sociable and lively place, thoroughly recommended for groups, families and the more gregarious kind of holidaymaker.

Accommodation The estate is divided into three sections – The Villas (exclusive; some of the units are beautifully appointed), Josmont Heights and Golden Terraces – that, together, form a cute little self-contained village. All the units are self-catering, fully furnished, equipped with stoves, microwaves, television sets and so on. Designs vary from charming Cape cottages to cabins on stilts and wooden bungalows; sizes range from four-bedroomed (and two-bathroomed) downwards.

Food, drink and service One usually does one's own cooking (indoors, or in your private braai area) but if you feel like a break, you're most welcome at the next-door Avalon Springs Hotel, which has full restaurant and bar facilities. There's also a pizza takeaway, and excellent homemade produce is sold from the office.

Amenities Plenty on offer, including three swimming pools (two of them reserved for specific categories of tenant); three tennis courts, and a children's playground.

There are horses for hire at nearby Lochie's farm; the Montagu golf club welcomes visitors (the course is about a kilometre away), as does the local bowls club. And, of course, there's the superb health spa at Avalon Springs. The countryside is generally ideal for rambling, walking and hiking.

Conferences: The air conditioned and fully equipped conference centre can accommodate 90 delegates; ceiling-mounted loudspeakers are linked to a recorder to enable each delegate to receive his own tape of the days's discussions. The centre opens onto the pool at Golden Terrace, and has excellent barbecue facilities.

MONTAGU SPRINGS in brief
How to get there: From Cape Town, take the N1 highway to Worcester, the R60 east to Robertson and the R62 to Montagu. Once there, follow the signs to the Springs and the Resort. **Tariff** *(See Authors' Note on page 4): Per chalet, F* **Official rating:** *Not applicable.* **Conference facilities:** *Available for 90 delegates (see text).* **Liquor licence:** *Unlicensed.* **Children:** *Welcome.* **Reservations:** *PO Box 277, Montagu 6720, Cape; telephone: (0234) 4-1050; fax: (0234) 4-2235.*

MOUNTAIN SHADOWS

Near Paarl

A most attractive thatched and gabled country homestead on an estate hidden away among the vineyards of the historic Drakenstein valley.

Mountain Shadows prides itself on its old-style hospitality. Indeed, the place is in some ways more like a large and luxurious private home than a hotel, an impression reinforced by the family pictures that decorate the walls, the fresh flowers, the well-used, well-cared-for antique furniture, the general air of conviviality and, above all, by the informally attentive way in which owner-managers Basie and Sandy Maartens look after you and even spoil you. Here, one can relax completely, and in supremely elegant surroundings.

The homestead has its own vineyard, a Jonkershuis (traditional home of the farming family's eldest son), and a lovely rose garden. The complex is now a national monument.

Accommodation There are only ten rooms, four in the old wine cellar, four in the Jonkershuis and two in the main house. Each has individual charm; all have private bathrooms; eight have rather attractive private patios; three have four-poster beds.

My room (one with a four-poster) was a pleasing affair of muted greens and polished wood; small bathroom but big bath, plenty of hot water, complimentary bottles of bath foam and so on. Very nicely done.

Food, drink and service Mealtimes are enjoyably sociable affairs: the guests may sit at one large table in the main dining room, or at individual tables in the conservatory.

The Maartens usually dine with their guests, and Basie is a genial and informative host. The menu is table d'hôte. There are two fulltime chefs (Silwood graduates) and as a consequence the food is both innovative and delicious.

Mountain Shadows has an extensive wine cellar (over 5 000 bottles, among which are some superb vintages).

Amenities A swimming pool, from where there are lovely views of vineyard and mountain, and a dam stocked with black bass.

Basie has had a great deal of experience in the safari world and will, if you're inclined, take you on a sport- or trophy-hunting trip to a game farm (ten species of buck; guns may be hired), or organize a deep-sea fishing expedition.

The hotel, or rather, its Cape Safari Programmes offshoot, lays on a variety of inviting tours – to Cape Town, Table Mountain, around the Peninsula and further afield, (for instance to Arniston and Agulhas).

For the more energetic, there are some appealing farmland and mountain walks in the area (picnic hampers provided), and of course plenty of most pleasant wineland day-drives. Paarl golf course is only minutes away.

Guests travelling on the prestigious Blue Train or by air are transported to and from D.F. Malan airport and Cape Towns railway station respectively.

Conference facilities are laid on for up to 18 delegates; exclusive occupancy (and of course special menus) may be arranged.

MOUNTAIN SHADOWS in brief
How to get there: From Cape Town, take the N1 past Paarl to the 'Drakenstein' turnoff, turn left before the tollgate; left again at the top of the bridge, in the direction of Klein Drakenstein to BP garage at the second stop street. Turn right; proceed 2 kilometres to the 'Mountain Shadows' signboard on the right. **Tariff** (See Authors' Note on page 4): D **Official rating:** Not applicable. **Conference facilities:** For up to 18 delegates. **Liquor licence:** Full. **Children:** Mountain Shadows does not cater for children under 12. **Reservations:** PO Box 2501, Paarl 7620; telephone: (02211) 62-3192; fax: (02211) 62-6796.

NEW BELMONT HOTEL

Ceres

The very best of the old-style South African country-town hotel, a favourite family getaway set among large and lovely gardens on the banks of the Dwars River in Ceres (see page 80). The New Belmont, which opened its hospitable doors just over a century ago, is owned and managed by the Caballero family, who run it in attractively relaxed (though highly professional, let it be said) fashion. Comfortable and friendly: the staff go out of their way to make your stay enjoyable.

This is a substantial, very well-appointed establishment which offers all the standard amenities and some more. In physical terms, the most impressive part of the place is probably its pillared entrance/reception area, a splendid foyer with stone fireplaces, grand piano and clusters of plush seating – a popular gathering place for afternoon tea.

Accommodation A total of 45 units, four of which are suites, all recently and tastefully renovated, decorated and furnished in a nice blend of the modern and the old-fashioned. Each room has its private bathroom, television (with second channel), heater/air conditioner. The two honeymoon suites are plush and rather fun: their bathrooms are carpeted; pink and green accents on the picture tiles depict cupids, bows and roses.

Food, drink and service The hotel has five bars and two restaurants. The main dining room offers a table d'hôte menu of good, unpretentious, imaginatively presented food; the barbecued pork ribs and the roast lamb went down a treat; the vegetables were beautifully fresh. The Oom Ben se Vat grillroom, which you enter through an enormous wine-vat, serves rather more upmarket à la carte fare in an intimate atmosphere. Light meals are available at the poolside snack bar and in the reception area.

We enjoyed our pre-dinner drinks in the Oulap se Rooi cocktail bar, which is located in the corner of the main dining room (under an awning connected to the vat). The Bok se Klok, a traditional men's bar open to the public, has a more robust atmosphere; the Blou Oog offers snooker, pool, darts and amiable sociability. There's also the pool bar (outdoors) and spa bar (indoors).

Amenities Plenty laid on: the hotel boasts a mini-zoo and an aviary; a health spa (heated indoor pool, sauna, jacuzzi, fully equipped gym, squash court); an outdoor pool; tennis courts (racquets can be hired); badminton and table tennis; boutique; hairdressing and beauty salons. We went for walks and picnics (hampers are provided) in the Ceres nature reserve. In winter there's skiing in the mountains (though one more or less has to belong to a club before taking to the slopes). The Dwars River beckons the trout-fisherman; the hills the rambler, hiker and climber. Golf, bowls and horse-riding are available in the area.

Conferences: four venues can accommodate 250 delegates between them.

NEW BELMONT in brief

How to get there: Ceres lies 180 km northeast of Cape Town. Take the N1 national highway to Worcester; turn off onto the R43 west and bear right (just before the town of

Wolseley) over Michells Pass. *Tariff (See Authors' Note on page 4):* C *Official rating:* ★★ *Conference facilities: Available for up to 250. Liquor licence: Full. Children: Welcome. Reservations: Porter Street, Ceres 6835, Cape; telephone: (0233) 2-1150.*

THE OLD MILL HOUSE LODGE

Near McGregor

A two-hour drive from Cape Town brought us to this charming cluster of 19th century buildings on the lower slopes of the Riviersonderend mountains, near the village of McGregor. It was worth the trip.

The Old Mill House is a Victorian homestead hidden away in another and more elegant time, in an age of long dresses and picture hats, blazers and straw boaters and leisurely teas on the lawn. You approach the house through grounds graced by shade trees and emerald turf, multicoloured flowerbeds and festoons of golden shower; inside there are uneven yellowwood floors, doorways that are a bit narrower and lower than you're used to, a beautiful period-style drawing room bright with rich and cheerful fabrics, and fresh flowers everywhere, their scent mingling with the enticing aroma of good, strong coffee and home-baked bread. A truly inviting place.

Adjacent to the homestead, set in five hectares of vineyard and rose garden, are the four guest-cottages; behind the house is the old watermill, to which local farmers once brought their wheat for grinding. The waterwheel, drivegear and millstones are still in good condition and Peter and Helaine Shand, the charming couple who now own and manage the property, aim to restore the machinery to full working order.

Accommodation The four cottages are end-gabled, stable-doored, whitewashed, thatched in traditional style; each has two bedrooms, *en suite* bathrooms with stone floors, ceramic basin (crafted by a talented local potter) and an old-style claw-footed bath. Oil heaters warm the rooms in winter. No TV, no radio, no telephone – which is quite in keeping with the character and intent of the lodge.

Food, drink and service Dinner is served in the exquisite dining room; the cutlery is solid silver, the glassware crystal. A set menu offers three courses of good home cooking: we had butternut soup, lamb casserole, apple-pie and cream. Vegetables come from the garden. Breakfast is English (plus fresh fruit and muffins); lunch is a light meal (cold meats and salads, cheeses, pickles, homemade bread); Helaine's delicious carrot cake makes its appearance at tea, taken on the millstone table-top under the shade trees.

Before-dinner drinks are enjoyed in the adjoining and pleasantly sociable bar, which is licensed to serve wine and beer. The village co-op presses its own grapes to produce very pleasant wines.

Amenities Guests laze by the sunlit pool; they embark on drives, hikes and rambles through the most attractive fynbos countryside. You may picnic by the waterfall, go bird-watching (the McGregor area is known for its bird life) or fish for bass and carp in the local dam. The lovely Breede River is fairly close, and a tour of the valley's wine farms fills a few pleasant hours. Sixteen kilometres from the Lodge, along the 'road to nowhere', is the start of the Boesmanskloof hiking trail (between McGregor and Greyton); the renowned cactus-farm at Klaasvoogds is 20 minutes' drive away (on the road to Ashton and Montagu); the Montagu Spa and its healing waters a half-hour's car journey.

THE OLD MILL HOUSE LODGE in brief
How to get there: The Lodge is off Voortrekker Street – the last property on the right, just outside the village of McGregor. **Tariff** (See Authors' Note on page 4): B **Official rating:** Not applicable. **Conference facilities:** None. **Liquor licence:** Wine and malt. **Children:** The Lodge is not suitable for young (under 12) children. **Reservations:** PO Box 25, McGregor 6708, Cape; telephone: (02353) 841.

ROGGELAND

Near Paarl

If tranquility in a setting that is both historic and charming is what you want from a holiday, then Roggeland Country House comes close to the ideal.

The homestead, in the Dal Josephat valley beneath the lovely Drakenstein Mountains near Paarl, was built in 1778 on land first farmed in 1691, and has been restored to its original thatched, limewashed and gabled gracefulness.

The grace is carried through to the inside. Roggeland's entrance hall, with its high beamed ceilings and its polished yellowwood, is unusually impressive; other reception areas are notable for their elegance and easy comfort, for their grand old fireplaces (marvellously inviting in winter) and their stunning fresh flower arrangements. Of special interest is the outside staircase that winds up to the roof (goats once used it to make their way to their attic manger), and the magnificent diamond-panelled yellowwood and stinkwood *porte visite* that divides entrance hall from dining room.

Just eight guest rooms: an exclusive place, aristocratic in a way but, because it's small and because it has a high management profile, also friendly, relaxed and undemanding.

Your hosts are Mildie Malan and Topsi Venter, who look after the guests most amiably. Topsi's special talents lie in the kitchen.

Accommodation Two splendid bedrooms in the main house and six in the outbuildings, individually and appropriately named (Jonkershuis, Kelder, Melkkamer, Voerkamer and so on); beautifully appointed. We stayed in the Jonkershuis (part of the house originally built for the farming family's eldest son) and the adjoining Pannevis, and we couldn't have asked for more pleasing surrounds. Each room has a Spanish reed ceiling, wall-to-wall carpeting, big double-bed, spacious *en suite* bathroom and deep casement windows flanked by solid shutters. The décor is soft and comforting; there are down duvets and crisp, hand-made linen on the beds, an abundance of fleecy towels in the bathrooms and, again, fresh flowers everywhere. A nice touch was the silver tray with glasses and small complimentary bottles of Paarl Rock brandy provided by a thoughtful management.

Food, drink and service Topsi used to run, in association with John Jackson (see the Peninsula Hotel, page 41), the acclaimed Rosenfontein restaurant in Cape Town; she is an examiner for the Silwood cookery school, and she knows all about good food. Her menus are imaginative; the dishes – with undertones of traditional Cape, Provençal and *cuisine moderne* – are stylishly prepared. A typical summer meal would include Brie and spring onion soup, red roman with wild sorrel dressing, chicken breasts stuffed with apricots and almonds, pomegranate gateau; in winter: cauliflower and cashew nut soup, smoked trout with olives and peppers, roast lamb with quinces, brandy pudding.

Vegetables and fruit are fresh from the farm; herbs from the garden.

Breakfast time (either full English to order or healthy affairs of wholewheat breads, local cheeses, muesli, fresh fruits and yoghurts) varies from very early, for keen hikers, to late, for the more idly inclined. No-one hurries you.

Service: courtesy with a smile. Topsi herself serves the meals, and chats most informatively, and entertainingly, about Paarl, the history of the area, wine and the culinary arts.

Amenities Roggeland is close to Paarl (see page 78) in the heart of the Cape's wine country. Guests sight-see, explore, follow the wine-routes, ramble through the fertile farmlands, picnic or birdwatch – or simply laze around this most pleasant of country hotels.

ROGGELAND in brief
How to get there: Take the N1 national highway from Cape Town and, just before the Huguenot tunnel, the exit to the R101, 'Drakenstein'. Go up the ramp, turn left at the first stop street. At the second stop street, look for the first sign (brown background) reading 'Roggeland Gastehuis' – follow the signs thereafter. *Tariff* (See Authors' Note on page 4): D **Official rating:** Not applicable. **Conference facilities:** Not available. **Liquor licence:** Unlicensed. **Children:** Roggeland is not suitable for children. **Reservations:** PO Box 7210, Noorde Paarl 7623; telephone (02211) 62-7501; fax: (02211) 62-0113.

STELLENBOSCH HOTEL

Stellenbosch

A small, historic and wholly charming little hotel in the heart of this time-honoured town (it's on the corner of Dorp and Andringa streets). The complex has two distinct parts, each of which once served as a private home – the first built at the end of the 17th century and restored in the 1800s in traditional limewash-and-thatch Cape Dutch style; the second a Victorian house with a pleasant terra cotta façade.

Both buildings have been proclaimed as national monuments.

For all that, though, the hotel offers the full complement of modern amenities – plus some special assets that set it well apart from the run-of-the-mill country inn. Not least of its attractions is the unusually attentive, helpful and kindly way in which guests are received and looked after. Thoroughly recommended.

Accommodation Just 20 rooms at the time of our visit (future extensions will provide a further 16).

You have a choice of four different types of unit. There are four Victorian rooms: frills and flounces, well-polished wood, a brass four-poster, period prints (of old magazine covers) and other Victorian embellishments, and, in one, a second doorway, discreetly masked from the outside by plants, that leads through to the attractive terraced courtyard. Ideal for honeymooners and romantic weekenders.

Almost as comfortable but quite distinct in character are the Courtyard rooms (they face onto but don't actually have direct access to the courtyard); the Classic rooms (Grecian spaciousness, and a tiny balcony overlooking the courtyard) and the Studio rooms, which are smaller upstairs units. The Studio's bathroom has a sitz (or hip) bath – a practical space-saver, but rather more comfortable than it sounds.

All rooms have *en suite* bathrooms (each with its hairdryer and little basket of soaps, shampoo, foam bath, shower cap); direct-dial phone (with bathroom extension); colour TV; radio-clock; well-stocked mini-bar and air conditioning.

Food, drink and service The Jan Cats Brasserie, named after an early Dutch barber-surgeon, then one of the town's more prominent residents', is a pleasantly decorated room, its most notable feature a rather lovely semi-circular solid-oak bar (at which pre-meal drinks and excellent pub-lunches are served, though of course there are separate tables as well). On balmy days the Brasserie extends out to a courtyard ornamented by pool, fountains, waterfalls, decorative little bridges, coloured umbrellas and a profusion of plants potted in half wine-casks. Very attractive.

More formal is the Victorian dining room, where *haute cuisine* is enjoyed in stylish surrounds. Upstairs in the thatched and wood-beamed loft is the pub, sometimes crowded with noisy students but nevertheless a pleasant venue for pre-meal drinks.

Amenities There's a swimming pool (rather oddly positioned at the entrance), and an inviting rooftop terrace where guests sip drinks and, some of them, play chess with a giant-sized set. The Stellenbosch Hotel is an ideal base from which to explore the charms of the town and the surrounding winelands; the reception staff are knowledgeable, and will point you in all the right directions.

STELLENBOSCH HOTEL in brief
*How to get there: The hotel is in Stellenbosch, on the corner of Dorp and Andringa streets. **Tariff** (See Authors' Note on page 4):* E **Official rating:** ★★★ **Conference facilities:** *None.* **Liquor licence:** *Full.* **Children:** *The Hotel is not suitable for children under 12.* **Reservations:** *P.O. Box 500, Stellenbosch 7600; telephone: (02231) 7-3644; fax: (02231) 7-3673.*

SWISS FARM EXCELSIOR
Franschhoek

A luxurious hotel and time-share complex is set in the lovely Franschhoek Valley just three kilometres from the historic town and, as the name suggests, very

Swiss in character: the buildings have sloping Alpine roofs, quaint weathervanes, bright-flowered window boxes and a tranquil mountain setting. Inside, there are cuckoo clocks, a lot of carved wood, and the female staff members dress in mob-caps and prettily-embroidered aprons.

The ethnic theme may sound contrived, but it's expressed stylishly, and it has appropriate antecedents: the land was originally granted, in 1699, to a Swiss immigrant named Muller, who established both a farm and a guesthouse-type hostelry on it. Over the long decades the place became a favoured stop-over of travellers making their way through the high hills to the north. It became a hotel proper in 1875.

The present proprietors, the Moutons, also have a long and distinguished lineage: they descend from Huguenot settlers who arrived in the Groot Drakenstein area in 1689. The family now own – in addition to the hotel – a prosperous fruit farm and a wine estate that produces fine vintages under the Le Moutonne label.

Swiss Farm Excelsior is especially noted for its health club, its wine club, and for its conference facilities.

Accommodation There are three different accommodation sections: the Swiss-chalet hotel, the modern Annexe (for conference delegates) and the timeshare units.

The hotel is a mixture of single and double *en suite* rooms and balconied family rooms, all nicely panelled in wood. Then there are the suites, which also have balconies but are more feminine in décor (frills are prominent, and they're popular with honeymooners). Most luxurious is the Mouton suite, which features a closed fireplace, broderie anglaise linen and a dining/sitting area.

All rooms have TV with M-Net, telephone, hairdryer, air conditioner and heater.

The Annexe features twin-bedded rooms with balcony, bath and shower, and all the mod cons mentioned above. They're all upstairs, and they command lovely views of the fruit orchards and mountains.

Food, drink and service The main dining room – The Excelsior (set menu and buffet) – is a large, high-ceilinged, most attractive place that looks out onto lawns and, farther away, the farm. Breakfast taken at a window table, with squirrels at play just outside, is a delight. Generally, top-quality cuisine in sophisticated surrounds.

Lunches and teas are served in the La Vue coffee shop. The terrace is a pleasant place in summer; braais are held on a fairly regular basis.

Drinks are taken on the terrace or in the elegantly restful cocktail bar, which is open to the public and features live entertainment in summer and on busy week-ends. A wine steward does duty by the pool in summer, and there's a non-alcoholic bar in the sports complex. Service is friendly and efficient throughout.

Amenities A huge pool, a short distance from the main building, is sited on a natural terrace that slopes down to a stream and the fruit farm. Again, magnificent views. There are changing rooms close by.

Guests are of course free to use all facilities of the hotel's magnificent health club: pool, gym, sauna, jacuzzi, aerobics, plunge pool, bowls, tennis and squash courts.

There's also Die Binnehof, the wine club (separate from the hotel, but membership is open to guests).

The original cellar was built in 1875; members are invited to taste the vintages, and are entitled to an annual quota of splendid limited-edition Binnehof, Le Moutonne and other rare estate wines at club prices.

Conference facilities are modern and extensive; the hotel can cater for up to 250 delegates at a time. Largest of the venues is the spacious ballroom (floor-to-ceiling windows, sprung floor) which also does duty as a functions- and banqueting-centre.

The dances held here in summer and over holiday periods are lively and thoroughly enjoyable affairs.

For the rest, there are some lovely rambles in the area (picnic hampers provided); bicycles can be hired by the more energetic, and of course there's the wine-route (the Vignerons de Franschhoek: see page 74).

SWISS FARM EXCELSIOR in brief
How to get there: Take the N1 from Cape Town; turn off at Exit 18 (Wemmers-hoek/Paarl/Wellington) and follow the signs to Franschoek. The R45 exit to Franschoek is a scenic alternative, once again from the N1. Drive through the town and turn right at the Hugenot Monument. The hotel is 3 km from Franschhoek, on the right of the road. Tariff (See Authors' Note on page 4): C Official

rating: ★★★ *Conference facilities: Up to 250 delegates (see text). Liquor licence: Full. Children: Welcome. Reservations: PO Box 54, Franschhoek 2071, Cape; telephone: (02212) 2071; fax: (02212) 2177.*

VAN RIEBEECK HOTEL
Gordon's Bay

A largish, good-value three-star establishment in Gordon's Bay, deservedly popular for its superb setting: it's right on the beachfront of this pretty little resort village; to sit on the terrace in the early evening, with a glass of cheer in your hand and the splendour of the sunset all around you, is a delight indeed.

The Van Riebeeck offers comfort, good food, all the standard amenities, and excellent conference facilities. We recommend it as a pleasant base from which to explore, and enjoy, this most attractive part of the Cape south coast.

Accommodation All 66 rooms have fine views of either the shoreline and sea or of the backing mountains. All are comfortable, pleasantly decorated in pastel shades. Each has a private bathroom, direct-dial telephone, radio and TV (with video channel).

Food, drink and service The Waterfront Restaurant, which overlooks the ocean, offers a nice selection of à la carte and carvery fare; the seafood is rather special. A lively dinner-dance is held on Saturdays. Service is efficient and courteous.

The two cocktail bars, the Robert J. Gordon and the Calypso, are casually congenial places popular with both visitors and locals. The pool bar is open during the summer months.

THE CAPE WINELANDS

Amenities The pool is set in a pleasant, wind-sheltered courtyard. The Gordon's Bay area offers sea and freshwater fishing (in the Steenbras dam). There's golf at the Strand (5 km away) and Somerset West (12 km); squash, tennis, bowls and horse riding facilities are available in the general area.

The Helderberg nature reserve (see page 77) is splendid walking country. The circular routes take you over the lower slopes of the mountain; recommended is the 8 - kilometre hike to the Disa Gorge, where, in summer (December to February), you can see displays of lovely disa orchids.

A more strenuous walk leads to the summit of Helderberg Peak.

Conferences: as mentioned, first-class facilities. Up to 200 delegates can be accommodated in the modern, self-contained centre, which is linked to the hotel by an overhead walkway. The centre comprises a pre-assembly area, a cocktail bar, and a large conference room divisible into three smaller, sound-proofed venues, each of which can accommodate 60 people.

VAN RIEBEECK in brief

How to get there: The hotel is on Beach Road, Gordon's Bay. From Cape Town, take the N2 to and through Strand/Somerset West and turn right at the Gordon's Bay signpost. Tariff (See Authors' Note on page 4): E **Official rating:** ★★★ *Conference facilities: Available for up to 200 delegates (see text).* **Liquor licence:** *Full.* **Children:** *Welcome.* **Reservations:** *PO Box 10, Gordon's Bay 7150; telephone: (024) 56-1441; fax: (024) 56-1572; telex: 5-24944 SA.*

WATERKLOOF GUESTHOUSE

Near Wellington

For those who enjoy uninterrupted peace, amiable company and the most healthy of foods.

Waterkloof is a rambling, homey, very unpretentious place in pleasantly pastoral surrounds near the town of Wellington and adjacent to the unusual Bloublommetjieskloof Farm, an enterprise that has taken what is known as the bio-dynamic approach to cultivation and stock-rearing.

This method of farming, pioneered by the celebrated Rudolf Steiner, seeks to preserve the soil's health and vitality with natural fertilizers by sedulously avoiding the use of synthetics of any kind and by rotating crops – in short, by cherishing the land, its crops and its cattle. The results, as we can testify, are little short of amazing. Waterkloof's dairy produce is fresh from the farm; wholesome vegetarian meals are served to guests (though meat-eaters are welcome to bring their preferred supplies).

The guest house is set into the hillside and commands lovely views, best enjoyed from the terrace that flanks two sides of the house. Inside, there's a comfortably homely lounge-cum-dining room (open fire, Lazi-Boy armchair, board-games), and a larger, even more informal room for communal living and relaxation which also serves as an informal venue for workshops and small-group discussions. Up to 22 people can be seated here. No television; only one telephone (with meter).

Your hosts are Joe and Heather Snyman, a charming couple with a great love for the outdoors generally and for this striking patch of Cape countryside in particular.
Accommodation Nothing luxurious, but the rooms are comfortable, and spotless; each has an *en suite* shower; other ablution facilities are rather reminiscent of a youth hostel, but for a certain type of holiday, and to a certain type of holiday-maker, it doesn't matter at all. One has a choice of terrace room, a room in the main house or self-contained cottage with open fireplace and gas fittings.
Food, drink and service Heather prepares the food, Joe serves it, and the menus are vegetarian though, as mentioned, you're welcome to 'bring and braai'. Dinner is the main winter meal in the cosily fire-warmed dining room and usually comprises three hot dishes; supplementaries include delicious home-made breads, jams, preserves, yoghurts, fruit juices, and superb farm cheeses that range from light to rich and creamy. No preservatives whatsoever are used; water comes from the natural spring on the property.
Amenities Among these is a swimming pool (a small dam, actually, fed by the spring). A visit to Bloublommetjieskloof Farm, which is run by Jeanne Malherbe with the help of enthusiastic volunteers helped by a core of permanent labourers, is recommended. . Heather keeps ducks and geese, though more as pets than providers – they're great favourites with the children.
Walks in the spectacular Bain's Kloof area are a must.

Waterkloof, in fact, is very much a place for families with youngsters, for quietly sociable groups, and for city-stressed weekenders who need to wind down in the gentlest of environments or work on projects in the tranquil surroundings.

WATERKLOOF in brief
How to get there: Take the N1 national highway from Cape Town, and then the R44 (Exit 16) or R303 exit to Wellington, past the cemetery and animal hospital after 1st Avenue. Turn right into Blouvlei Road at the Guest House signpost (this is the sixth right turn within the built-up area). After a little more than 3,5 km you'll see, on your right, the Bloublommetjieskloof and Waterkloof sign. Follow the signs to the parking area. **Tariff** *(See Authors' Note on page 4):* B **Official rating:** *Not applicable.* **Conference facilities:** *Informal workshop facilities.* **Liquor licence:** *No. Waterkloof is not licensed to serve liquor, although you're welcome to bring your own.* **Children:** *Welcome.* **Reservations:** *PO Box 217, Wellington 7655; telephone: (02211) 3-2374.*

WHIPSTOCK FARM
Near McGregor
One of the most hospitable of the region's guest farms – a rambling, stone-flagged homestead eight kilometres (along a dirt road) from the small country town of McGregor.

The house dates from the mid 19th century, has a thatched roof, sturdy whitewashed walls and sash windows; its 20 guests (maximum) are hosted by David and Marianne Bernhardi, a caring couple with a flair for making you feel at home.

Whipstock makes no claims to luxury, but it's an undemanding and very sociable place. Focal point of the hospitality is the lounge, a room full of country furniture, some antique pieces, a piano, a music system that provides the full range from rock to classical, books and magazines and relaxed conviviality. And, of course, there's the farm itself, and the pleasant countryside around, both of which offer holidaymakers the gentler kinds of distraction.

Accommodation Guests are housed in separate outbuildings, which are unpretentious but comfortable. Each has its bath or shower and there's plenty of hot water. Rietvlei, the original farmhouse, has a reed ceiling, patchwork duvets and oil lamps; The Annex is a Georgian country-style family room with two connecting bedrooms and its own *voorstoep*.

Food, drink and service There's no menu: Marianne cooks, David serves; guests sit at separate tables in a room with mismatched (but quality) furniture and a huge open fire.

The food is home-style, and very good: our dinner consisted of homemade mushroom soup (and homemade bread) followed by a melting chicken pie (with broccoli, roast potatoes and sweet butternut) and a wickedly creamy trifle to end the meal.

Amenities The farm, like Waterkloof (see page 109), practises traditional – natural – methods of conserving and enriching the soil; crops include citrus and almonds (the orchards are being re-established) and Steen and Hanepoot grapes. Among the residents are a herd of Jersey cows, some pigs, honey-bees, all kinds of chickens and ducks (the pond is a child's paradise); dogs and cats; a hand-reared calf called Blommetjie; and Banjo and Beauty, two horses who need experienced handling. A nice ride is to the dam, where there's canoeing and fishing.

This is good rambling country; David will advise you about or take you on walks and cycle rides lasting from two hours to a full day; the Boesmanskloof trail from Greyton ends at McGregor, the hikers invariably spending the night at Whipstock (David drives them back in the morning). Birdwatchers also find the area rewarding; the raptors are especially notable.

WHIPSTOCK in brief
How to get there: From Cape Town, take the N1 national highway to Worcester, the R60 east to Robertson and then the short (signposted) road south to McGregor. Drive through the village and continue south towards the mountain for a further 8 km of good gravel. The 'Whipstock' sign is on your right.
Tariff (See Authors' Note on page 4): A **Official rating:** *Not applicable.* **Conference facilities:** *None.* **Liquor licence:** *Unlicensed.* **Children:** *Welcome.* **Reservations:** *PO Box 79, McGregor 6708; telephone: (02353) 733.*

THE WEST COAST

❏ WHAT TO SEE AND DO

❏ WHERE TO STAY

THE WEST COAST

☐ WHAT TO SEE AND DO

The Olifants River rises in the hills of the southern Karoo, gathering volume as it flows north-westwards, past the pleasant country towns of Citrusdal, Clanwilliam and Vredendal, before entering the Atlantic Ocean 250 kilometres north of Cape Town. Its valley is green and pleasant, and enormously fertile, sustaining splendid harvests of wine- and table-grapes, fruit, vegetables, tobacco, rooibos tea, great fields of wheat and, most especially, grove upon grove of Washington and Naval oranges. Beyond the Olifants' is Namaqualand, a 48 000 square kilometre, narrow belt of increasingly arid countryside stretching to the lower reaches of the Orange River and the southern extremity of the Namib desert.

Most of the maritime strip comprises what is known as 'sandveld', up to 50 kilometres wide in parts, elevated above sea level and characterized by 'raised beaches'; sandy terraces that are the legacy of the time, 60 000 years ago, when the ocean's surface was some 100 metres higher than it is today. The terrain is bleak, sparsely populated, dry, largely devoid of surface water, seldom blessed by rains (precipitation averages less than 50 milimetres a year in places), though the interaction of the cool Benguela current and the warm onshore air often produces dense fogs.

To the traveller driving north through Namaqualand, the terrain seems harsh, barren; incapable of sustaining any but the hardiest, least attractive forms of life. Yet the land has its bounty. Here, in the sandveld and in the broken country of the Hardeveld to the west, there is an enormous profusion of succulents and flowering plants: the region is home to an incredible 4 000 and more floral species, most of which belong to the daisy and *mesembryanthemum* ('vygie') groups – though aloes, lilies, perennial herbs and a host of other families are represented. Most of the plants are small, low-growing; all are drought-resistant. The seeds lie dormant during the long dry months and then – after the modest rains and before the onset of the burning desert airs – when they sense the warming of the earth and the promised arrival of the pollinaters, they burst into life, maturing in a matter of days to mantle the countryside in glorious carpets of wild flowers.

This lovely springtime show is not restricted to the semi-arid areas north of the Olifants. Patches of daisies and vygies mingle with the proteas, ericas and pincushions of the Cape Floral Kingdom's fynbos vegetation (see page 19) far to the south.

CAPE TOWN TO PIKETBERG

The main highway north (the N7) will lead you, in its initial 150-kilometre stretch, through the Swartland, or 'black country', so named for the rich darkness of its soils. Other colours, though, would perhaps be more descriptive: about a sixth of the national wheat crop is produced in the region, and, in spring, the fields are bright green with the young harvests – in summer, a ripe gold.

The Swartland's principal town is Malmesbury, founded in the shallow valley of the Diep River in 1743. Once famed for the curative properties of its mineral springs (in recent years the waters have been sadly neglected), it's now most notable as a grain and wine-producing centre. Of interest in the general area is the Oude Kerk, first of the region's formal places of worship and today an interesting little museum; the wagons and wagon-building displays on the farm Spes Bona; the Kalbaskraal nature reserve south of town. Jan Christiaan Smuts was born here (he retained the distinctive Malmesbury accent throughout his life; his childhood home has been lovingly restored and is open to the public), and, close to the village of Riebeeck Kasteel to the north east, is the Kasteelberg, or 'castle mountain', a fine place for walking.

The next port of call on the highway north is Moorreesburg, a small and rather ordinary place, though it does boast one of the world's three wheat museums. Thirty kilometres beyond is the town of Piketberg, modestly notable for its Edwardian-style museum, its fruit-cooling and grain-packing complex, and for its backdrop of impressive sandstone mountain. An upland area that once gave sanctuary to a section of the Khoikhoi (formerly known as Hottentot) people, a tribe that took up arms against the very early Dutch colonists. During the ensuing hostilities, which lasted from 1674 to 1677, the Dutch established a military outpost, or 'piquet', on the high slopes and it was from this that the village's name was taken.

Some way to the east of Piketberg – follow the R44 for 26 kilometres – is Porterville, over which looms the high and rugged Great Winterhoek wilderness area, a 20 000-hectare expanse of mountain and forest that beckons the hiker and the climber: the Winterhoek peak itself rises 2 078 metres above sea level; a network of pathways, 90 kilometres of them in all, has been established.

CITRUSDAL

A pleasant little town set in the fertile Olifants River valley, some 45 kilometres north of Piketberg. The last ten kilometres of highway cuts through the Olifants River Mountains via the Piekenierskloof Pass, a name recalling the days when Dutch pikemen guarded the entrance to the valley from the hostile Khoikhoi. The region is renowned for its bountiful, and venerable, orange groves: the first trees were planted from seedlings nurtured in Jan van Riebeeck's Cape Town garden. One particular specimen, on the farm Hexrivier near town, has borne good fruit for the past 250 years and is now a national monument. Visitors are welcome to tour both the estates and the Goede Hoop co-operative's packing sheds, the country's largest (they handle nearly 70 000 tons of oranges during the season).

The Olifants River is popular among serious canoeists, and within the angling fraternity: its waters are home to the largest variety of indigenous fish south of the Zambezi, among them the Clanwilliam yellowfish (*Barbus capensis*), a species unknown elsewhere. Much of river valley constitutes the Clanwilliam wild flower area, whose springtime displays rival those of Namaqualand far to the north. The river has been dammed some 50 kilometres north of Citrusdal to irrigate the farmlands of the Hantam district, and to supply the needs of:

CLANWILLIAM

The town is one of the country's ten oldest (white settlers began moving into the area as early as 1732), and one of the most attractive. Of architectural and historical note are the 'Drostdy' (1808), the Dutch Reformed church (1864) and the Anglican church, one of 50 designed by the talented Sophie Gray, wife of Cape Town's first Anglican bishop. This remarkable woman, incidentally, helped establish some of the province's best-known schools, including Bishops, Zonnebloem College and St Cyprian's, and still found time to administer her husband's vast diocese.

Clanwilliam is the headquarters of the country's rooibos tea industry: the needle-shaped shrub (*Aspalathus linearis*) grows wild throughout the western Cape but is especially prolific in the uplands to the east of town. The local packing sheds, again, welcome visitors.

The area is also noted for its springtime wild flowers, perhaps seen at their best in the Biedouw Valley, where the blooms cover the slopes from roadside up to high mountain (local sheep farmers are admirably aware of this precious floral gift, moving their flocks to alternative pastures during the flowering season), and in the 125-hectare Ramskop nature reserve, whose displays – a mix of Karoo succulents and coastal fynbos – are especially colourful between June and October. You can't take your vehicle into the reserve, but the area is criss-crossed by footpaths; the circular route leads you up to a high point (and to a pleasant roof-top tearoom) from which there are lovely views of the Olifants River, Pakhuis Pass, Clanwilliam dam, the town itself and of the grand hills of the Cederberg to the east. Within the reserve is the charming Clanwilliam wild flower garden, a fenced-off 7,5-hectare area in which some 200 species indigenous to the Clanwilliam and Namaqualand regions are cultivated. Bulbs and seeds are on sale within the reserve.

If you're interested in Bushman rock-art, take time off to visit the Agter-Pakhuis area to the north-east.

The more sportily inclined are well catered for at the Boskloof and Kranskloof swimming spots, the Bulshoek recreational dam and the nearby river-bathing area and, most especially, at the Clanwilliam dam, 18 kilometres long and said to be the finest of the country's water-skiing venues.

WUPPERTAL

The road through the Pakhuis Pass (the R364) will lead to the turn-off to this picturesque, terraced cluster of white-walled, thatch-roofed cottages in a secluded valley 75 kilometres from Clanwilliam. The village, on the northern bank of the quaintly named Tra-Tra River, was founded in 1810 as the country's first Rhenish mission farm and 'technical school': the villagers were taught to work the land and to become expert in such trades as thatching, millinery, tanning, woodwork, bricklaying – and shoemaking, at which they excelled. Today the area is noted for its tobacco and rooibos tea and, especially, for the fine *veldskoene* – tough but comfortable walking shoes – that are made in the village. The place has changed little since the early decades of the 19th century; the houses are as they were, and donkey carts still ply the winding main street. If you happen to be in the general vicinity over Christmas, make a point of attending the carol service: it's an occasion you'll remember.

THE CEDERBERG
This scenically superb mountain range, lying to the east of the Citrusdal/Clanwilliam axis, takes its name from the beautiful, rare and at one time almost extinct Clanwilliam cedar (*Widdringtoni cederbergensis*). The species suffered grievously from the woodman's axe and from veld-burning in the early years of white settlement, but a few specimens managed to cling to life on the higher slopes. These, now carefully nurtured, will hopefully be the nucleus of new generations. Another, even rarer plant is the pure-white snow protea (*Protea cryophila*), which survives precariously above the snow-line and occurs nowhere else on earth. For the rest, these enchanted uplands are home to the large red disa (*Disa uniflora*), the charming pincushion and to numerous other endemic plants ranging from spring annuals to handsome indigenous tree species.

The Cederberg is a vast (80 000 hectare) controlled area of starkly eroded rock formations and magnificent vistas; of caves and overhangs, peaks and ravines, of clear mountain streams and waterfalls. The region is well-watered – it enjoys up to 1 000 mm of rain a year – and the higher places are often snow-capped in winter. Rock features of particular note are The Maltese Cross, The Wolfberg Arch and the three-metre cleft known as The Wolfberg Cracks; also The Tafelberg and its Spout. Bird life is prolific and fascinating: sunbirds and orange-crested sugarbirds are common; some fine raptors – black eagle, rock kestrel, jackal buzzard – can be seen. About 30 mammal species are present, among them klipspringer, steenbok, baboon and wild cat.

This splendid region is criss-crossed by over 250 kilometres of unmarked but well-defined paths, and it attracts hikers and ramblers, climbers, photographers and nature-lovers from afar. Arm yourself with a forestry map before entering, which you'll do on foot (no cars allowed), probably via the Algeria forest station, where there is an unusually fine camping ground and picnic area.

**CLANWILLIAM
TO VANRHYNSDORP**
There's very little of tourist interest on the long, 75-kilometre stretch north to the sheep-farming centre of Vanrhynsdorp – except of course in springtime, when the countryside is bedecked to the far horizons with wild flowers. The Vanrhynsdorp region is famed for the profusion and beauty of its blooms; the succulent nursery in town, where there are some rare species on show, is worth a visit. Vanrhynsdorp lies just to the north of the Olifants River, at the southern end of a desolate, semi-desert region known as the Knersvlakte. In the general vicinity are the Gifberg and Kobee gorges, the 125-metre Ouberg waterfall and, to the north-east (along the R27 highway) the grandeur of Vanrhyn's Pass, one of ten major mountain throughways built by

the renowned 19th-century road engineer Thomas Bain. It cuts through the Bokkeveld escarpment to lead the motorist into a quite different world: the parched wilderness of the Knersvlakte quite suddenly gives way to a relatively well-watered and pleasantly green land of sweet grasses and tall trees. But seemingly a lonely one, too: the celebrated author Laurens van der Post wrote of 'farms hidden behind rare puritanical hills guarding secret water, so that [the countryside] appears totally unpeopled'. The village of Nieuwoudtville lies just beyond the pass: an attractive little place of rather unusual sandstone buildings and an inviting wild-flower reserve. Nearby are the splendid 100 metre-high Nieuwoudtville falls.

To the east of Vanrhysdorp are two small towns, each with its modest attractions. Vredendal, 24 kilometres distant, prospers from the generous waters of the Olifants River irrigation scheme and is the centre of a 'Wine of Origin' area (five co-operatives). It is also attracting a growing number of industries (furniture, dried fruit, mineral waters). Lutzville, a flourishing little agricultural settlement, lies to the north.

CLANWILLIAM TO THE COAST

The highway north from Vanrhynsdorp will take you into the arid depths of Namaqualand, to the town of Springbok and the magnificent new Richtersveld National Park beyond, and, if you digress eastwards, to Port Nolloth and Alexander Bay in the sandy wastes of the west-coast diamond country. These places, intriguing though they are, lie outside the parameters of this book: they're just too far from Cape Town, or indeed from anywhere, to be considered as weekend venues.

Turn left off the N7 at (or rather, near) Clanwilliam, follow the R364 for 64 kilometres and you'll reach the coast at Lambert's Bay, a largish fishing village that is fast gaining favour among the more casual type of holidaymaker. Some make the journey for the sun and sand (though the water tends to be cold, and the beach windswept), others for the fish and rock-lobsters that can be caught in the sea – and tasted at Die Muisbosskerm, an open-air, rough-and-ready and genially hospitable eatery.

And for the bird life of the area: the Bay's Bird island – something of a misnomer since you can walk to it – is haven to a vast colony of Cape gannets and to cormorants, penguins, seagulls and others. Altogether, the island plays host to a full 150 different seabird species. Other ornithological treasure-houses in the general area are the Lonvlei dam where, after good winter rains, the flamingoes gather in their thousands, and the Wadrif salt pan, along the coast to the south and also home to vast congregations of aquatic birds. Farther along 48 kilometres from Lambert's Bay – is Elands Bay, where the surfing is superb when the south-easter blows, which is often. Here you'll find the west coast's only large river-estuary and, upstream, Voorvlei, another splendid sanctuary for the seabird and the wader. The route from Lambert's Bay to Cape Town, around 250 kilometres in all, keeps the motorist in sight of the sea for most of the way and it is a pleasant enough drive. It leads along a scenically uncluttered, even stark but in places strikingly beautiful coastline of heath, sandveld, jagged cliff and wide beach. The region is becoming increasingly popular among Capetonian (and other) holidaymakers, despite the unremitting fierceness of the sun, the chilliness of the Atlantic waters and the gusty offshore wind that sweeps stinging eddies of sand before it.

ELANDS BAY TO SALDANHA
This is a comfortable two hours' journey, the first stretch taking you along the coast of St Helena Bay, 'discovered' and named by the Portuguese navigator Vasco da Gama on that saint's day (7th November) in 1497, and to the Berg River. The bay is one of the country's premier commercial fishing grounds: the upwelling of the cool Benguela current here provides the nutrients that sustain massive shoals of pilchards, anchovies and mackerel. The water's edge is lined by fish factories – and, unusually, by wheatfields that extend down to the shore.

The harbour village of Velddrif lies at the mouth of the Berg river, serving among other things as celebratory venue for completion of the annual Berg River canoe marathon, which starts at Paarl in the winelands north of Cape Town (see page 78). The estuary is a magnet for large numbers of flamingoes, avocets, spoonbills and, sometimes, for the otherwise seldom seen glossy ibis. Even more inviting to the bird-lover is the nearby Rocher Pan nature reserve, sanctuary for 150 different species, among them huge numbers of waterfowl. Amenities include hides, observation towers, picnic sites and pathways.

A little farther south, halfway across the peninsula, is the largish commercial centre of Vredenburg, from which roads lead to Stompneusbaai at the southern extremity of St Helena Bay; to the picturesque little hamlet of Paternoster, and to Cape Colombine and its nature reserve, a pleasant place for strolling, for crayfishing and for rock-angling.

Sweeping down the coast from the southern rim of the peninsula is Saldanha Bay, one of the world's finest natural harbours but, until fairly recently, little used by shipping: it was bypassed by the early navigators in favour of Table Bay which, though it offered poorer shelter, could provide an abundance of fresh water. Today, though, the port of Saldanha is both the principal centre of the west-coast fishing industry and a deep-sea terminal for the export of iron ore, capable of accommodating the largest of bulk carrier vessels and geared to handle a massive 33 million tons of ore a year. The iron is brought down from Sishen, in the northern Cape, over an 860-kilometre electrified railway line in ore trains that can be up to two kilometres long.

Local tourism has been slow to develop – fish factories clutter the shores of the bay, and the countryside around has few immediately apparent attractions – but the area has some powerful drawcards: yachtsmen and watersports enthusiasts, in particular, are drawn to the area in increasing numbers. Visitors may tour the harbour and its loading terminal. Ten kilometres south-east of Saldanha is:

LANGEBAAN LAGOON

The 16 kilometre-long channel of water that opens into Saldanha Bay is both one of Africa's finest wetland areas and the focal point of the west coast's tourism industry. For bird-lovers, the lagoon offers an Aladdin's cave of delights: the clear, shallow waters (six metres deep at most), the mud and sand banks and the rocky shores and islands of the bay are a magnet for huge numbers of curlew sandpipers (migrants from the breeding grounds of the Arctic and sub-Arctic regions), of cormorants, flamingoes, gannets, gulls, herons, plovers, knots, turnstones, sanderlings and other species. Nearby Schaapen Island is home to the largest known colony of kelp (or southern black-backed gulls). In the hot summer months there are around 55 000 birds in residence, all drawn to the lagoon and its environs by the shelter they provide and by the abundance of easily available food: marine algae, molluscs, crustaceans and other nutritious mud-loving organisms.

Langebaan, the islands and some 20 000 hectares of coastal countryside are the components of the recently proclaimed West Coast National Park, which is still being developed and which will eventually – once the local landowners are tied into the conservation scheme – cover a much larger area. The terrain is, like most other parts of the west-coast region, virtually treeless, but the ground cover has points of interest and in spring, when the annuals come into bloom, its enchantment. For the most part vegetation comprises succulents and succulent-type plants, dwarf bushes, sedges and some coastal fynbos, or heath. Postberg nature reserve, which lies within the park's boundaries, contains bontebok and eland, blue and black wildebeest; other species are being reintroduced.

There are conservation displays at Langebaan Lodge, which serves as the information centre for and headquarters of the national park as well as a fine commercial hotel (see page 122). From here, short guided walks lead to the saltmarshes and driftsand areas. Other hiking trails (including a beach walk) and horse-trails are planned, one of which has an overnight stop at Geelbek, a dignified old farmstead now restored to its original (1860) condition. The lagoon is a very popular venue among sailors and other watersportsmen, many of whom stay at Club Mykonos, just outside the park and the nearest thing you'll get to a Greek Island village this side of Suez (see page 121).

LANGEBAAN TO CAPE TOWN

Continue down the R27 and you'll get to the junction with the east-west R315 which, if you turn towards the coast, will take you to the charming seaside hamlet of Yzerfontein. This is reckoned to be one of the country's finest surfing spots; other visitors come for the good fishing; still others for the excellent seafood served at Die Pan, a marvellously sociable open-air restaurant.

From the shore at Yzerfontein one can discern the low shape of Dassen Island, named for the rock-rabbits, or dassies, that number among its residents. Dassen is one of about forty submerged mountains that lie off southern Africa's south and west coasts. Collectively they are known as the Guano Islands, a reference to their enormous and valuable deposits of bird-manure, used commercially over the centuries as fertilizer and at one time the focus of the so-called 'guano wars' between fiercely competing interests. Bird Island in Lambert's Bay (see page 117) is one of them; Saldanha Bay encompasses five (Vanerling, Jutten, Malgas, Marcus, Schaapen, Meeu, Jacob's Rock and North-west Rocks).

Dassen, nearly five kilometres long and two kilometres wide, is one of the larger and, in conservation terms, most important of the islands: it supports a great number of seabirds, serving as the principal breeding ground of the Cape penguin, more commonly known as the jackass penguin for its harsh, braying call. Nearly 100 000 of these birds congregate here during February, and again in September. One authorative scientist has ranked Dassen among 'the naturalist's wonders of the world'.

Fifteen kilometres inland from the intersection is the pleasant town of Darling, set in a countryside renowned for its springtime flower displays, for its wheat and wine-grapes, for the milk, cheese and butter (one of Darling's more unusual features is its Butter Museum) and other products of a most bountiful land; also for the lovely lupins and Chincherinchees grown locally for export. The farm Oudepost boasts the country's largest orchid nursery. The wild flowers are best seen in the Tienie Versfeld reserve, a botanical sanctuary that preserves a typical fragment of sandveld environment.

The final stretch of the coastal route will take you to the seaside villages of Melkbosstrand and Bloubergstrand.

Melkbosstrand ('milkbush beach') plays host to discerning anglers and crayfishermen and, each New Year, to large and energetic *Boeresport* gatherings. Close by is Koeberg, the country's first and to date only nuclear-power plant (a second is planned): designed and built by a French consortium, its two 922 mW pressurized water reactors began generating electricity in 1985, using local uranium enriched by an efficient process developed by South African scientists.

Bloubergstrand translates as 'blue mountain beach', a name taken from the nearby 330-metre hill but more appropriate, perhaps, to a far better-known feature – Table Mountain, of which there are stunning views from the village. Bloubergstrand is a fast-growing residential area, and also something of a gourmet's paradise: among a bevy of outstanding seafront restaurants is the acclaimed Ons Huisie, a charmingly restored fisherman's cottage.

◻ WHERE TO STAY

CEDARBERG HOTEL
Citrusdal
A smallish, well-appointed, friendly and generally exceptionally pleasant country hotel situated in Citrusdal, in the heart of the fertile valley of the Olifants. The place is a convenient and most comfortable base from which to explore the lovely countryside of river and hill and sweet-

scented orange grove, and to take in the splendours of the nearby Cederberg wilderness area (see page 116).

Accommodation The 26 rooms are attractively furnished; each is air conditioned and has its private bathroom, television and telephone. Fairly unpretentious but most comfortable.

Food, drink and service The hotel has two bars, one of them an especially inviting venue, and a restaurant whose set menu offers good, homely cuisine: sweet-corn soup, roast beef, a nice selection of salads from the buffet, apple crumble and so on. The pub lunches (shepherd's pie, mutton chops) are similarly unpretentious.

For conferences and groups, the hotel will lay on a wine-tasting session and an excellent theme dinner.

Amenities At the hotel there's a swimming pool, volleyball court, croquet lawn, snooker and billiards tables; nearby: golf and tennis.

A little farther afield are Bushman art sites, mineral springs, and the scenic delights of the wine and citrus farms, and of the Cederberg.

Conferences: the hotel can accommodate up to 45 delegates.

CEDARBERG HOTEL in brief

How to get there: Citrusdal is just off the N7 highway, 174 km north of Cape Town. Tariff (See Authors' Note on page 4): B Official rating: ★★ Conference facilities: For up to 45 delegates. Liquor licence: Full. Children: Welcome. Pets: Welcome. Reservations: PO Box 37, Citrusdal 7340, Cape; telephone: (02662), ask for 82; fax: (02662), ask for 334.

CLUB MYKONOS

Langebaan

Greece away from Greece – right here on the Cape's rather wind-swept west coast. The late Lawrence Darrell once said that 'being in Mykonos is the nearest man can come to living in a rainbow', a piece of imagery that could well have inspired the founders of the Club.

Mykonos is not just a hotel, it's a whole village. Your accommodation is a whitewashed, colourfully trimmed *kaliva*; when you emerge from it, you walk along cobbled alleys and through attractive public squares, to and past coffee shops, bars, bakeries, boutiques and delicatessens. If it wasn't for the wind, you could easily imagine yourself beneath the Aegean sky.

The concept is imaginatively grand, and staying there is a lot of fun.

Accommodation The 256 self-catering *kalivas* are staggered along the beach to maximize the view. Each is simply but attractively decorated. The five blocks have evocative Greek names – Eurania, Clio, Thalia, Calliope and Erato.

The *kalivas* vary slightly in design. Smaller units are available for couples and small families; all have television and telephones, bright, cheerfully-coloured fabrics, white walls. A luxury unit comprises a large living room with a lounge and dining section, separated from the modern kitchen by a breakfast counter. A balcony with shade-awning and a magnificent sea view leads off the living room; down a passage is a bathroom and three bedrooms with built-in cupboards. The main bedroom has a bathroom *en suite* and its own small and attractive balcony.

Though Club Mykonos is primarily a timeshare project, units may be rented on a casual basis. The new Athene Cascades Hotel will open in 1992 to accommodate both holidaymakers and conference delegates.

Food, drinks and service The village is generously served by coffee shops and *tavernas*, and we didn't manage to try them all. We did, however, eat in the open-air Strandloper restaurant, where traditional west-coast specialities – for instance fish braais (we particularly enjoyed the barbecued crayfish) and potjiekos – are on offer. At the Aegean Taverna we fed on *moussaka* to the sound of smashing plates and the warble of bazoukis, while two adventurous revellers did a reasonable facsimile of Zorba's dance. Onlookers hurled reject plates specially provided for the purpose. If you find this culturally swamping, there's also live entertainment in the waterfront bar, with a special entertainment pub a short distance away.

Amenities Club Mykonos has a vast gymnasium complex that offers aerobics, air-baths, saunas, a heated pool, four squash courts, five tennis courts and a weights area to help fight the battle of the bulge. You can go parasailing with your heart in your mouth, or take yachting lessons. Launch trips took us around Langebaan Lagoon and out to the crayfish beds, beyond the sanctuary, where we lowered nets and struggled to get them back on board. We were thrilled to have netted two crayfish. And there's the beach, a long, long stretch of white sand beyond the rocks along which the buildings sprawl; and a 140-berth marina graced by expensive-looking yachts. The marina is part of the Venetian Quarter, a waterfront cluster of shops, pubs and restaurants (of the latter, the Ariadne is said to be superb).

Conferences: the R6-million conference centre includes the 483 square-metre Athene Room (up to 500 delegates), which can be divided into four. The Plato and Socrates rooms are smaller, for between 30 and 50 people in schoolroom or cinema format. All these areas are richly carpeted, air conditioned and have full audio-visual facilities.

CLUB MYKONOS in brief
How to get there: The resort is just north of the Langebaan lagoon mouth. From Cape Town, follow the N1 past Paarden Island and take the R27 exit. The R27 will lead you to Langebaan. **Tariff** (See Authors' Note on page 4): Varies per unit. **Official rating:** Not applicable. **Conference facilities:** Available for up to 500 delegates (see text). **Children:** Welcome. **Reservations:** Private Bag X2, Langebaan 7357; telephone: (02287) 2101; fax: (02287) 2303.

LANGEBAAN LODGE

Langebaan

The Lodge – the old Hotel Panoramic – was taken over by the National Parks Board in 1988 and radically refurbished to provide an attractive, pleasantly informal and very welcoming haven for visitors to the splendid West Coast National Park, centrepiece of which is Langebaan Lagoon (see page 119). The place has been very pleasantly appointed and decorated (in natural colours; cane and wood are much in evidence), and the public areas – lounge, terrace, dining room, breakfast room, pub – are beautifully designed and positioned to allow the broadest of views. What appealed to us most especially, though, was the way in which we were received and looked after: the uniformed NPB staff are knowledgeable, friendly, courteous, helpful, take an obvious pride in their work; all in all, we couldn't have asked for better hosts.

Accommodation Each of the 24 rooms in the upgraded part of the hotel has its own private bathroom, television, telephone, comfortable cane furniture and floor-to-ceiling French windows. Thirteen of them have lagoon views.

Food, drink and service Homely à la carte fare. The menu offers seafood as well as standard meat dishes. Sunday lunch caters for the larger appetite. The hotel's coffee shop specializes in delicious milk tart and chocolate cake.

Drinks are served on the pleasant terrace, and in the smartish cocktail bar, a cheerfully nautical venue.

Amenities Resident guests have exclusive use of the swimming pool. The Lodge also runs a nice little gift shop, and an excellent information centre: the static displays tell you all about the park, the marine ecosystem, bird migration and so on. Established walks such as the three-day 13- to 16-kilometre Strandveld educational trails (hikers are accommodated at the historic Geelbek homestead) are great fun; there's game- and flower-viewing in the Postberg section of the park, which is open from August to September. Sailing, boardsailing, angling and other watersports take place on the lagoon. Just to the north is Club Mykonos, which, among other things, has an impressive number of inviting restaurants (see page 121).

LANGEBAAN LODGE in brief
How to get there: Langebaan is 115 km north of Cape Town; take the R27 coastal route to the signposted turnoff. ***Tariff*** *(See Authors' Note on page 4):* **C** *Official rating:* Not applicable. *Conference facilities:* Groups of up to 50; catering for 120 is possible. *Children:* Welcome. *Reservations:* PO Box 25, Langebaan 7357; telephone: (02287) 2144; fax: (02287) 2607; telephones: Cape Town (021) 419-5365; Pretoria (012) 343-1991.

MARINE PROTEA

Lambert's Bay

The historic century-old Marine, close to the beach in the small coastal town of Lambert's Bay, was recently renovated and is now a most attractive medium-sized seaside hotel, spick and span, brightly decorated, nicely furnished in vaguely Victorian/colonial style: it has black-and-white tiled floors, and lots of latticework, white wicker furniture and potted palms. Very comfortable and pleasing to the eye. What makes the place special, though, is the welcome you get: everyone from the manager down really does seem to want you to enjoy your stay, and goes out of his or her way to make sure you do.

We went at the very best time, in the spring, when Namaqualand showed all its fabled finery and we drove through kilometre after kilometre of flower-carpeted countryside. Food for the soul.

Accommodation The 47 rooms were newly and cheerfully decorated; mine was done out in pleasing tones of blue and white, and it looked out to the bay. Each unit has its private bathroom, radio, TV and telephone.

Food, drink and service Superb food on both the four-course table d'hôte and the à la carte menus.

Lambert's Bay is crayfish country and the Marine makes the most of its location. You have a choice of crayfish pâté, crayfish bisque laced with cream and brandy, crayfish deep fried in a beer batter with fresh tomato butter, grilled crayfish with lemon butter, crayfish with cheese and herb sauce (flavoured with mustard and gratinated), cold crayfish with salad and herb mayonnaise, sliced crayfish in mild curry cream on saffron rice, crayfish with feta and fettucine... what more could a mortal desire? We wondered, though, after glutting ourselves for a few days, if we wouldn't be led to intone a substitute grace:

'For crayfish young and crayfish old, for crayfish hot and crayfish cold, for crayfish tender, crayfish tough, we thank thee Chef – we've had enough'.

There were of course other things on offer, other fish and meat dishes (splendidly matured and sauced steaks, homemade chicken pie, and a nice boiled lamb with caper sauce). But when in Rome ...

Drinks: Good wine list, and a most pleasant bar area. Service is courteous, efficient and, as mentioned, genuinely friendly.

Amenities A few minutes' walk from the Hotel is Bird Island (see page 117); we saw thousands of cormorants, gannets, gulls and penguins crammed together on the same rocky outcrop. Trawler cruises and guided tours of the crayfish factory are arranged by the hotel. There is a golf course nearby.

Conferences: Two large air conditioned conference rooms, divided by an acoustic sliding door, each equipped with sound systems, triple-lens porta-jet overhead projectors, wide screens, VHS video machines and monitors. Total capacity: 120 delegates (60 per room) There are two venues for smaller groups (up to 15 people). The conference package also includes (weather permitting) a crayfish trawler cruise.

MARINE PROTEA in brief
How to get there: Lambert's Bay is 280 km from Cape Town. One can either take the inland highway (the N7) to Clanwilliam and then west on the R364, or the coastal route (the R27) through the Langebaan area, Velddrif and Eland's Bay. **Tariff** *(See Authors' Note on page 4):* D **Official rating:** ★★★ *Conference facilities:* Available for up to 120 delegates (see text). **Liquor licence:** Full. **Children:** All are welcome. **Reservations:** PO Box 1, Lambert's Bay 8130; telephone: (026732) 49; fax: (026732) 36.

THE OVERBERG

❏ WHAT TO SEE AND DO
❏ WHERE TO STAY

THE OVERBERG

❐ WHAT TO SEE AND DO

The name translates as 'the other side of the mountain', which is how the early white settlers at the Cape thought of the lands to the east, beyond the high and lordly Hottentots-Holland range – a vaguely defined area that, for the purposes of this book, stretches from the foothills of the mountains, Betty's Bay and Cape Hangklip in the west to Still Bay and the inland centre of Swellendam in the east.

The Overberg is a scenically attractive and varied region known for the rugged cliffs, the coves and embayments of its shoreline, for its rich wheat and barley fields, its green pastures and forest plantations, for its wild flowers, for the gentleness of its hinterland countryside. The ocean, too, can be gentle, but is not always so: over the centuries the winds and currents and the jagged rocks of the seashores have claimed a great many ships, and their wrecks, some of them visible, most of them submerged beneath the shallow waters of the great Agulhas Bank, testify to the ferocity of the storms that sometimes lash this part of the southern coast. But most summer days are kinder, the waters warm and placid, and they play host to thousands of holidaymakers, to yachtsmen and anglers, sunbathers, surfers and skiers.

If you glance at the map you'll see that the marine resorts tend to be rather isolated from each other. There is, for much of the way, a coastal road, but it's rather serpentine and, generally speaking, one is advised to take the N2 national highway from Cape Town, negotiating the spectacular Sir Lowry's Pass and then turning south at the appropriate inland intersections.

This is the route we shall be following for most of the way, though for the first stage of the journey we digress southwards, on the R44, before reaching the pass. The turn-off is just beyond the Strand/Somerset West complex (see page 77), and it leads along the eastern shores of False Bay, past the village of Gordon's Bay to:

CAPE HANGKLIP AND KLEINMOND
The cape is the dramatically high southern extremity (460-metre) of the Hottentots-Holland mountains, a windswept and hauntingly lonely place, once the refuge of runaway slaves and cattle-rustlers and now the location of a lighthouse, a hotel and a modest scatter of cottages. This stretch of the False Bay coast is much favoured by serious fishermen, and by those who delight in profusions of wild flowers: here, among the hills, one can see magnificent displays of proteas and everlastings. Just to the north of Hangklip, at the mouth of the Buffels River, is Pringle Bay, a tranquil and timeless little village whose beach and lagoon entice the quieter kind of weekender.

To the west of Hangklip, beyond a trinity of small lakes (they were once river-estuaries, long since cut off by the dunes) is Betty's Bay, another sleepy little resort area, popular among anglers, lazers in the sun and, most especially, among nature lovers. The nearby Harold Porter botanical garden, a delightful 190-hectare expanse of fynbos (of both the coastal and mountain types), is renowned for its ericas: it is haven to about 50 species, many of which are rare. Most charming of the floral residents is the red disa (*Disa uniflora*). A nice place for walking (dogs are allowed, provided they're kept on the leash) and for picnicking (there's an especially inviting spot near the waterfall).

Kleinmond, farther along the coast to the east, lies at the mouth of the Bot River and at the foot of the 600 metre-high Palmietberg. Nearby is the Palmiet River lagoon, whose waters, and those of Sandown Bay, beckon the fishermen. About 600 hectares of the surrounding land have been proclaimed as the Kleinmond coastal and mountain reserve, an attractive patch of countryside criss-crossed by short walking trails.

The reserve's marshland is home to some 1 500 plant species, to a variety of buck and great numbers of waders and other birds, and to the rare and endearingly tiny micro frog.

SIR LOWRY'S PASS AND BEYOND

If you stay on the N2 after leaving Strand/Somerset West you'll reach, after five or so kilometres, the base of the precipitous mountain range and the start of the winding pass that was named after Sir Lowry Cole, an early 19th century Cape governor. This is one of the region's most spectacular drives – and, incidentally, train journeys as well: the steep gradients, the tunnels and cuttings and the magnificent vistas that unfold attract railway enthusiasts from afar. The views are quite stunning: from the summit one gazes over the flat plains below and the whole southward sweep of False to Cape Point in the remote distance.

Once over the pass, you descend in gentler fashion to the Overberg proper to reach the small centres of Elgin and Grabouw, headquarters of the country's apple-growing industry. The fertile land here nurtures huge orchards of Granny Smiths, York Imperials and Golden Delicious, and of pears and peaches. Elgin in fact scarcely ranks as a 'centre': it is really little more than a railway siding, though there are two large packing houses in the area (visitors welcome, though formal tours are only conducted during the slack season). Also of note is the Orchard Elgin Country Market, billed as a 'fresh new concept in country shopping' that offers fruit and other local produce, preserves and handcrafts, a 'haute deli', a continental bakery and excellent breakfasts and lunches. Grabouw has a small museum given over to the story of the apple.

After 20 or so kilometres the highway runs through the Houw Hoek ('glen pass') to the small town of Botrivier and the wheatlands beyond. South of the town, reached via the R43, is:

THE HERMANUS AREA

The seaside resort of Hermanus and its surrounds are enormously popular among privileged retirees, among weekending Capetonians and holidaymakers from farther afield. The town itself is a fairly substantial place of shops and hotels and widely spread scatters of affluent-looking holiday homes, all attractively set between mountain and the blue waters of Walker Bay. The area is a paradise for anglers, crayfishermen and perlemoen (abelone) divers, for sailors, watersportsmen and sunsworshippers drawn to beautiful beaches and a sea that is warm and safe for bathing. The nearby Kleinsriviervlei lagoon is a most pleasant stretch of water that plays host to the local yacht club.

Hermanus once served as the bustling centre of prosperous fishing and whaling industries and it has a charming old harbour, now preserved as a museum (and national monument) where vintage and veteran fishing boats, and an evocative collection of reconstructed buildings, are on display. The quayside no longer echoes the sirens of the incoming boats and the cries of the mongers, but there's another harbour next door, a fine new one that accommodates a collection of modern craft used by both commercial and sporting fishermen. Some of the boats can be hired for deep-sea tunny and marlin expeditions.

There are a number of rewarding walks in the vicinity of Hermanus. Especially recommended is the route along the top of the cliffs, from the harbour to the lagoon, along which there are lovely views of the rocky shoreline and its coves. Even grander are the vistas that unfold along the Rotary Mountain Way, a scenic drive that cuts through the backing Kleinrivier mountains, hills that rise abruptly from 60 to nearly 900 metres above sea level. Much of this grand upland area (some 1 450 hectares) has been proclaimed as the Fernkloof nature reserve, an attractive tract of fynbos (heath) countryside that shelters some exquisite wildflower species. About 35 kilometres of walking trails have been established within the reserve. Also in these hills (though the location isn't advertised) is the Orothamnus reserve, a 12-hectare patch set aside specifically to protect the rare marsh rose *Orothamnus zeyheri*. This lovely species has happily responded to grafting experiments and can now be propagated in nurseries.

Across Walker Bay, to the east of Hermanus and inland along the Klein River, is the small village of Stanford, notable for its pretty setting and for the local pottery and craft centre (glazed-clay items, copperware, hand-spun jerseys, traditional raw-hide whips). On the other (western) side of Hermanus, and now almost extensions of the town, are the hamlets of Hawston and Onrus, small and pleasant resorts that tend to be crowded with campers during the holiday season. The latter is at the entrance to a peaceful lagoon; its restaurant, the Onrus Kitchen, is held in high esteem by connoisseurs of good food.

South of Stanford, on the eastern shore of Walker Bay, is the fairly large village and harbour of Gansbaai, where you can buy fresh fish at the quayside, and walk along a breakwater from which there are splendid views of the coastline and the well-named Danger Point to the southwest. It was off this promontory that the British troopship HMS *Birkenhead* came to grief in February 1852 with the loss of 445 lives. Most of those who perished were soldiers bound for the eastern Cape frontier, and they died – heroes to a man – standing to rigid attention as the vessel foundered, so enabling the civilians to climb aboard the three serviceable lifeboats. Their gallantry, exemplified in the phrase 'women and children first', is honoured both in the annals and in the language: the 'Birkenhead Drill' was to become synonymous with unyielding discipline in the face of disaster.

THE CALEDON AREA

Inland, just off the national highway to the north-west of Hermanus, is the town of Caledon and its sequence of seven superb mineral springs. Recorded by white travellers as early as 1689, they yield two million litres of irradiated water a day, and in late-Victorian times they served as the centerpiece of the southern hemisphere's most fashionable spa, boasting pools, a grand pavilion, a sanatorium and a fine hotel. Much of the old splendour disappeared with the great fire of 1946, but imaginative efforts have recently been made (and others are on the drawing board) to restore resort and town to their former and most impressive glory (see page 135).

The Caledon museum, comprising two small historic buildings, is well worth a visit for its fascinating displays of Victoriana and for its textile section. So too is Victoria Park, otherwise known as the Caledon nature reserve and wild flower garden, which is famed for its marvellous springtime floral show. The park covers 214 hectares of Swartberg hillside, 56 hectares of which have been quite beautifully landscaped and adorned with shrubs and trees and colourful fynbos species, among them the exquisite Caledon bluebell (*Gladiolus sparthaceus*). Scenic pathways criss-cross the reserve; wooden bridges have been built; picnic sites established. The annual Caledon Wild Flower Show, held each September, draws thousands of visitors.

As attractive in its own, rather more spectacular way is the Salmonsdam nature reserve, something over 50 kilometres to the south-east (take the R316 from Caledon). Here, within an 850-hectare proclaimed area, there are rugged hills, deep kloofs, streams, waterfalls and a wildlife population that includes 130 bird species and several varieties of buck.

THE GREYTON AREA

The road that branches off the N1 a few kilometres before Caledon will take you north-east to Greyton, one of the Cape's most tranquil and charming villages (though, let it be said, it was 'discovered' fairly recently by press and public and its character could be threatened). The local nature reserve sprawls along the southern slopes of the Riviersonderend mountains – a range that takes its name from the river that rises in the Hottentots-Holland and flows eastward, seemingly (to the early white settlers) 'without end'. The reserve covers 2 220 hectares of rugged hills that rise, at their highest, to 1 465 metres above sea level: a splendid place for walking, especially in springtime when the wild flowers are in bloom. Greyton itself is a pretty little village with an oak-lined main street and three hotels, two of which are featured further on (see pages 137 and 142). As enchanting, though in quite a different way, is Genadendal, a short distance to the west and founded, in 1737, as South Africa's very first mission station by Georg Schmidt, the 'Apostle of the Hottentots' and later taken over by the Moravian missionaries. The place is frozen in the past, its church, parsonage, school building and neat, beautifully thatched cottages little changed by the decades.

South of the Riviersonderend range of mountains is:

THE CAPE AGULHAS AREA
The cape is the Africa's southernmost point, its name derived from the Portuguese word for needles – not a reference to their physical appearance but to their position on the map: the early navigators found that, here, their compasses were not affected by magnetic deviation but rather bore 'directly upon the true poles of the earth'.

Otherwise, Agulhas holds little of interest. The cape itself is the southern segment of a fairly large inland plain which, after the modest interruption of a small range of hills, slips quietly under the ocean to become the vast, shallow Agulhas Bank, the most extensive part of southern Africa's continental shelf. The bank is 250 kilometres wide and its waters, warmed by the westward-flowing, tropical Agulhas current, comprise some of the world's richest fishing grounds, sustaining huge numbers of kabeljou (kob), sole and other bottom-dwellers. Most notable feature of the Agulhas promontory is its lighthouse: it was built in 1848 and generates some 18 million candlepower.

The general region is an agriculturally prosperous one (wool, grain, dairy products), its principal centre the pleasant inland town of Bredasdorp, 24 kilometres north of the cape. Worth visiting is the local Maritime Museum, which features (among other things) relics of many of the vessels wrecked along the rugged, gale-swept coast over the centuries. Among these was the *Birkenhead*, which came to grief in 1852 off Danger Point, 70 kilometres to the west (see page 128). Bredasdorp's Cape Gothic-style Dutch Reformed church is also of note.

Just to the south of town is the Bredasdorp mountain reserve, an 800-hectare expanse of mountain and coastal fynbos countryside which offers walking trails, and fine views from its highest point (360 metres), some lovely plants in its 86-hectare cultivated area (among them giant proteas, ericas and the brilliantly red Bredasdorp lily), and a wild-flower show each August.

Similar to Genadendal in some respects (see page 129) is Elim, a picturesque and much-photographed Moravian mission station 37 kilometres to the south-west of Bredasdorp. The settlement was founded in 1824 in a rural setting that is graced, in summertime, by great numbers of everlastings and other wild flowers; its cottages are thatched and whitewashed; its old watermill is a national monument, and its German-made church clock, which first started ticking in 1764, still keeps good time.

But to return to the seaside. The tiny village of Struis Bay, next door to Agulhas, is a holiday resort popular for its excellent fishing and, off the splendid 16-kilometre beach that stretches westwards, safe bathing and good surfing. There's also a small harbour and, at nearby Hotagterklip, a cluster of nicely restored fishermen's homes.

Even more charming are the cottages at Waenhuiskrans, a small fishing village farther along the coast, on the shores of Marcus Bay. The place, also known as Arniston, takes its Afrikaans name from the huge sea-cave carved out of the nearby cliffs, a cavern that seemed, to the early white settlers, to be quite wide and tall enough to serve as a coach-house ('waenhuis') able to accommodate several wagons and their spans of oxen. Not that it could ever have been put to this use: the entrance, circular and under two metres in diameter, is only accessible at low tide. The great hall of the cave is a product of marine erosion, a process that has sculpted many other strange and often impressive rock formations along this particular part of the south coast. Also of interest in the cavern and along the shoreline to either side are the giant pods of the *Entada gigas* sea-bean, and a number of stone fish-traps built by the 'Strandloper' ('beachranger') people in prehistoric times.

The village's alternative name commemorates one of the most tragic maritime disasters to have occurred in these notoriously treacherous waters. On 30 May 1815 the British troopship *Arniston*, on its way home from Ceylon, was driven ashore by the southerly wind and a strong current and foundered in the bay. Of the 378 people on board, all but seven were drowned, including Major-General Lord Molesworth and his wife, 25 children, 14 women and a number of sick-listed servicemen. Why no lifeboats were launched remains a mystery. The stranded survivors – a carpenter and six sailors – managed to sustain themselves for the next two weeks on the ship's biscuits and military provisions that had been washed ashore, and were eventually rescued by a local farmer out looking for lost cattle. He stumbled on the forlorn little party near a beach on which 300 corpses lay rotting.

The beaches and their surrounds now have more pleasant associations. To the north-east lies the De Hoop nature reserve, one of the Cape's most important proclaimed areas: together with its marine section, it sprawls across 60 000 hectares of endangered coastal fynbos (the largest remaining expanse of this indigenous Cape vegetation) and species-rich waters. The reserve is haven for 230 species of bird, fully 1 500 plant species – 50 of which grow only in this particular place and 70 of which are classed as either endangered or rare – and to 70 mammal species, including Africa's largest population of the once-threatened bontebok (see page 133).

Of the 13 types of marine mammal to visit the area, the southern right whale is perhaps the most distinguished.

On the other side of Arniston is the much smaller but in its way just as interesting De Mond nature reserve, an utterly unspoilt 300-hectare area of dunes, heath, milkwood, mountain cypress and other indigenous forest patches, kloofs, rock-pools and ecologically significant river-estuary. Here, birdlife is also prolific (the uncommon Knysna woodpecker and the martial eagle have been recorded). Among the various charted walks in and through the area is the 30-kilometre, scenically outstanding Grootberg-Horingberg trail.

THE ST SEBASTIAN BAY AREA

Well to the east of Arniston is Cape Infanta, a promontory that flanks the Breede River and its wide estuary, beyond which is St Sebastian Bay. This is something of an angler's paradise: some magnificent catches have been recorded from both the bay and the estuarine waters, and the area is renowned for its oysters and other shellfish. The river is navigable for some 35 kilometres upstream; at its mouth is the popular little resort of Witsand and, next door, Port Beaufort, once a bustling harbour village but now given over to a quieter, more relaxed lifestyle. Today the old customs house serves as a hotel; the thatched church, built in 1849, is a national monument.

At the inland extremity of the river's navigable reaches is Malgas, which also did duty as a harbour of sorts: before the railway was built the village was used as an outlet for wheat and wool and for the ostrich feathers that were exported – at enormous profit – from the Little Karoo during the boom years of the late 19th and early 20th centuries.

Much of the quaintness of the past remains here, perhaps most charmingly in the vehicle pont, powered by two men and the last such working contraption in South Africa.

THE SWELLENDAM AREA

Farther inland, on the N2 national highway a little over 100 kilometres beyond Caledon, is Swellendam, the country's third oldest white settlement (after Cape Town and Stellenbosch). The place has an interesting past: it was founded in 1747 in what was, at the time, the far extremity of colonial encroachment, developed peacefully for a while and then, in 1795, declared itself independent of Dutch East India Company rule – the burghers complained that they had 'for too long been under the yoke of slavery' (though ironically many of them were slave-owners themselves). The 'republic' lasted just a few months before submitting to the newly-installed British regime later that year.

Swellendam rests in the tranquil valley of the Koringlands River and is graced by some lovely old buildings. Of these, the most notable by far is the Drostdy (the early magistrate's court and residence), completed in the town's first year and preserved as a structure of great charm and historical importance. It now serves as a museum housing period furniture, household implements, wagons and an unusual collection of early paper money. Other places of interest are the cluster of 18th century craftsmen's premises nearby; the old prison and the next-door post office (in those days the jailer was also the postmaster); the burghers' Oefeninghuis (a place for meeting and worship), and the Auld House, which once belonged to the locally prominent and very wealthy Barry family. One enters the town from the east, along a splendid avenue of stately oak trees. Forming its backcloth are the Langeberg's Clock Peaks (the twelve o'clock is the closest), a series of heights whose summits, on sunlit days, cast shadows from which one can tell the approximate time of day.

Well worth visiting is the Marloth nature reserve, which covers over 11 000 hectares of high mountain and deep ravine to the north of Swellendam. Wildlife includes buck and some fine raptors; among them is the black eagle, but this is primarily a place for the hiker. The six-day Swellendam trail crosses the reserve, and there are several other rewarding walks in the area.

More environmentally important perhaps – and certainly better known – is the Bontebok National Park, seven kilometres south-east of Swellendam. The park was established, in the 1930s (near Bredasdorp to the east; it was moved to its present and much more suitable location 30 years later) on the initiative of a group of concerned local farmers: by the 1920s only 22 of these sturdy, medium-sized antelope remained in the region and it seemed the species would suffer the same fate as the bluebuck, its now – extinct cousin. The 2 800-hectare area – through which the Breede River runs – is now sanctuary for the country's second largest herd, smaller only than that in the De Hoop reserve (see page 131). It also sustains grysbok, grey rhebok, steenbok, red hartebeest, duiker and a modest number of Cape mountain zebra. Some 200 types of bird, nearly 30 reptile and ten amphibian species and 500 plant species, many of them rare. Notable are the yellowwood, wild olive and milkwood trees. For visitors, there are game-viewing roads, walking trails, picnic spots, a caravan-camping site (self-catering accommodation is being developed), information centre and shop. Best time to visit the park is during the spring and early summer (September to November), when the ground cover is fresh from the winter rains.

❐ WHERE TO STAY

ARNISTON HOTEL
Waenhuiskrans

Deservedly renowned as one of South Africa's finest private coastal hotels. The Arniston was a rather ruggedly informal fisherman's inn until the early 1980s, when it was taken over by Nicky and Steve Fitzgerald (who also, recently, launched The Bay in Cape Town; see page 23). It is now known for its low-key luxury, its fine cuisine, its beautifully appointed reception areas (Cape furniture, natural materials, open fireplaces), and for its splendid hospitality. The building, an old and picturesque one, overlooks beach and bay.

Accommodation Two dozen rooms, some standard, some luxurious, some (the sea-facing ones) with shower, the rest with bath (my bathroom was rather small, but perfectly adequate); all individually and brightly decorated, each with a telephone, and an electric blanket in winter. No television. The upper rooms have balconies, and to sit out at sunset and watch the sea-and-sky colours change is a joy indeed. Other rooms fringe the ground-floor poolside, and are popular with older guests.

Food, drink and service A smallish but imaginative table d'hôte menu; superb food in Cape and French styles. Try the baked Cape salmon with fresh garden salad followed by the creamiest of ice-creams, or the Karoo lamb marinated in rosemary sauce. For breakfast – taken in the main dining room, from which one can view the sea, the sands and early-morning joggers – one has a choice of hot or cold menu; the bran muffins are recommended.

Service is impeccable, and friendly. Drinks are enjoyed in the crisply appointed cocktail bar overlooking the beach and in the rather more casual Strandloper's public bar, much favoured by visiting anglers and the locals. The wine cellar is excellent.

Amenities There's plenty to see and do in Arniston and the surrounding countryside (see pages 130 – 131); the coastline, and its caves, are well worth exploring. Small boys catch huge octopuses in the rock pools; commercial fishermen hawk their catches (which include fine fresh oysters) in noisily amiable fashion; one can walk, bathe, sunworship, and generally relax.

The hotel has a pool but little else in the way of laid-on recreational amenities: it sets out simply to provide quietness, privacy and quality cuisine, and succeeds admirably in doing so.

ARNISTON HOTEL in brief

How to get there: From Cape Town, take the N2 national highway east to Caledon, then the R316 to Bredasdorp and beyond to the coast at Arniston. Bear in mind that the town is officially known as 'Waenhuiskrans', and may be signposted as such. Follow the signs to the hotel, 220 km from Cape Town. **Tariff** *(See Authors' Note on page 4):* E **Official rating:** ★★★ *Conference facilities: Available for up to 20 delegates.* **Liquor licence:** *Full.* **Children:** *No children under 10.* **Reservations:** *PO Box 126, Bredasdorp 7280, Cape; telephone: (02847) 5-9000; fax: (02847) 5-9633.*

BEACH HOUSE

Kleinmond

Not too long ago James and Gaila Borland renounced the city rat-race for idyllic Greyton, where they bought, transformed and ran the hugely – and deservedly – successful Post House country inn (see page 142). A couple of years later, seeking a new challenge, they took over the old Sandown Hotel in Kleinmond, on the False Bay coast to the east of Cape Town, giving it a new name – the Beach House – and their own, distinctive and most imaginative touch.

The Beach House is a very special place. From the outside it has the look of an old-style, rather unexceptional seaside establishment – low-profiled, many-windowed and balconied. Inside it's something of a revelation, a visually delightful compound of sweeping stairway, gleaming wood, rich carpet, bright lemon-yellow and powder-blue Caribbean décor. Cheerful, elegant – and beautifully positioned. Here, the beach is literally on your doorstep; the ocean views wide and wonderful. In winter and autumn (June through November, the migrating season) you can sit beside a log fire with a warming glass of cheer in your hand and watch the whales sporting in the chilly waters of the bay.

The Beach House offers stylish comfort, fine cuisine and a rare brand of hospitality, and it is highly recommended.

Accommodation A total of 23 rooms (22 in the main building and the Garden suite separate) – all individually and beautifully decorated in soft pastels, lime green and blues – of which several have canopied double beds; the upstairs, sea-facing rooms have furnished balconies and panoramas that seem to stretch for ever. Most of the other rooms also enjoy splendid views of either ocean or mountain. Each unit has its private bathroom, its telephone, hairdryer and decanter of complimentary sherry, which we thought was a very nice touch. No radios or TVs (a deliberate omission: one comes here to get away from such things).

Food, drink and service The Whistling Whale restaurant is a large, simply furnished, most attractive room with huge windows looking out to the seascape. Dinner is a stylish meal; the seasonal menu is particularly strong on seafood (fresh linefish is bought in either the village or in Hermanus each day) but, of course, it also features other delectables.

Lunches (served in the Whistling Whale and the Ball and Anchor pub) are lighter: salads, pâtés and so on, though you can also order a nicely sauced steak. Sunday lunch is a bigger and very popular affair.

Morning or afternoon tea are taken in either the Winter Lounge (which has TV and a log fire) or the Summer Lounge (cane furniture and pot plants). Bar service is available in both. Breakfast: full English or continental.

The Ball and Anchor is a nicely-decorated and congenial place in which to meet, and to sample the ever-improving wines of the region.

Amenities The Beach House has a pleasant swimming pool. We also played board games in the lounge; browsed in the library and generally enjoyed ourselves in idyllic surrounds.

The Kleinmond area has a lot to offer nature lovers. There's birdwatching around the Beach House; walks in the local nature reserve, more strenuous hikes farther afield, in and through the mountains; tennis in the village; boat trips – and winter sightings of the endangered southern right whale – in the bay. Among other marine species to be seen are seals and sea otters and, along the coast at Betty's Bay, a colony of Rockhopper penguins. Bikes and canoes can be hired in the village.

Conferences: Facilities are offered for groups of 40 (cinema seating) and 30 (U-shape classroom format). There are also four small breakaway rooms.

BEACH HOUSE in brief
How to get there: Take the N2 highway east from Cape Town; turn right on the R44 just beyond Strand/Somerset West (Gordon's Bay route). Alternatively, travel over Sir Lowry's Pass, then take the Botrivier/Hermanus turnoff after Houw Hoek and right onto the R44 to Kleinmond. **Tariff** (See Authors' Note on page 4): D **Official rating:** ★★ *Conference facilities:* Available for groups of up to 40 (see text). *Liquor licence:* Full. *Children:* No special rates for children. *Reservations:* PO Box 199, Kleinmond 7195, Cape; telephone: (02823) 3130; fax: (02823) 4022.

DE OVERBERGER

Caledon

Caledon's original Victorian Bath – the rather quaint pavilion with a row of benches on one side and change-rooms on the other – slipped sadly into decay after the great fire of 1946, but has recently risen phoenix-like from the ashes, and is now the centrepiece of the brand-new and extensive De Overberger hotel complex. Here, in the grand tradition of Baden-Baden and Carlsbad, we 'took the waters'.

The springs, 'discovered' by the Dutch settlers in 1689, yield 1,7 million litres of warm, health-giving water a day, and they once enjoyed high standing in the ranks of international pleasure-seekers. Samples sent over to the Chicago Fair of 1893 won top honours (they 'sparkled like champagne to the eye' and were adjudged the most 'potent') and fashion-conscious Europe was soon beating a path to this rather unlikely spot. People came for the Baths and lingered to enjoy civilized sociability and fine cuisine. *La belle époque* in the colonial backwoods.

De Overberger is part of the 'Caledon 2000' scheme, an impressive attempt by the civic authorities and private enterprise to return the town to its former glory. On the drawing board are the development of the nature reserve and wild flower garden (see page 129), and the expansion of the local museum; the restoration of some splendid Victorian buildings (37 have been identified as prospective national monuments) and more resorts and amenities will follow.

The hotel is in a pleasant woodland setting: it's been built in front of the old pavilion, on a site that looks over to the mountains and down to the grain silos in the green valley below. It's a large place, well equipped for weekenders *en masse* and for conference delegates, and it now belongs firmly in the 1990s.

Accommodation The complex comprises three double-storeyed blocks; a combined total of 100 comfortable rooms. Those on the ground floor feature pastel floral fabrics with a leaning towards blue; pink predominates on the second floor. All rooms have private bathrooms, TV, telephones.

Food, drink and service The large Lady Anne dining room serves a good à la carte meal; we enjoyed refreshments and snacks on the terrace (nice views; there was a small pond, with its resident ducks, just below us). Light lunches are served by the pool. There is a cocktail bar.

Amenities There's a lot laid on in the way of recreation, and, of course, this is a premier health spa. The air is fresh, the countryside attractive; the combination of hot springs, exercise and massage is a sure-fire recipe for physical wellbeing.

For those who prefer the invigoration of cold water, there's a very large cloverleaf-shaped swimming pool surrounded by sloping lawns. Next door is a volleyball court; nearby is a charming wood-and-glaze gazebo: it's filled with plants and houses a spa bath into which the hot-spring waters are pumped. After wallowing in the healing waters one undergoes a spell of self-indulgent aromatherapy massage in the health-and-beauty centre or, more energetically, a work-out in the gym. There's also horse-riding *in situ*, squash, bowls and golf in the area, and walking paths through lovely fynbos countryside.

Conferences: Facilities for 150 people in a series of separate centres. The conference rooms are modern, well equipped and comfortable.

DE OVERBERGER in brief
How to get there: From Cape Town, take the N2 national highway east to Caledon. The total distance is about 115 km. **Tariff** *(See Authors' Note on page 4): C* **Official rating:** ★★★ **Conference facilities:** *Available for 150 delegates.* **Liquor licence:** *Full.* **Children:** *Welcome.* **Reservations:** *PO Box 480, Caledon 7230; telephone: (0281) 4-1271; fax: (0281) 4-1270.*

GREYTON LODGE
Greyton

We visited some truly exceptional country hotels during our travels but Greyton Lodge, in our view, is in a class of its own.

The inn, on the main street of this picturesque little village (see page 129), has had a chequered career: initially a gaol (two of the old cell windows now serve as bedroom air-vents; the garden gate is also an original) and then, like Topsy, 'it just growed', becoming in turn a trading store, a homestead (the present bar and reception area were once the onion shed and stables respectively), a police station and (again) a gaol; finally – a house, lovingly restored to its charming 19th century character by owner-manager Leonard Glass, who took over the property at the end of 1984.

In the years since then he has created an outstanding little European-style *gasthaus* that offers old-style hospitality in elegantly comfortable surrounds, attentive personal service, cosmopolitan company and superb food. Leonard prefers to leave the kitchen to chef Elsa van der Nest, a cordon bleu.

On his trips abroad, Leonard has promoted the country generally and Greyton Lodge in particular, and at any given time, but especially between December and March, overseas visitors are prominent among the guests.

Accommodation Sixteen individually and very nicely styled rooms of various sizes from smallish to suite, in buildings linked by garden walkways. Antiques and other legacies of the past are a pleasant feature of the appointments. The main suite has its own lounge and is wonderfully decorated in black and gold, but otherwise the overall feel is of cottagey comfort. 'People, particularly professional people', says Leonard, 'come here to relax, to unwind', so telephones and TVs have been banished from the sleeping areas.

Food, drink and service Simple but delicious food is served with consummate style in a cosy, intimate dining room, which is warmed by log fires in winter. In spite of the Lodge's exclusivity – big names in the business and professional world are invariably on the guest list – the atmosphere is friendly and casual: people gather in the pub for a chatty pre-dinner drink, which Leonard dispenses.

A set menu, delightfully different each day; cordon bleu country cuisine and a choice of two main courses; the Lodge is known for its pear soup and pink rack of lamb with strawberry wine sauce. There's also an excellent wine cellar. During summer, breakfast is served outside, in a garden full of fruit trees. Tea on the terrace, with the lawns spreading before you, is a delight.

Amenities There's television and a good selection of books in the main lounge, which used to be the old kitchen – the stove has been retained but it's now an elegant, rather English, supremely comfortable room of soft couches, brocade and massed flowers. The original duckpond has been enlarged and converted to create a pleasant willow-shaded swimming pool. The more energetic visitor has a splendid selection of hill-country walks to choose from (recommended is the 16 kilometre hike to McGregor, through the Riviersonderend mountains, and the fairly strenuous clamber up the 1 466-metre Kanonberg), and there are horses and cycles for hire. The nearby Greyton nature reserve encompasses some spectacular scenery, a number of different kinds of buck and, in springtime, a lovely array of wild flowers. Greyton village, with its attractive cottages, antique shop, coffee shop and pub, will fill a pleasant few hours of your time.

The recently built conference centre can accommodate 25 delegates, and is equipped with video, overhead projector, flip charts, film screen and so forth.

GREYTON LODGE in brief
How to get there: From Cape Town, take the N2 national highway for 112 km; turn left at the Greyton sign. The village is 32 km farther along; follow the signs to the Lodge. **Tariff** *(See Authors' Note on page 4):* C **Official rating:** *Not applicable.* **Conference facilities:** *Available (see text).* **Liquor licence:** *Wine and Malt.* **Children:** *Children under 12 are not accommodated.* **Reservations:** *PO Box 50, Greyton 7233, Cape; telephone: (02822) 9876/9800; fax: (02822) 9672.*

HOUW HOEK INN
Elgin/Grabouw

The Inn, on the Houw Hoek Pass road, is the oldest licensed hotel in the country – a charmingly rustic cluster of buildings looking onto a duckpond and a lawn over which Shetland ponies, ducks and geese wander at will. At the bottom of the garden is a river, beyond which are lovely hills. In the grounds are mature oaks, poplars, and a blue gum which is apparently the largest of its kind south of the Limpopo (it stands at the door of the pub, and according to travel-writer T.V. Bulpin, is said to thrive on the aroma of good cheer and on the sociability inside, rustling its leaves appreciatively when patrons tell their jokes).

The ground floor of the main house dates from about 1779; the upper storey was added in 1860, and since then the place has been progressively extended to include old adjoining farm buildings and rondavels. The effect is truly and attractively ranch-style – long and low and spreading – though some of the parts at the back, added on 25 years ago, are double-storeyed.

The Inn is on the site of a toll-gate and staging-post established, in Dutch East Indian Company days, on the old cattle-trail to the interior. An early guest was the writer, socialite and social commentator Lady Anne Barnard, who stopped over in 1798, pronouncing the boiled chicken 'fit for an emperor'. The food is still excellent, and much of the rural heritage has been preserved – though there are all the modern conveniences (including a helipad).

Houw Hoek Inn is very popular over weekends (one usually has to book well in advance); conferences take up most of the weekdays.

Accommodation The 33 units include centuries-old stone rondavels and some upstairs rooms that incorporate pleasant roof balconies. All have private bathrooms, telephone, and TV with a video channel. The general standard is reasonable. The bridal suite has a splendid canopied bed.

Food, drink and service The Inn is now under French management and meals can be invitingly elegant affairs, though there's also good, plain country fare: we enjoyed home-made bread, farm-fresh milk, cream, eggs and deep-dish pies as well as cordon bleu cuisine. The cellar is stocked with a fine selection of wines.

Two dining rooms: a small one in the main building and the large Barn, where there's a dinner-dance with a set menu on Saturday evenings.

The Barn can accommodate 150 people for Sunday lunch.

Good pub lunches are served in The Hitching Post, and thereby hangs a tale. Some decades ago a young man stuck a ten shilling note on the ceiling before he went overseas, saying that when he returned broke, he would still be able to buy himself a drink or six; others followed suit – and the ceiling now sports over 200 banknotes from different countries, some very old.

Amenities Strolling around the grounds and fishing in the river, or simply sitting on the veranda surveying the pleasant scene, helped us pass the time very enjoyably. We also played snooker in The Hitching Post and walked in the surrounding mountains. For the energetic there's squash, badminton, volleyball, bowls and a swimming pool in which to cool off afterwards.

There are conference facilities for 100, full AV equipment is provided; as the hotel sleeps only 60 people, however, seminars tend to be smaller.

HOUW HOEK INN in brief
How to get there: The Inn is just off the N2 national highway east of the Elgin/Grabouw area. Distance from Cape Town: 75 km. *Tariff* (See Authors' Note on page 4): E **Official rating:** ★★ **Conference facilities:** Available for 100 delegates (see text). **Liquor licence:** Full. **Children:** Welcome. **Reservations:** PO Box 95, Grabouw 7160; telephone (02824) 4-9646/4-9696; fax: (02824) 4-9112.

KLEIN RIVER LODGE
Stanford

The lodge, in the pleasant little Overberg village of Stanford, offers tranquility, unpretentious comfort, good food and the warmest kind of country hospitality – in the most pleasant of surrounds. The garden is very English, very lovely; from the wide terraces of the sturdy old house we looked across lawns and arbors of roses to the river and the mountains beyond.

Owners David and Angela Bednall are hooked on Victoriana: they spent years in the building business and have collected, fitted and displayed a splendid array of old windows, doors and every other kind of Victorian relic they could find. They also restore furniture, keep poultry, grow vegetables and cook fine food – classic Jacks-of-all-trades and, quite evidently, master of all. The Bednalls are amiable and caring hosts; the routines are undemanding – the comfortable lounge is well supplied with books – and the enticement, in winter, is to put soft music on the stereo and settle down by the fire to read; to relax completely.

Stanford is a quarter-hour's drive from the seaside town of Hermanus, one-and-a-half hours from Cape Town.

Accommodation I had Room One, very spacious, with a high ceiling, full-length windows, two easy chairs, large cupboards, a two-metre square bed and a private bathroom (the water's almost hot enough to make tea). A bonus was the electric blanket – Stanford can be cold in winter.

There are seven rooms in all, five with *en suite* bathroom and shower-room; the others so close to bathrooms that it doesn't make much difference. All the rooms are different; all are filled with Victorian and Edwardian bric-a-brac. One is at the top of a rather attractive winding staircase that leads up from the pub, and it feels a bit like a tree house when you're inside (the views from the windows are splendid).

Food, drink and service Before-dinner drinks are served in the aptly named and most congenial Potting Shed, a Victorian-style pub complete with horse brasses, open fireplace and gleaming woodwork. The bar was created by David from the original floorboards of the house.

The tariff at Klein River Lodge includes breakfast, and dinner is provided by prior arrangement. The food is prepared by David, served *en famille* in either the kitchen or the dining room (depending on the number of guests). It's superb: creative, wholesome. Vegetables, herbs, fruit and nuts are harvested from the garden, the Bednall's free-ranging chickens supply the eggs, the fish comes fresh from Hermanus and Gansbaai.

Breakfast is taken in the kitchen, another bric-a-brac-filled room where we chatted to David while he prepared a full English meal.

Amenities Stanford is the centre of one of the country's most prolific protea-growing regions. It's also fine bird-watching, hiking and rambling country. There's horse-riding, canoeing and good fishing in the vicinity.

A full range of recreational facilities is available in and around Hermanus (including an excellent golf-course).

KLEIN RIVER LODGE in brief
How to get there: The Lodge is in Stanford's King Street. To get to the village from Cape Town, take the N2 highway to the Hermanus turn-off at Bot River and the R43 through Hermanus. Stanford is 15 minutes on from Hermanus. **Tariff** (See Authors' Note on page 4):D **Official rating:** Not applicable. **Liquor licence:** Pending. **Children:** The Lodge does not cater for children. **Viewing:** By appointment only. **Reservations:** PO Box 96, Stanford 7210, Cape; telephone: (0283) 30-0689; fax: (0283) 30-0987.

MARINE HOTEL HERMANUS
Hermanus
A hotel in the grand Victorian tradition: lofty ceilings, enormous rooms; wide, arched corridors; long, broad verandas,

a huge balcony; capacious, columned dining hall, extensive sitting room and bar (both of these have imposing Cape colonial fireplaces), generous interior courtyard, space, space and more space, and a general atmosphere of quiet dignity, – all combining to recall the glory of *la belle époque*. And pools everywhere – an outdoor bath, an indoor plunge, a jacuzzi and, beneath the cliff, a generously proportioned tidal pool.

The original hotel opened its doors in 1902, closed in 1981 for four years of renovations and re-opened, in pristine splendour, in December 1985. It belongs to and reflects the exquisite taste of David Rawdon of earlier Lanzerac (page 93) and Matjiesfontein (page 95) fame. The turn-of-the-century flavour is still there in the *chinoiserie* (the original mustard and brown dragon-patterned plant pots) and the antique furniture, but the rooms have been redecorated, floors recarpeted or retiled, for contemporary comfort.

The building, and its décor, belong in the five-star class, though the hotel officially rates only two stars – apparently because it has a comparatively small staff complement. Yet lunch came with such alacrity that it astonished us; indeed the service was generally quite outstanding.

Accommodation 55 individually decorated suites, and bedrooms, and, again, a welcome generosity of space.

The sumptuous bedsitters are the size of what most hotels call suites, and the suites are palatial. The 'ordinary' bedrooms overlooking the mountain at the back are not in the least ordinary: they lead out onto the glorious upper-floor terra cotta-tiled sundeck, adjacent to the indoor pool room. These units are available at very reasonable rates. One of our bedsitters had a soft champagne-coloured carpet in the bedroom, complementing large white tiles in a sitting room that was up a step higher and ran through to the sea-facing windows. Bedspread, curtains and upholstery were in a jade-green, oriental-patterned fabric depicting birds and exotic plants. The large bathroom had one of those old-fashioned towel warmers, of the kind that doubled as a hot-water pipe.

The resplendent honeymoon suite has an upstairs bedroom, a sitting room below, and a jacuzzi in the bathroom. Executive suites have a sitting room, bedroom and sea-facing bathroom with a jacuzzi. All rooms have TV, fridges, phones and clock radios.

Food, drink and service We had a pub lunch in the very comfortable bar, where, in winter, lunches and Sunday suppers are served by the fireside. The large public bar has a 10-metre-long teak counter, and behind it a gracious arched nook where drinks are displayed. It's a place of elegance and style, though the mood is casual and relaxed.

The Mediterranean dining room is large and airy, extending from the inside courtyard on two levels to overlook the sea. A wooden table in the centre carries a mouthwatering spread of dishes. On calm and sunny days the terrace outside is used for alfresco meals.

There can be no more pleasant place to sip afternoon tea than in the resident's lounge, a room of antiques, Persian rugs and wingback chairs. The room overlooks a spectacular seascape.

Amenities We've already mentioned the many and varied bathing pools. For the rest, there's a large, sea-facing billiard room with leather furniture and a magnificent old full-sized table.

The hotel is close to the harbour and town of Hermanus (see page 127), which has an excellent golf course. There's sailing, fishing, some beautiful beaches in the vicinity, and several interesting walks, one of which leads along the path in front of the hotel. For the less energetic: benches, donated in memory of people who knew and loved Hermanus in years gone by, have been placed along the top of the cliff above the sea – a very pleasant place to sit, ponder and commune with your favourite muses.

MARINE HOTEL in brief

How to get there: The hotel is on Marine Drive, near Hermanus. Take the N2 out of Cape Town, turn right at Botrivier and follow the signs. The R44 coastal road is a slightly longer but scenically more pleasant alternative. (See directions for The Beach House, page 134) **Tariff** (See Authors' Note on page 4): C **Official rating:** ★★ **Conference facilities:** Available. Contact the Hotel for details. **Liquor licence:** Full. **Children:** No children under 12. **Reservations:** PO Box 9, Hermanus 7200, Cape; telephone: (0283) 2-1112; fax: (0283) 2-1533; telex: 526722.

THE POST HOUSE

Greyton

A small country inn with a big reputation, one of two that lend distinction to the small and charm-loaded village of Greyton (see page 129). The original building was erected (in 1860) to serve as the local post office, later fell prey to neglect but was lovingly restored and furnished with an eclectic combination of antiques by previous owners. Quaintness and quality are the keynotes, the former element most visible in the fine yellowwood ceilings and the old-style fireplaces that grace the building. Hosts Craig and Pam Miller, who have inherited a tradition as 'purveyors of food and lodging to the gentry', maintain a homely and welcoming establishment.

Accommodation There are 13 bedrooms, bathrooms *en suite*, each named after a Beatrix Potter character (I stayed in Peter Rabbit), each furnished with a mix of Edwardian antiques and cottagey pieces. All face onto a grassy courtyard bordered by a rose garden, each has its private veranda. Crackling fires heat many of the rooms in winter, and all are cool and airy in summer. No TV or radio (one doesn't really need either in this marvellously tranquil place).

Food, drink and service The old-world Ball and Bass pub is the most convivial of the rooms, and here we relaxed with the other guests, in front of a splendid open fire, to await dinner. Table d'hôte menu: steaming soup, entrée and either fresh Hermanus kabeljou or a beautifully prepared rare fillet with chive Béarnaise. Sweets, coffee and port are served in front of the fire to end a most enjoyable evening. On balmy summer days light lunches and teas are taken in the garden.

Amenities In the grounds there's a secluded swimming pool, a fishpond and an aviary of budgies and cockatiels. Activities on offer include horse-riding, cycling, angling, bird-watching, tennis and croquet. And there are some most rewarding walks and rambles, and one notable hike, in the area.

A recent addition is the fully equipped 12-seat conference room, complete with telefax, overhead projector and flip chart.

THE POST HOUSE in brief
*How to get there: Greyton is 135 km from Cape Town. Take the N2 highway to the R406 turn-off just before the town of Caledon. The road is in good condition and tarred all the way. Tariff (See Authors' Note on page 4): C **Official rating:** Not applicable. **Conference facilities:** Available for up to 12 delegates (see text). **Children:** Welcome by prior arrangement. **Reservations:** PO Box 42, Main Road, Greyton 7233; telephone: (02822) 9995; fax: (02822) 9920.*

WILDEKRANTZ

Elgin/Grabouw

A pleasant Cape Dutch-style guesthouse surrounded by 185 hectares of pear orchards in the lovely Houwhoek Valley, close to the historic Houw Hoek Inn (see page 138) and half-an-hour's drive from the seaside resorts of Hermanus and Gordon's Bay. Established in 1820, the homestead was recently and very nicely, even elegantly, restored. It's especially popular among honeymooners and with people in search of the quietest, most restful of weekends.

Accommodation Seven rooms/suites, individually and beautifully decorated (period furniture is a feature) by the respected interior designer Jay Smith. Mine had a four-poster bed, a balcony, a sitting room and a bathroom with opulent brass taps. All the rooms are *en suite*; all have tea and coffee-making facilities.

There's television and a stereo in the sociable sitting room.

Food, drink and service Wildekrantz serves a good breakfast and will provide picnic lunches and suppers. Guests otherwise take their other meals at the Houw Hoek Inn. Children are subject to a varied tariff schedule, depending on age and it's best to check before booking.

Amenities There's a strikingly attractive black-marble swimming pool in the terraced gardens; country walks to be walked and birds to be watched. Houw Hoek Inn, next door, has a most congenial pub. Golf, beaches, sailing and so on at Hermanus and Gordon's Bay.

WILDEKRANTZ in brief
*How to get there: From Cape Town, take the N2 highway to and through Grabouw, turn left at the Houw Hoek Inn sign (opposite the farm stall), and bear left at the Inn. Follow the signs to the hotel. **Tariff** (See Authors' Note on page 4): D **Official rating:** Not applicable. **Conference facilities:** Available for small groups of up to 5. **Liquor licence:** Wildekrantz is not licensed to sell liquor. **Children:** Only children over 2 can be accommodated (see text). **Reservations:** Private Bag X24, Elgin 7180; telephone: (02824) 4-9042; fax: (02824) 4-9872*

WINDERMERE LODGE

Elgin/Grabouw

'The most English house in South Africa' is how host Ken Kidd describes the lodge that nestles among the apple-orchards of

THE OVERBERG

the lovely Elgin Valley. And indeed Windermere is very much like one of the more attractive corners of rural England, in spirit as well as in reality: Ken is an unashamed Anglophile who owned a restaurant in Cornwall and he brought the essence of the West Country – its down-to-earth honesty, its humour and its hospitable ways – with him to his new home.

This colonial-style home was built in the 1920s on a commanding slope above terraced gardens; the trees behind have been a long time a-growing; inside, all is frilled and flounced, spick, span and cosily comfortable. A warm and welcoming place, full of books and bric-a-brac, polished wood and fresh flowers. From the sun-parlour you look over the orchards to the Hottentots-Holland and Groenland mountains in the distance – a lotion for the eyes: it's one of the finest views in the Elgin valley. Windermere is a member of Relais du Cap's group of selected country houses.

Accommodation Five pleasant rooms and a luxury suite – four *en suite* (two with shower only), one with a private bathroom. All are most comfortable and pleasingly done out in cottagey style, with soft fabrics, flowered wallpaper and plenty of plump pillows. Each room has tea- and coffee-making facilities, heater, fan and hair-dryer. No telephone to hand (there's one in the hall); TV in the lounge (portable sets are supplied on request).

Food, drink and service The dining room is timber-beamed, smallish, intimate; Sheila Kidd, London trained, produces fine food in the best English tradition. Her roasts, centrepieces of the five-course dinner, are superb, as are her delectable home-made soups and sweets. Bread and butter are also home-made; milk and eggs come from Windermere farm, vegetables and fruit are also of the very freshest.

Incidentally, the tariff covers bed and breakfast; the dinner is extra.

Ken serves drinks in The Cabin (named after his Cornish pub), a marvellously convivial place that gleams richly with glasses, bottles and brasses and nautical collectables – a ship's bell, a genuine John Hastie ship's wheel and an ornately gold-trimmed, hundred-year-old cash register. The Cabin is fully licenced.

Service: your charming hosts go well out of their way to make your stay enjoyable and memorable.

Amenities For lazers in the sun, there's a swimming pool (on the lower lawn); for ramblers, fine stretches of woodland countryside (you can walk around the surrounding farm for two hours without crossing its boundaries). Nearby is a beautiful dam where one may picnic, row, fish or swim. Cape Town is 50 minutes' away. Recommended excursions: the magnificent 'forestry mountain drive' to Kleinmond, to the coast (Hermanus, Strand), to Stellenbosch and the winelands, and along the spectacular Four Passes drive. The newly opened Fruit Route offers an interesting diversion; on the Lodge's doorstep is the well-appointed Elgin/Grabouw Country Club, where there is squash and tennis.

WINDERMERE LODGE in brief

How to get there: From Cape Town: follow the N2 towards Caledon, take the Viljoenshoop turn-off (right) at the second Grabouw/Elgin intersection. Windermere Lodge is 2 km from the highway; look for the entrance opposite the Andrag tractor garage; follow the signs to the lodge. **Tariff** *(See Authors' Note on page 4):* D **Official rating:** Not applicable. **Liquor licence:** Full. **Children:** Windermere is not suitable for children, exceptions may be made for older offspring. **Reservations:** P.O. Box 120, Elgin, Cape 7180; telephone: (024) 59-2503; fax: (024) 59-3016.

VISITORS' ADVISORY

❏ CLIMATE

❏ TRAVEL & TOURING

❏ SPORT & RECREATION

❏ SPECIAL EVENTS

❏ USEFUL ADDRESSES
 & TELEPHONE NUMBERS

VISITORS' ADVISORY

CLIMATE

The south-western Cape is a winter rainfall region and enjoys a Mediterranean-type climate. Summers are warm to hot, though the air is often cooled by strong south-easterly winds; winters are characterized by cold, wet periods interspersed with warmer, sunny spells and occasionally, when the 'berg wind' blows in from the interior, with stiflingly hot days. The best weather is experienced in the springtime (September), and in autumn and early winter (March to June).

Cape Town's climate is discussed in general terms on page 7. Specific indicators include:

Temperature: January average daily maximim: 26,2°C; daily minimum: 16,4°C; June average daily maximum: 18,5°C; daily minimum: 9,0°C; maximum temperature ever recorded: 40,8 °C; minimum -0,3 °C.

Rainfall: January average monthly rainfall is 17 mm; June average monthly rainfall is 109 mm; the highest daily rainfall on record is 77 mm.

TRAVEL & TOURING

Cape Town is 1450 km from Johannesburg, 1461 km from Pretoria, 1 654 km from Durban, 1 024 km from Bloemfontein, 753 km from Port Elizabeth, 1 038 km from East London and 1 500 km from Windhoek.

The region is served by an excellent system of roads. The major highways leading to and from Cape Town are the N1 through the Great Karoo to Johannesburg, Pretoria and the Zimbabwean border in the far north; the N2 along the southern coastal belt to Port Elizabeth and beyond to Durban; and the N7 through Namaqualand to the Namibian border and Windhoek.

Rail passenger, semi-luxury coach and regional air services connect the city with major southern African centres. There are direct airline flights between Cape Town and London (twice-weekly at the time of going to press). Other international services are planned. The D.F. Malan airport is 22 km from city centre.

Rail enquiries: at the station information desk or Tel: (021) 940-2667/8/9; rail tours (021) 21-6274; Blue Train (021) 218-3871.

Coach enquires: a number of firms, including Autonet, Greyhound, Connex, Inter Cape and Translux, operate services. Contact Captour or Satour for details.

Air enquiries: Tel: (021) 93-6223 (SAA passenger services); (021) 418-1525 (SAA international); (021) 25-4610 (SAA domestic).

VISITORS' ADVISORY

The Automobile Association The AA of South Africa provides a wide range of services: advice on touring, camping and places of interest (it keeps a range of excellent maps and brochures); help in preparing itineraries; insurance, car hire and accommodation booking facilities; assistance with breakdowns and other emergencies, and so forth. These amenities are available to visitors who belong to a motoring organization affiliated to the AA of SA through the AIT (Alliance Internationale de Tourisme) or FIA (Federation de l'Automobile).

The AA's Cape Town headquarters are in AA House, off Oswald Pirow Street on the Foreshore. Tel: (021) 21-1550; breakdown: (021) 419-4378; medical hotline: dial toll free 0800 - 111 - 995.

Local travel Rail, bus and taxi services within Cape Town and the Peninsula are generally adequate.

Buses: Regular services link the city with all the major suburbs. The main bus terminal is behind (to the west of) the Golden Acre complex.

Taxis: Cape Town's cabs do not cruise the streets in search of fares. They are to be found in a number of designated city ranks and at several but by no means all railway stations, and the companies are listed in the Yellow Pages. If your journey is anything more than a cross-city hop, ask the driver for an estimate of the cost, and make quite sure that he can locate your destination precisely (some cabbies are surprisingly unfamiliar with their own city and its suburbs).

There are also the so-called 'black taxis' – minibuses that cruise the main thoroughfares. They are relatively cheap, fast (sometimes too fast), often crowded, and they will stop if you hail them. A Tuk-Tuk three-wheeler service was introduced to the city in 1991.

Trains: Regular rail services connect the city with the southern, south-eastern and northern suburbs and towns, but not the central and western parts of the Peninsula; the main rail terminus is in Lower Adderley Street. During 1991 criminals were active on some stretches of the line; security has been tightened, but it's suggested nevertheless that you seek advice (from hotel reception or Captour) before embarking on a trip beyond the nearer suburbs.

Car hire: The major, internationally- known rental companies maintain offices in Cape Town, at the airport and at other points throughout the region. A kilometre charge is levied; tariffs vary according to the type of vehicle. For one-way (city-to-city) rentals there are no 'drop-off' charges; delivery and pick-up services within the city are usually free of charge. Local firms provide similar (and often highly competitive) services; other companies offer for hire fully equipped caravans, campers and campmobiles (or dormobiles), four-wheel drive vehicles, micro- and mini-buses. Consult the Yellow Pages.

VISITORS' ADVISORY

Parking: On-street parking within the central area is a problem during business hours (the peripheral areas are more accommodating). However, there's usually space at one or other of the many open squares (outside the railway station for instance), at the various 'pay-and-display' lots and vacant building sites, and in the half-dozen or so multi-storeyed and underground 'parkades'. Consult your city street-plan or ask hotel reception.

Trips and tours The visitor has a wide choice of local coach and minibus tours. Also on offer are sea cruises, steam train excursions and helicopter trips. City Tramways provides special 'Sunshine Rover' tickets which enable visitors to reach, via the scheduled bus routes, the Peninsula's more popular tourist areas; other (private) firms, between them, cover the scenic, historic, maritime and culinary attractions of the entire south-western Cape in half-day, one-day and longer excursions. Among the operators are:

Hylton Ross, Tel: (021) 438-1500; Pat's Adventures, Tel: (021) 794-4140 (yacht charter also available); Plusbus Touring, Tel: (021) 218-2191/2/3; Rodeon Tours, Tel: (021) 419-6150/1; Safari esCape, Tel: (021) 794-4832; Sealink, Tel: (021) 25-4480 (cruises, helicopter trips and charter); Springbok Atlas, Tel: (021) 45-5468; Specialised Tours, Tel: (021) 25-3259; Sun Tours, Tel: (021) 689-1232; Tales of Africa Tours, Tel: (0282) 2-3702; Top Tours, Tel: (021) 551-2904; Welcome Tours & Safaris, Tel: (021) 434-3890.

The wine routes To date, nine wine-ways have been established, seven of which fall within the ambit of this book (see pages 59 and 74). Information from Captour or from the appropriate information offices, namely: ❏ Constantia, Tel: (021) 794-5178/9 (Groot Constantia), (021) 794-5191 (Buitenverwachting) and (021) 794-5188 (Klein Constantia) ❏ Stellenbosch, Tel: (02231) 4310 or (02231) 3584 ❏ Paarl, Tel: (02211) 2-4842 ❏ Vignerons de Franschhoek, Tel:(02212) 7-2086 ❏ Worcester, Tel: 0231) 7-1408 ❏ Robertson, Tel: (02351) 4437, and ❏ Swartland and Olifantsrivier, Tel: (02724) 6-1731/3.

Other routes Speciality, or thematic, excursions include the Fruit Routes (winelands), the Cheese Route (winelands), the Crayfish Route (west coast), the Wool Route (southern Cape), the Afrikaanse Taal (Language) Route (winelands), the French Huguenot Farms Route, the Arts and Crafts Route (Peninsula, winelands), the Antique Route (Peninsula, Stellenbosch, Somerset West and Paarl), the Wreck Route (south and west coasts) and the Whale Route (False and Walker Bays). Information from Captour or the various local publicity offices (see further on).

Steam train excursions. A number are planned; one of the more inviting is the Champagne Express, which runs along the little-used 30-km track between Paarl and Franschhoek, stopping at wine farms and a newly-established art centre *en route*; Tel: (02211) 2-4842/2 or (02212) 2055.

VISITORS' ADVISORY

SPORT & RECREATION

The Cape Peninsula has nearly 150 km of coastline, much of it ideal for beach leisure, bathing, boating, surfing, fishing and other watersports.

Beaches Best of these are probably Muizenberg's on the east coast and Clifton's on the west (see pages 54 – 58). Among other splendid stretches are Milnerton and Blouberg-strand, to the north; Camps Bay, Bakoven, Llandudno, Hout Bay, Sandy Bay, Noordhoek, Kommetjie and Scarborough along the west coast; Maclear Beach in the Cape of Good Hope nature reserve, and a number of other sandy strips both to the north and south of Muizenberg on the False Bay coast.

The Cape south and west coasts also offer much to the beach-lover, the sportsperson and the lazer-in-the-sun. See Chapters 4 (pages 112 – 124) and 5 (125 – 145).

Bird watching The Peninsula is home to more than 300 species; some of the more rewarding venues are the city's public gardens (just to the south of the central area), Kirstenbosch (Newlands), Rietvlei (a coastal-bird sanctuary north of Milnerton), Ronde-vlei (east of the Constantia – Tokai area), the World of Birds (Hout Bay) and the Cape of Good Hope nature reserve. For more information, contact the Cape Bird Club, Tel: (021) 686-6393 (afternoons).

Bowls Numerous clubs, most of which welcome visitors. Contact the WP Bowling Association, Tel: (021) 24-1919.

Cycling A splendid way to explore the Peninsula and hinterland. The premier fun-ride is the Argus tour. The WP Pedal Power Association organizes recreational rides, Tel: (021) 794-2268; for information on the regular Sunday excursions, telephone 'Dial-a-Ride' on 61-2415. To cycle in the Cape of Good Hope nature reserve, contact Cape Cycle Ventures, Tel: (021) 780-1353. A useful publication is *Cycling in and around Cape Town* by Tim Anderson and Colin Dutkiewicz: it features 36 rides and is available from larger bookshops.

Fishing Sea-anglers have the freedom of the Peninsula's coastline (but not of the harbour area); prominent species include white steenbras, red roman, snoek, elf and kabeljou (kob); deep-sea anglers also catch marlin, tunny (three tuna species are to be found off Cape Point) and swordfish. No permits are needed, but there are strict catch limits. Crayfish (rock lobster), oysters and perlemoen (abelone) may not be taken out of season.

Radio Good Hope (the local station) broadcasts information on fishing conditions at 18h15 each day; local newspapers run angling columns. For detailed advice, contact the Department of Environmental Affairs, Tel: (021) 402-3911.

Boats may be chartered from, among others, Big Game Fishing Safaris, Tel: (021) 64-3837; Bluefin Charters, Tel: (021) 83-1756; African Fishing Safaris, Tel: (021) 72-1272; Falcon Charters, Tel: (021) 790-3619; Condor Charters, Tel: (021) 47-0741, and Seaboard Yachting Ventures, Tel: (021) 25-4292.

Freshwater angling: catches are limited to 10 per person per day; there are also size restrictions, and permits are required. Open season for trout is from 1 September to 1 June. Information: contact the WP Artificial Lure Society, Tel: (021) 24-5613 or the Cape Piscatorial Society, Tel: (021) 24-7725.

Golf Peninsula golf clubs welcome visitors; among the best courses are those at Green Point, Milnerton, Mowbray, Rondebosch, Wynberg, Simon's Town, Westlake and Clovelly. Contact the WP Golf Union, Tel: (021) 531-6728.

Health and fitness Among the more prominent health studios are the Cape Town Health and Racquet Club, Tel: (021) 419-6600; Heerengracht Health and Fitness centre, Tel: (021) 25-2929; Capetonian Health Spa, Tel: (021) 25-3163, and the Townhouse Health and Fitness centre (see page 46).

Horse-racing Regular meetings (Saturdays and Wednesdays) are held at the Ascot course (Milnerton), Durbanville and Kenilworth (where the prestigious Metropolitan Handicap concludes the season).

Horse-riding The Peninsula's riding schools and stables welcome visitors. Contact Captour for a list and directions. For more adventurous exploratory rides, contact Horse Trail Safaris, Tel: (021) 73-4396, or Vineyard Horse Trails, Tel: (021) 981-2480. The Cape Hunt and Polo Club, at Durbanville, is the southern hemisphere's oldest hunt; it meets on Sundays (at various venues) for a chase without blood-letting; Tel: (021) 96-3968.

Squash Numerous venues in and around Cape Town; contact the WP Squash Racquets Association, Tel: (021) 461-4107.

Swimming The two largest public pools are at Newlands (Olympic standard) and that adjacent to the Sea Point Pavilion. There's also a heated indoor pool at the top of Long Street, in the city.

Watersports The Peninsula offers virtually limitless opportunities for boating, yachting, boardsailing, waterskiing, diving, surfing and so forth. Useful contacts include the WP Sailing Association, Tel: (021) 64-2972; Cape Sailing Academy, Tel: (021) 86-1640; Ocean Divers International, Tel: (021) 23-5898, and the Cape Peninsula Aquatic Club, Tel: (021) 73-1150.

VISITORS' ADVISORY

Walking and hiking There are some splendid walks and trails on the Peninsula and in the hinterland. Ask Captour for information on city walks. Rewarding areas a little farther afield include Table Mountain and surrounds; along many stretches of both the east and west coast; in the Cape of Good Hope nature reserve; around Hout Bay and Constantia, in the Silvermine reserve and the Cecilia, Tokai and and Newlands forests.

Useful publications include David Bristow's *Exploring the Western Cape*; Maxwell Leigh's *Pocket Guide to Cape Town*; Tim Anderson's *Day Walks in and around Cape Town*; Shirley Bossy's *A Walking Guide for Table Mountain*; the Mountain Club of South Africa's *Table Mountain Guide: Walks and Easy Climbs*; the Western Cape Forestry Branch's *Teacher's Guide to Tokai* and *The Tokai Nature Trail*; Shirley Bossy's *A Walking Guide for the Hout Bay to Simon's Town Mountains*, and Mike Lundy's *Twenty Walks around Hout Bay*.

Useful contacts: the National Hiking Way Board, Tel: (021) 402-3093; the Trails Club of South Africa, Tel: (021) 72-9189; the Mountain Club, Tel: (021) 45-3412, and the Cape Natural History Club, Tel: (021) 24-6967.

SPECIAL EVENTS

Cape Peninsula Minstrel (Coon) Carnival: first week in January ❏ Metropolitan Handicap, Kenilworth: 3rd Saturday in January ❏ Cape Festival: variable in recent years; usually April, for two weeks ❏ Two Oceans Marathon: Easter Sunday ❏ Snoek Derby, Hout Bay: July/August ❏ Spring Wild Flower Show, Kirstenbosch: September ❏ Rothmans Sailing Week: December.

Winelands Worcester Agricultural Show: January ❏ University of Stellenbosch Carnival: March ❏ Paarl Vineyard Festival: mid-March ❏ Nederburg Auction, Paarl: mid-April ❏ Boland Agricultural Show: end April ❏ Worcester Wine and Food Festival: August ❏ Robertson Spring Show: September ❏ Ceres Agricultural and Wild Flower Show: 1st week in October ❏ Van der Stel Festival, Stellenbosch: October ❏ Stellenbosch Food and Wine Festival: last weekend in October.

West coast Saldanha Sailing Championships: Easter weekend ❏ Lutzville Valley Carnival: April/May ❏ Sandveld Potato Festival, Clanwilliam: August ❏ Vredendal Agricultural, Food and Wine Festival: August ❏ Clanwilliam Wild Flower Show: last weekend in August ❏ Citrusdal Citrus and Agricultural Festival: early September ❏ Saldanha Harvest of the Sea Festival: 2nd Saturday in September ❏ Darling Wild Flower Show: 3rd weekend in September ❏ Clanwilliam Angling Festival: October/November ❏ Olifantsrivier Young Wine Show, Vredendal: October.

VISITORS' ADVISORY

Overberg Hermanus Festival of the Sea: June ❏ Caledon Wild Flower Show: September ❏ Caledon Beer and Bread Festival: September ❏ Bredasdorp Foot of Africa Marathon: October.

USEFUL ADDRESSES & TELEPHONE NUMBERS

Sources of information
Satour (South African Tourism Board). Shop 16, Piazza level, Sanlam Golden Acre, Adderley Street, Tel: (021) 21-6274.

Captour Head Office, Tel: (021) 462-2040; Visitors' Information Bureau, Strand Concourse, Adderley Street, Tel: (021) 25-3320; Johannesburg office, Tel: (011) 331-8494. The Bureau produces street and other maps, a number of very useful brochures, booklets (covering accommodation, restaurants, shopping, the Winelands, special-interest routes and so forth) and the Cape Town *What's On*. The organization will also handle tour, car hire and emergency accommodation reservations.

Winelands Tourist information offices include: Ceres, Tel: (0233) 2-1177; Franschhoek, Tel: (02212) 2440; Gordon's Bay, Tel: (024) 56-2321; Montagu, Tel: (0234) 4-2471; Paarl, Tel: (02211) 2-4842; Robertson, Tel: (02351) 3112; Somerset West, Tel: (024) 51-4022; Stellenbosch, Tel: (02231) 4310; Tulbagh, Tel: (0236) 41; Wellington, Tel: (02211) 3-1121, and Worcester, Tel: (0231) 7-1408.

West Coast Tourist information offices include: Langebaan, Tel: ((02287) 2115; Vredenburg/Saldanha, Tel: (02281) 4-1276 or 3-2231; the Olifants River and West Coast Tourism Bureau, (Klawer) Tel: (02724) 6-1731/3, and the West Coast Tourism Bureau, (Lambert's Bay) Tel: (026732) 516.

Overberg Tourist information offices include: Hermanus, Tel: (0283) 2-2629, and Swellendam, Tel: (0291) 4-2770.

Table Mountain
The Kloofnek bus departs from Adderley Street, outside OK Bazaars. Bookings for cableway and guides: Tel: (021) 24-5148.

National Parks Board
Head Office: P.O. Box 787, Pretoria 0001; Tel: (012) 343-1991. Cape Town: P.O. Box 7400, Roggebaai 8012, Tel: (021) 419-5365. The Board's central Cape Town offices are in St George's Mall.

VISITORS' ADVISORY

Theatre and other bookings
Through Computicket. No telephonic bookings, but for information call (021) 418-3409. Computicket offices are located at the Strand Gallery in the Strand Concourse; the Golden Acre Cine in the Golden Acre; the Nico Malan theatre complex on the Foreshore; Garlicks in Claremont; the Gardens shopping centre, Gardens; the Baxter theatre complex, Rosebank; the Adelphi Centre, Sea Point; Accent in Constantia Village, and at A.P. Jones on Main Road, Fish Hoek.

Diplomatic representatives
These are listed in the Yellow Pages under Consulates and Embassies. Among countries with representatives in Cape Town (telephone code 021) are Australia 419-5425; Austria 21-1440; Belgium 61-7376; Canada 23-5240; Denmark 25-1025; Finland 23-7240; France 21-5617; Germany 24-2410; Greece 23-1354 (Embassy) and 24-8161 (Consulate); Israel 45-7207; Italy 23-5157 (Embassy) and 24-1256 (Consulate); Japan 25-1695; Netherlands 21-5660; Norway 25-1687; Portugal 21-4560 (Embassy) and 24-1454 (Consulate-General); Spain 25-1468; Switzerland 25-4838 (Embassy) and 21-7633 (Consulate); Taiwan (Republic of China) 21-7633 (Embassy) and 21-4267 (Consulate-General); United Kingdom 461-7220 (Embassy), 25-3670 (Consulate passport section) and 25-3670 (commercial section); United States 21-4280 (Embassy and Consulate).

Emergencies
If in difficulty, dial the exchange on 1022. Specific emergency numbers include:

Ambulance: national ambulance number 1-0177; **hospital casualty departments:** Groote Schuur (Observatory) 47-3311, New Somerset (Green Point) 21-3311, Conradie (Pinelands) 531-1311, Red Cross Children's (Rondebosch) 685-5011, Victoria (Wynberg) 797-8131, Tygerberg (northern areas) 931-6129; **poisoning centres:** Red Cross Children's 685-5011; Tygerberg 931-6129; **after-hours pharmacies:** consult Yellow Pages, or dial 461-8040 or 82-1101; **police:** headquarters 561-4326; flying squad 1-0111; **fire brigade:** (Cape Town) 461-5555; **sea rescue:** 218-3500; **mountain rescue:** 218-3500; **Lifeline** (local equivalent of the Samaritans) 461-1111.

INDEX

INDEX

Establishments featured in the text and the page numbers on which they are reviewed appear bold in the index.

A

Adderley Street 10
Alphen Hotel 60
Ambassador by the Sea 22
Arniston 100,131,133
Arniston Hotel 133
Arumwood Lodge 85
Assegaaibosch nature reserve 76
Avalon Springs Hotel 86,99,100

B

Badkloof Mineral Springs 85
Bain's Kloof 79,110
Bantry Bay 22
Baviaan's River 96
Baxter theatre 18,19
Bay Hotel, The 16,20,**23**
Beach House 134
Betty's Bay 126
Biedouw Valley 115
Bird Island 117,120
Bloubergstrand 120
Bo-Kaap 12
Boesmanskloof Hiking Trail 98,104,111,138
Boland open-air museum 82
Bontebok National Park 133
Botrivier 127

Bredasdorp 130
 mountain reserve 130
Breede River 132

C

Cableway 8
Caledon 129,135
Caledon Area 129
Caledon nature reserve
 see Victoria Park
Caledon Springs 129,136
Camps Bay 23
Cape Agulhas 100,130
Cape Doctor 7
Cape Floral Kingdom 19,54,113
Cape Hangklip 56,126
Cape Infanta 132
Cape of Good Hope 58
Cape of Good Hope nature reserve 54,56,58
Cape Peninsula 52 – 71
 Eastern Seaboard 56
 Western Seaboard 55
Cape Point 56,58
Cape Sun, The 10,20,**27**
Cape Swiss Hotel 28
Cape Town 6 – 51
 Church Street 11
 Long Street 11
Cape Town Symphony Orchestra 20
Cape Winelands 72 – 111
Capetonian, The 29

Castle of Good Hope 10
Cecilia Forest 59,63
Cedarberg Hotel 120
Cederberg 116
Centenary nature reserve 85
Ceres 80,91,102
Ceres nature reserve 100
Chapman's Peak Drive 56
Citrusdal 113,114,120
Clanwilliam 113,115
Claremont 31,48
Clifton 16
Club Mykonos 121
Cogmans Kloof 85
Constantia 60,62,70
Constantia Nek 55
Cultural History Museum 11
Cumberland Hotel 87

D

D'Ouwe Werf 89
Danger Point 128
Darling 120
Dassen Island 119
De Hoop nature reserve 131,133
De Mond nature reserve 131
De Overberger 135
De Tuyn Huys 13,61
De Waal Sun, The 30
Devon Valley Protea 88

INDEX

District Six 16
Don, The 30

E

Elands Bay 118
Elgin 127,138,143
Elim 130

F

False Bay 6,56,126
Fernkloof
 nature reserve 128
Fish Hoek 57
Foreshore, The 9,29
Four Passes 77
Franschhoek 77,106

G

Gansbaai 128
Gardens
 12,28,30,36,40,114
Geelbek 119,123
Genadendal 129,130
**Goedemoed
 Country Inn 90**
Gordon's Bay 78,108
Government Avenue 13
Grabouw 127,138,143
Great Karoo 95
Green Point 15
Greenmarket Square 11
Greenways 31
Greyton 129,137,142
Greyton Lodge 137
Greyton
 nature reserve 129
Groot Constantia
 59,62,63

Groot Drakenstein
 Valley 77,100
Groot Moddergat 63
Groote Kerk
Groote Schuur Estate 8,17
Groote Schuur
 Hospital 17
Guano Islands 120

H

Harold Porter Botanical
 Garden 126
Hawston 128
Heerengracht 9,10
Helderberg reserve
 77,86,95,109
Helshoogte Pass 76
**Herberg Guest House,
 The 91**
Hermanus 127,140,142
**High Rustenberg
 Hydro 92**
Hotagterklip 130
Hotel Metropole 34
Hottentots-Holland
 nature reserve 76
Houses of Parliament 13
Hout Bay 55,63,64
 Museum 55
Houtkapperspoort 64
Houw Hoek 127,143
 Pass 127
**Houw Hoek Inn
 138**,143
Huguenots, The 73

I

Ida's Valley 92
Inn on the Square 11,32

J

Jonkershoek Valley
 76,93
Josephine Mill 18

K

Kalbaskraal
 nature reserve 114
Kalk Bay 57
Karoo 81
Karoo National Botanical
 Gardens 82,88
Karos Arthur's Seat 33
Kirstenbosch 18,62,63
Khayelitsha 6
Klaasvoogds cactus
 farm 104
Klein River Lodge 139
Kleinmond 126,134
Koeberg 120
Kommetjie 56
Koo, The 83
Koopmans-De Wet
 House 12
KWV 78

L

Lambert's Bay 117
Langebaan 121,122
Langebaan Lagoon
 119,123
Langebaan Lodge 122
Lanzerac, The 93,141
Little Karoo 83,98
Llandudno 55
Long Beach 56
**Lord Charles Hotel,
 The 94**

INDEX

Lord Milner, The 95
Lord Nelson Inn 66
Lutzville 117

M

Malay Quarter
  see Bo-Kaap
Malgas 132
Malmesbury 113
Marina da Gama 57
Marine Hotel
  Hermanus 140
Marine Protea 123
Mariner's Wharf
  see Hout Bay
Marloth
  nature reserve 132
Martin Melck House 12
Matjiesfontein 81,95,141
McGregor Country
  Cottages 97
McGregor 83,97,103,110
Melkbosstrand 120
Metropolitan
  Methodist Church 11
Michell's Pass 80,81
Mitchell's Plain 16
Mijlof Manor 35
Mimosa Lodge 98
Monkey Valley 67
Montagu 83,86,98,99
  Mineral Springs 85,99
Montagu Springs 99
Moorreesburg 114
Mosterts Mill 17
Mount Nelson Hotel,
  The 36
Mountain Shadows 100
Muisbosskerm 117
Muizenberg Area 56,69

N

Namaqualand 113
Namib Desert 113
New Belmont Hotel 102
Newlands 18,38
Newlands Sun, The 38
Nico Malan theatre 9,19
Noordhoek 56,67

O

Observatory 17
Old Mill House Lodge,
  The 97,103
Olifants River 113
Onrus 128
Orange River 113
Oranienstein Guest
  House 39
Oranjezicht 48
Overberg 125 – 145

P

Paarl 78,90,100,104,105
Paarl wine route
  see Wine Routes
Paarlberg
  nature reserve 79
Park Avenue 40
Peninsula, The 41
Planetarium 14
Porterville 114
Post House, The 142
Postberg
  nature reserve 119
President Hotel, The
  15,**42**
Prince Alfred Hamlet 81
Pringle Bay 126

R

Ritz Protea Hotel 20,43
Riviera, The 15
Robben Island 15
Robertson 83
Robertson wine route
  see Wine Routes
Robin Gordon Hotel 68
Rocher Pan
  nature reserve 118
Roggebaai 10
Roggeland 104
Rondebosch 44
Rondevlei nature
  reserve 60
Rooikat Ring Trail 96
Rose House 44

S

Safariland game park 76
Saldanha Bay 118
Salmonsdam nature
  reserve 129
Sandvlei 57
Sandy Bay 55
Scarborough 56
Schaapen Island 119
Sea Point 16,30,33,41-43
Shrimpton Manor 69
Silvermine
  nature reserve 60
Silvermist Mountain
  Retreat 70
Silwerstrand 83
Simon's Town 57,67
Sir Lowry's Pass 127
Somerset West 77,85,94
South African Library 13
South African Museum 13

INDEX

South African National Gallery 13
St George's Cathedral 11
St George's Mall 11
St George's Hotel 11,45
St Helena Bay 118
St James 57,68
St Sebastian Bay 132
Stanford 128,139,140
Stellenbosch 75,88,89,93,105
Stellenbosch Hotel 105
Stellenbosch wine route *see* Wine Routes
Stompneusbaai 118
Strand 77
Strand Street 12
Struis Bay 130
Swartland 113
Swellendam 132
Swiss Farm Excelsior 106

T

Table Mountain 8,54
Tamboerskloof 35,39
Tavern of the Seas *see* Cape Town
The Cellars Country House 62
The West Coast 112 – 124
Theatre on the Bay 20
Tienie Versveld reserve 120
Tokai 60
Townhouse, The 46
Tulbagh 80
Tygerberg Zoo 76

U

University of Cape Town 17

V

Van Riebeeck Hotel 108
Vanrhynsdorp 116
Van Ryn brandy cellar 76
Velddrif 118
Victoria and Alfred Hotel 14,47
Victoria and Alfred Waterfront 14,47
Victoria Drive 55
Victoria Park 129,136
Vignerons de Franschhoek *see* Wine Routes
Villa Lutzi 48
Vineyard Hotel, The 18,20,**48**
Visitors' Advisory 146 – 153
Vlottenberg 76
Voorvlei 117
Vredenburg 118
Vredendal 113,117

W

Wadrifsoutpan 117
Waenhuiskrans *see* Arniston
Wagenmakers Vallei 79
Walker Bay 127
Waterfront *see* Victoria and Alfred Waterfront
Waterkloof Guesthouse 109
Wellington 79,109
Wemmershoek 77
Westbrooke 17
Whipstock Farm 110
Wiesenhof Wildpark 76
Wildekrantz 143
Winchester Mansions Hotel 50
Windermere Lodge 143
Wine Routes 59,73 – 75
  Constantia 59
  Paarl 74
  Robertson 75
  Stellenbosch 74
  Vignerons de Franschhoek 74
  Worcester 75
Winterhoek 114
Witsand 132
Witsenberg 80
Wolseley 81
Wolwenskloof 79
Worcester 82,87
Worcester wine route *see* Wine Routes
World of Birds 55
Wuppertal 115
Wynberg 16

Y

Yzerfontein 119

Z

Zonnebloem *see* District Six